Outlawed Pigs

Outlawed Pigs

Law, Religion, and Culture in Israel

∾ Daphne Barak-Erez

THE UNIVERSITY OF WISCONSIN PRESS

The University of Wisconsin Press
1930 Monroe Street, 3rd floor
Madison, Wisconsin 53711-2059

www.wisc.edu/wisconsinpress/

3 Henrietta Street
London WC2E 8LU, England

Library of Congress Cataloging-in-Publication Data
Barak-Erez, Daphne.
Outlawed pigs : law, religion, and culture in Israel /
Daphne Barak-Erez.
p. cm.
Includes bibliographical references and index.
ISBN 0-299-22160-1 (cloth : alk. paper)
1. Food law and legislation—Israel. 2. Jews—Israel—
Dietary laws. 3. Muslims—Israel—Dietary laws.
4. Pork—Religious aspects—Israel. I. Title.
KMK1020.B37   2007
343.5694´07664—dc22   2006031811

A land whose cattle are sheep,
whose sheep are cattle,
and whose pigs are outlawed

—DAVID AVIDAN

Contents

Preface

I grew up in Israel in a secular Jewish family. My grandparents left their religious homes in Eastern Europe and emigrated to what was then Palestine in order to live as modern Jews. My family still preserved some religious traditions, however, mainly as cultural signs of national identity. Although we disregarded many traditional dietary rules, one salient feature of the family fare was that we did not eat pork. Pork was different.

Some steakhouses at which I used to dine with my family as a child in the 1970s featured "white" steak in their menu. It was some time before I understood this was a euphemism for pork, a euphemism that was also used by people who were not observant and even ate pork—a food taboo for Jews for millennia. At the secular government school I attended, I learned about "Hannah and Her Seven Sons," the story of a family killed by an ancient Greek ruler because its members bravely resisted an edict forcing them to eat the flesh of swine. Now, I tell my children that "Jews don't eat pork," although this is certainly no longer accurate. More explanations will follow as they grow up.

When I began my law studies, I found that the traditional taboo against pigs had been incorporated into Israeli law that, aside from the domain of family law and a few other exceptions, is generally a secular system. Specific legislation prohibits pig-breeding and commercial pork-trading in Israel. When I began teaching and specialized in public law, I was amazed to discover the amount of cases dealing with prohibitions on pig breeding and pork-trading and their application, interpretation, and circumvention. Many important principles of Israeli administrative law were generated in this marginal area.[1] In fact, one could venture a claim that basic principles of Israeli public law "piggybacked" (no pun intended) on these restrictions,[2] perhaps as much as the national prohibition of alcohol in the early twentieth century shaped the norms of criminal law doctrines in the United States.[3] Brian Simpson's comment on ducks in English case law appears fitting in this context: "The contribution of ducks to the common law system has been limited, but significant; they have concentrated the minds of lawyers upon fundamental issues of timeless principle."[4]

At first, pig-related law in Israel seemed amusing—so much energy invested in such a rare and discrete topic! Only later did I realize that the intensity surrounding this litigation goes beyond the merely anecdotal and tells a fascinating story about the mark of culture on law, and about the law as a mirror of cultural changes. More specifically, this litigation projects the changing attitudes of Israeli society on issues of religion and national identity. This book seeks to tell the story by analyzing the pertinent legal debates from historical and cultural perspectives.

I owe thanks to many. Let me begin with those friends and colleagues who followed the course of my research for this book and contributed helpful advice, especially Yishai Blank, Tom Green, Assaf Likhovski, Bill Miller, Frances Olsen, Gideon Sapir, Ronen Shamir, Ernest Weinrib, Lorraine Weinrib, Elimelech Westreich and Stephen Wizner. Joel Migdal provided support and inspiration. I had several assistants who helped me through the research, and I am particularly grateful to Assaf Porat and Keren Izsac. I am indebted to Batya Stein for her excellent editing of the text.

Thanks to the Cegla Center for the Interdisciplinary Research of Law, which supported the research for this book.

I also take this opportunity to express my gratitude to Stewart and Judy Colton for their support and friendship over the years, beginning with my doctoral dissertation and through various research projects.

My family has a significant share in this book, through their proverbial love and understanding. I am grateful to my parents, Judith and Elazar, and to my husband Chen, who also helped in my search for historical and cultural sources. I lovingly dedicate this book to our sons, Eran and Yuval. May they have good life as proud Jews in a decent world.

Outlawed Pigs

CHAPTER 1

Religious Symbols and Culture in Israeli Law

T HIS BOOK EXPLORES how the historical sensitivity of Jewish culture to pigs was incorporated into Israeli law. More specifically,
it traces the course of two Israeli laws that sought to give concrete
formulation to the abhorrence of pigs: the Local Authorities (Special
Enablement) Law of 1956, which authorizes municipalities to ban the possession of and trade in pork within their jurisdiction, and the Pig-Raising
Prohibition Law of 1962, which forbids pig-breeding throughout Israel,
except for areas populated mainly by Christians.[1] My focus will be on
the processes that culminated in the adoption of prohibitions against pig-
breeding and pork trading, and on the resistance they provoked. I argue
that the controversies surrounding these issues provide a key to changing
attitudes toward religion and tradition in Israeli society. Although these
laws were also controversial at the time they were enacted, closer scrutiny
of the debate surrounding them points to a growing detachment among
the Israeli secular public from traditions that had previously also been
respected by non-religious Jews, together with a declining willingness to
view religious elements of the culture as having national significance.

A legal prohibition against pork in the context of Islamic rule was one
of the hypothetical examples John Stuart Mill discusses in his classic *On
Liberty:* "To cite a rather trivial example, nothing in the creed or practice of Christians does more to envenom the hatred of Mahomedans
against them, than the fact of their eating pork. There are few acts which
Christians and Europeans regard with more unaffected disgust, than
Mussulmans regard this particular mode of satisfying hunger. It is, in

the first place, an offence against their religion; but this circumstance by no means explains either the degree or the kind of their repugnance. . . . Suppose now that in a people, of whom the majority were Mussulmans, that majority should insist upon not permitting pork to be eaten within the limits of the country."[2]

Notwithstanding the almost prophetic character of this example, some differences between Mill's hypothetical example and the actual prohibitions against pork in Israeli law must be noted. First, the traditional Jewish aversion to pigs is not restricted to the eating of their flesh.[3] Second, prohibitions against pork in Israeli law never applied to actual consumption, but rather to preparatory activities such as pig-breeding and the sale of pork.[4] Third, Mill refers to pork as an instance of the dangers inherent in a law that limits liberty by invoking the protection of personal feelings (given the "repugnance" and "abhorrence" that Muslims feel when they see people eating pork).[5] By contrast, legislation on these issues in Israel was originally justified on grounds of national pride and culture rather than on preventing offense to religious sensibilities.

Pig-related legislation in Israel is an interesting instance of a basically secular legal system adopting a specific religious norm. The enforcement of religious norms is not particularly intriguing when religious law is also the law of the country. For instance, the import of pork is illegal in Saudi Arabia, where Islamic law is also state law.[6] The inclusion of specific religious rules in a secular legal system is of greater interest because of the need to reconcile these rules with such legal principles as freedom of religion with which they are in obvious tension. This inclusion is indeed absolutely precluded in a system such as the one prevailing in the United States, which upholds constitutional separation between religion and state in the form of a prohibition against the establishment of religion.

In principle, Israeli law is a secular system with few exceptions. In matters of marriage and divorce, it makes the law of the various religious communities binding on their individual members,[7] thereby preserving the approach of the British Mandate's legislation (after the end of World War I, the United Kingdom was granted a Mandate to control Palestine by the League of Nations). Seeking to avoid interference with the various communities inhabiting the Holy Land, British legislation stated: "Jurisdiction in matters of personal status shall be exercised . . . by the Courts of the religious communities."[8] At present, the main statute in this context regarding the Jewish population in Israel is the Rabbinical Courts Jurisdiction (Marriage and Divorce) Law of 1953, which states: "Matters of marriage and divorce of Jews in Israel, being nationals or residents of the State, shall be under the exclusive jurisdiction of rabbinical courts" (section 1), and "Marriages and divorces of Jews shall be performed in Israel in accordance with Jewish religious law" (section 2). Israel has also enacted several laws to accommodate the needs of observant Jews, like the Kosher Food for Soldiers Ordinance 1948, which dictates that Jewish dietary laws will be observed in IDF (Israel Defense Forces) kitchens.

Another law forbids the import of ritually prohibited meat (Meat and Meat Products Law, enacted in 1994). This law serves the interests of observant Jews because it makes kosher meat both accessible and relatively inexpensive, by limiting potential competition from cheap, imported nonkosher meat (although it also makes all meat more expensive).[9] This law was enacted under political pressure by the religious parties. These parties were opposing a Supreme Court ruling that had rendered invalid a government decision to postpone privatization of meat imports in order to prevent the import of nonkosher meat.[10] The government reached its decision after it became apparent that private importers, contrary to the policy that had guided concentrated government imports until then, would consider importing ritually prohibited meat. The purpose of the law was to give legal backing to the ban on imports of ritually prohibited meat.[11]

Note that, although these statutory prohibitions relate to ritually prohibited meat in general rather than only to pork, MK (Member of Knesset) Yehuda Gafni of the Yahadut ha-Torah ultra-Orthodox party described them in a Knesset debate as pig-related: "I wish to comment favorably on the late Prime Minister Yitzhak Rabin who, when in office, invested considerable effort in bringing about an amendment to the Basic Law that would preclude pork imports into this country."[12]

Contrary to some of the aforementioned examples of religious legislation, laws concerning pigs and pork-trading were not meant to serve the material interests of religious Jews, who will not consume ritually prohibited food whatever the Knesset legislation might state. These prohibitions were intended to reflect a cultural sense of the abhorrence of pigs that had evolved through the long history of Jewish persecution, first in the ancient Hellenistic world and then in Christian Europe. The ban was thus a legal norm intended to reflect a shared cultural characteristic rather than to merely enforce a particular religious doctrine. From the religious public's perspective as well, the motivation to introduce pig-related prohibitions derived mainly from an aspiration to make the traditional symbol system part of the evolving Israeli culture.

Why concentrate on the symbolism of the prohibition on pigs? First, this is one of the most powerful symbols of Jewish culture and practice. As detailed in chapter 2, abhorrence of pigs is a constitutive foundation of collective Jewish memory.[13]

Second, other dominant traditions that could also have made for interesting case studies were never enacted into law in Israel, and cannot be used to discuss the effects of culture on law. For instance, refraining from driving on the Day of Atonement (Yom Kippur) is a practice observed by an overwhelming majority of the Jewish population in Israel. Once a year, traffic stops and most of Israel's streets become pedestrian malls, except for emergency vehicles. No law, however, forbids driving on that day. Another commandment observed by a vast majority of Israeli Jews, even the non-religious, is the circumcision of boys, a practice that has singled out Jews throughout history and was sometimes used to identify them. This norm (naturally, if I may add) is not state law.

Third, some religious tenets that were enacted into law are not solely symbolic, but also entail significant economic implications as well. These tenets are therefore less suitable for discussion in the context of the present discussion, which focuses mainly on the cultural aspects of law, even though a clear-cut division between culture and its political and economic background is obviously a complex endeavor. For instance, the legal day of rest in Israel is the Sabbath, in accordance with Jewish tradition (with due exceptions for members of other religions).[14] The scope of the prohibition on labor and commerce on the day of rest has been marked by many controversies, as is true of other countries that have contended with their own "Sunday laws."[15] These disputes have obvious cultural implications, since the observance of the Sabbath has been a typical feature of Jewish life everywhere. In Israel, however, it also involves significant economic consequences. For instance, religious representatives who support legislation in this area are certainly motivated by their beliefs, but also by loyalty to their constituencies, including observant

merchants who suffer financial losses while their competitors sell on the
Sabbath—a day when many people have time for leisure and shopping.
As noted, dietary rules also involve considerable cost to the religious
public, due to their potential impact on prices. Kashrut laws have always
had significant economic implications. For instance, non-Jewish butchers in the Middle Ages engaged in a struggle against competing Jewish
butchers who would sell to non-Jews, at reduced prices, meat decreed
prohibited by ritual slaughterers, thereby undercutting their rivals.[16]
Admittedly, restrictions imposed on pig-breeding and on pork sales also
have economic consequences for those engaged in this industry. The
involvement of specific kibbutzim in this branch of the economy is a
background factor that cannot be completely dismissed when discussing their representatives' objection to legislation in this area.[17] Nevertheless, the economic importance of prohibitions concerning pigs is
definitely more limited, and therefore they serve as a better test-case for
analyzing the cultural dimension of law.

Indeed, Israel's legal system includes several other laws with defined
symbolic characteristics. These new laws, however, were enacted during
the rise of religious politics in the 1980s, and we still lack an appropriate
historical perspective of the debates that surrounded them. One example is the Festival of Matzot (Prohibition of Leaven) Law of 1986, which
forbids offering leavened bread for sale in Jewish areas during Passover.
By contrast, disputes over pig-related prohibitions have played a role
in Israeli law since the 1950s, allowing us to trace the changing attitudes
toward the pig symbol in the context of political and social developments.

My perspective concerning pig prohibitions in Israeli law touches on
law and culture in general, and on the symbolic function of legal norms
in particular. The cultural study of law shows that legal controversies
and legal reasoning often reflect underlying cultural perceptions.[18] This
book aims to expose the cultural perceptions that launched the legislation
on pig-breeding and pork trading, as well as those reflected in the ongoing public debates and the surrounding legal proceedings. The cultural
study of law is an especially suitable tool for analyzing these perceptions
because it focuses on communities.[19] More specifically, this book centers
on the implications of affirming through the legal system one of the chief
symbols of Jewish tradition—the prohibition on pigs. As Joseph Gusfield notes: "The fact of affirmation through acts of law and government

expresses the public worth of one set of norms, of one sub-culture vis-à-vis those of others. It demonstrates which cultures have legitimacy and public domination, and which do not."[20] At the same time, it has been argued that legislating symbols makes them less effective for the purpose of identifying their supporters as group members because, when backed by the force of law, symbols may also gain the respect of nonmembers.[21]

Similarities are evident between the controversies surrounding Israeli pig prohibitions and litigation associated with religious symbols in other countries regarding religiously motivated activities such as placing crosses in public places,[22] or acts of desecrating religious symbols.[23] In all these examples, disputes have overstepped narrow religious boundaries to reflect emotions and feelings of belonging. Clifford Geertz explained the significance of religious symbols:

> But meanings can only be "stored" in symbols: a cross, a crescent, or a feathered serpent. Such religious symbols, dramatized in rituals or related in myths, are felt somehow to sum up, for those for whom they are resonant, what is known about the way the world is, the quality of the emotional life it supports, and the way one ought to behave while in it. Sacred symbols thus relate an ontology and cosmology to an aesthetics and a morality: Their peculiar power comes from their presumed ability to identify fact with value at the most fundamental level, to give to what is otherwise merely actual, a comprehensive normative import. The number of such synthesizing symbols is limited in any culture, and though we might think that a people could construct a wholly autonomous value system independent of any metaphysical referent, an ethics without ontology, we do not in fact seem to have found such a people.[24]

Obviously, the notion of pig prohibitions as symbolic has no parallel in other Western legal systems, where legal controversies related to pigs were usually confined to tort law, veterinary inspection, or breeding regulations concerning the use of pigs in households, farm life, and industry. In these systems, pigs are part of the ordinary course of life. Accordingly, there are historic records dealing with everyday issues such as pigs as property or the damage caused by pigs.[25] During the Middle Ages, and even later, pigs were brought to criminal trials and sentenced for violence against people.[26] In English common law precedents, pigs are discussed mainly as sources of nuisance.[27] In fact, the best known description of "nuisance" in American legal annals relates to pigs. According to Justice Sutherland, a nuisance is "merely a right thing in the wrong place—like a pig in the parlor instead of the barnyard."[28] As urban life developed, conflicts developed around initiatives to prohibit pig-breeding in cities. The endeavor to keep pigs off New York's streets was the topic of Hendrik Hartog's famous article entitled "Pigs and Positivism."[29] On the other hand, several American cities became important centers for the "hog industry." In fact, the meat-packing industry began with pork, and Chicago's economic growth during the nineteenth century has been described as owing much to pigs.[30] Pig-breeding is now concentrated in agricultural areas, where it is considered both an important industry and a source of environmental problems.[31]

Even in Western Christian culture, however, and despite their economic impact, pigs have usually been associated with uncleanliness and bad character. The pig has tended to function as a symbol of repulsive personal conduct or characteristics: "Pigs seem to have borne the brunt of our rage, fear, affection and desire for the 'low.'"[32] In England, sweet or agreeable images of pigs began to appear in popular culture only toward the end of the nineteenth century, when pigs disappeared from the vicinity of people's homes.[33]

This change of image, however, did not completely erase the basic fund of imagery connected with the term "pig." Up to this day, the term "pig" is used mainly with negative connotations: "chauvinist pig," "capitalist pig," "pork barrel," and so forth. George Orwell's *Animal Farm* (1946), where pigs are the protagonists, describes them as base creatures lacking in conscience.[34] Contemporary British playwright John Arden called his play dealing with the lives of people on the fringes of society *Live Like Pigs*. The Beatles' *White Album* has a song by George Harrison entitled "Piggies" (first released in 1968), in which the last stanza goes: "Everywhere there's lots of piggies / Living piggy lives / You can see them out for dinner / With their piggy wives / Clutching forks and knives to eat their bacon."

The pig is also an abomination to Muslims, and the Koran expressly forbids the consumption of its flesh: "You are forbidden to eat carrion; blood; pig's meat; any animal over which any name other than God's has been invoked"[35]; "He has forbidden you only these things: carrion, blood, pig's meat, and animals over which any name other than God's has been invoked."[36] When Islamic countries enact prohibitions against pigs, however, they are enforcing religious doctrine rather than a norm known for its symbolic importance, as the national prohibition against alcohol in the United States was inspired by religious motivations.[37]

One valid equivalent to the Israeli situation could be the prohibitions on the slaughter of cattle in Indian law. Article 48 of the Constitution of India, considered one of the Constitution's Directive Principles of State Policy, requires the adoption of measures prohibiting the slaughter of cattle: "The State shall endeavor to organize agriculture and animal husbandry on modern and scientific lines and shall, in particular, take steps for preserving and improving the breeds, and prohibiting the slaughter of cows and calves and other milk and draught cattle." This article, inspired by the Hindu tradition that views cows as holy, was based on strong popular sentiment. The need to ban the slaughter of cows was debated in the Indian Constituent Assembly and explained by its supporters as not only a religious matter but also as a cultural and economic interest.[38]

Since India adopted the constitution, questions about the ban on slaughtering cattle have been raised on several occasions. In practice, laws prohibiting the slaughter of cattle have been gradually introduced in many Indian states. Given the protection of fundamental freedoms ensured by the Indian constitution, these laws have been attacked in the Indian Supreme Court.

The basic precedent in this matter was laid down in *Mohd. Hanif Quareshi v. Bihar,*[39] following a petition filed by Muslim butchers. The petitioners argued that the prohibition on slaughtering cattle infringed on their freedom of occupation as well as their religious custom of sacrificing cattle. The court held that the state is allowed to restrict fundamental freedoms in order to uphold the Directive Principles of State Policy. A restriction, however, must be reasonable. Insofar as this petition was based on the right to freedom of religion, however, it was rejected outright due to the lack of any evidence about cattle slaughtering being a religious duty in Islam. As for the infringement of freedom of occupation, the court found that the prohibiting legislation can be considered reasonable if it addresses cattle capable of yielding milk, or being used for breeding or for work. Yet, and as an exception to this limitation, the court did uphold the total prohibition on the slaughter of cows, in contrast to other other forms of cattle. In practice, therefore, judicial review introduced only a limited change in the scope of the prohibition.

Later cases approved the same principles with regard to legislative amendments that tried to circumvent even the limited scope of the legal slaughter of cattle recognized by the court. In these cases as well, the court upheld its main rulings on the constitutionality of legislation aimed at imposing significant restrictions on the slaughter of cattle.[40] In practice, this legal state of affairs encourages the illegal smuggling of cattle into states that do not prohibit slaughter or to illegal secret slaughterhouses, usually under conditions that inflict terrible suffering on the animals.[41]

Just as this ban on cattle slaughter reflects social norms and tensions in India, so do prohibitions on pig-breeding and pork-trading offer an interesting perspective for evaluating cultural and social processes in Israel. Israeli circumstances regarding pig-related laws, however, pose additional problems.

First, whereas the decision to place legal limitations on the slaughter of cattle was debated by the Constitutional Assembly of India and written into that country's constitution, initiatives to introduce traditional Jewish prohibitions on pork into Israeli law were confined to the legislative and administrative spheres. Hence, when Israeli courts are asked to review these initiatives, they lack a specific constitutional norm to guide them on this matter. Furthermore, pig prohibitions began to evolve in Israeli law before the Israeli system acknowledged constitutional limitations on legislative infringements of human rights. The enactment of basic laws on human rights in 1992 changed the constitutional background against which these prohibitions are now evaluated.[42]

Second, and this is another significant difference, whereas legal attacks on the cattle-slaughter ban in India came from Muslims, conflicts around the pig prohibitions in Israel emerged within the Jewish public. The chronicle of intensifying attacks against pig prohibitions in Israeli law, therefore, is one of changing values and conceptions within Israel's Jewish society rather than one of conflict between rival ethnic and religious communities. Muslim society in Israel accepts the legislation on pigs and pork, which in fact hardly affects it. Due to the high levels of traditionalism in this society, Israeli Muslims tend to abstain from pork in any event, regardless of the law.

This book, then, specifically traces changes in the perception of pig-related legal prohibitions in Israeli law, arguing that they can be seen as a microcosm of changes in Israeli society in general. Public and legal activities involved in the application and enforcement of pig-related norms were unusually intense during the 1950s and 1960s, abandoned in the 1970s, and resumed in full force during the 1990s—a renewed concern that may be explained in various ways.

One explanation is primarily sociological and claims that pig-related prohibitions were consensual for a few decades and reflected the dietary customs of Israeli Jews, including those who did not care to follow dietary laws in general but still abstained from the consumption of pork due to its symbolic status in Jewish culture. These prohibitions reemerged as a practical issue in the 1990s because of dietary practices characterizing immigrants from the former USSR and the growing detachment of the Israeli secular public from traditional Jewish culture.

A second explanation focuses on legal developments and points to constitutional changes in Israeli law during the 1990s with the legislation of new basic laws on human rights. This constitutional transformation allowed for judicial review of pig-related prohibitions from a constitutional perspective. Therefore, fifty years after the original debates, the constitutional Basic Laws have forced a rethinking of the prohibitions, exposing deep and fundamental changes in Israeli society.

A third explanation focuses on the political background of the legislation. Israeli politics in the 1950s was based on compromises between the religious and the secular, despite harsh disagreements. By contrast, the 1990s fostered the emergence of small parties promoting a religious or anti-religious agenda as an important feature of their political platform.

A fourth explanation worth considering hinges on a change in the hegemonic public view of the importance of individual rights and liberties. Whereas the 1950s were characterized by a high level of willingness to restrict individual rights for the sake of the communal good, Israelis today are inclined to oppose legislation that limits individual freedoms.

In sum, this book traces the rise and relative decline of pig-related prohibitions in Israel. The early proposals introduced in the 1950s to impose legal prohibitions on pig-breeding and the sale of pork came mainly from religious parties, but were backed, and to some extent encouraged, by secular representatives who had been reared on the historical Jewish taboo against pigs and shared the aspiration to develop a national culture, including a legal culture, based on Jewish heritage.

Over the years, the symbolism of pig-related prohibitions has progressively eroded within the secular Jewish public. As a result, prohibitions enacted in the 1950s and 1960s have come to be perceived by the legal system as reflecting only religious interests, and were interpreted and implemented accordingly. This book follows the course of this process, beginning with an account of pig prohibitions in Jewish history and culture. It focuses on their translation into legal arrangements in a Jewish political community, from the time of the British Mandate and up to the present ongoing public debate.

On 14 June 2004, the Supreme Court of Israel issued a long-awaited ruling on the legality of municipal bylaws banning pork sales.[43] The decision and the controversies around it, as discussed in chapter 8, indicate that the peculiar regulation of pig-breeding and pork-trading in Israeli law is not only an interesting chapter in Israeli legal history, but is also a living dilemma relevant to the understanding of current processes in Israeli society and politics. The pig controversy can be seen as a microcosm of larger developments, including the growing gap between secular and religious Jews and, chiefly, the crystallization of a new identity for secular Jews in Israel, one that is detached from traditional Jewish culture and draws its main inspiration from universal values.

CHAPTER 2

Pig Prohibitions in Jewish and Israeli Culture

RECOGNIZING THE UNIQUE STATUS of pig-related prohibitions in Jewish culture (mainly against breeding them and eating their flesh) is an essential starting point for any discussion of modern legislation said to be inspired by them. Biblical law only prohibits eating the flesh of pigs, but later sources include more extensive prohibitions on activities related to pigs, with special emphasis on breeding them. This chapter describes how the prohibitions evolved from a set of religious rules into a religious as well as a national symbol.[1] This description will not engage in a full or systematic discussion of the religious rulings on this matter, but will instead point to the significance of pig prohibitions and their symbolic status over time. The perception of pig prohibitions as a central characteristic of Jewish identity was initially developed by outsiders. In time, however, Jews adopted this view as well, and these proscriptions became a "key symbol" in Jewish culture.[2] They became associated with significant memories and a taboo developed around them.

Although the Torah includes many dietary prohibitions, those concerning pigs tower above all others in Jewish religious tradition and Jewish national history. Several anthropological and theological hypotheses have attempted to shed light on the reasons for the abhorrence of pigs in Jewish culture. In *Purity and Danger*, anthropologist Mary Douglas argues that biblical culture associated holiness with "completeness" and rejected as impure any apparent exception to the category to which it prima facie belonged. According to this explanation, the pig was rejected because it "deviated" from the category of the cloven-hoofed ruminants that were the typical farm animals of the time. Since the pig was incomplete, as it was not a ruminant, it could not serve as a metaphor for complete godliness.[3] From a different perspective, anthropologist Marvin Harris offers an ecological explanation, arguing that pig-breeding was expensive and wasteful in Middle Eastern conditions. Pigs need shade, an area in which to wallow in mud or water, and food much richer than the grass provided to animals that chew the cud.[4]

Other theories, originating in the study of religion, explained the rejection of the pig on the basis of its ritual status in other religious traditions prevalent in the area. James Frazer argued that the ban on the consumption of certain animals, including that on pigs, reflects a tradition that had perceived them as holy and attempted to obtain their protection.[5] Another theory states that the prohibition on pigs was aimed at differentiating the Israelites from their neighbors. More specifically, it was argued that the pig prohibition was linked to the attempt to eradicate the cult of the goddess Asherah, in which pigs were used as animals for sacrifice.[6]

Archaeologists have relied on this prohibition for classifying as non-Jewish materials unearthed in excavations that contain the remains of pigs. In a book discussing the relations between the biblical text and archaeological research, Israel Finkelstein and Neil Silberman described significant portions of biblical history as unfounded, but admitted there was strong evidence that the ancient Israelites had refrained from breeding pigs or consuming their flesh. They state: "Half a millennium before the composition of the biblical text, with its detailed laws and dietary regulations, the Israelites chose—for reasons that are not entirely clear—not to eat pork. When modern Jews do the same, they are continuing the oldest archaeologically attested cultural practice of the people of Israel."[7] Others have argued that ascribing to Jews excavation remnants without pig traces uncritically assumes that the taboo surrounding pigs dates far back, whereas evidence indicates that prohibitions on pigs acquired special meaning only later.[8] In any event, as regards later periods in which the Jews' loathing of pigs was already indisputable, any evidence of pig-breeding has become a sign that the remains date to the Roman era or to the time of the Christian Crusades.[9]

In Jewish sources, the pig is singled out from the beginning. Rather than letting the prohibition on pigs be inferred from the fact that they do not fit the criteria of ritual purity, Leviticus explicitly mentions the pig as a forbidden animal: "And the swine, though he divide the hoof, and be cloven-footed, yet he chews not the cud; he is unclean to you. Of their flesh shall you not eat, and their carcass shall you not touch; they are unclean to you" (Leviticus 11:7–8). The same rule is reiterated in Deuteronomy 14:8: "And the swine, because it divides the hoof, yet chews not the cud, is unclean unto you: you shall not eat of their meat, nor touch their carcasses." The pig is the only cloven-hoofed animal whose meat is forbidden: "There is no other beast whose hoof is cloven and is unclean, save the swine. Therefore, the Scriptures discussed it in detail."[10]

In various exegeses, the pig appears as a Janus-like character. In other words, it is an animal that purports to be pure because of its cloven hoof and yet is not, and is hence a symbol of guile and duplicity, usually describing fraudulent oppressors: "When the swine is lying down it puts out its hoofs, as if to say, 'I am clean'; so does this wicked state rob and oppress, yet pretends to be executing justice."[11] And elsewhere: "Like the boar which displays its cloven hoof, as if to say, 'I am clean,' so wicked Esau displays himself so openly on the seats of justice that the legal tricks whereby he robs, steals, and plunders appear to be just proceedings."[12]

The pig is often singled out as a symbol of abomination. It is the ultimate profanity.[13] Isaiah prophesied that those "eating swine's flesh, and the detestable thing, and the mouse, shall perish together"[14] and the Book of Proverbs uses the metaphor "like a jewel of gold in a swine's snout."[15] The sages made frequent references to the pig's impurity,[16] and Maimonides offers a graphic description: "The major reason why the Law abhors it is its being very dirty and feeding on dirty things. . . . Now if swine were used for food, market places and even houses would have been dirtier than latrines."[17]

The all-encompassing prohibition dates back as far as the Mishnah: "Swine may not be bred in any place whatsoever," unlike other animals, about which it is said they cannot be bred in Jerusalem or in the Land of Israel.[18] Likewise, the codex of halakhic law known as *Shulhan Arukh,* states: "Jews are forbidden to breed swine in any place, even for the purpose of greasing skins, and needless to say even for commerce."[19] In this context, the Talmud cites a story linking the prohibition on swine to a national catastrophe, when the struggle between Hyrkanus and his brother Aristobulus paved the way for a Roman siege on Jerusalem.

According to this story, a pig which was brought to the beleaguered people instead of the sacrificial sheep, dug its hooves in the walls of the city: "On the morrow they let down denarii in a basket, and [the Romans] hauled up a pig. When it reached half way up the wall it stuck its claws [into the wall], and the land of Israel was shaken for a distance of four hundred parasangs. At that time they declared: 'Cursed be a man who rears pigs.'"[20]

Nations that enslaved Israel have also been likened to swine in various Jewish sources: "'The boar out of the wood doth ravage it' (Psalms 80:14) refers to the Roman Empire. For when the people of Israel do not do the will of God, the nations appear to them like the boar out of the wood."[21] Many refer to the pig as "the other thing"[22] and avoid any specific mention of it. A similar avoidance pattern was adopted relative to various religious deviations, such as speaking of "the other" when referring to Elisha Ben-Avuyiah, a sage who became an apostate.

Both halakhic and non-Jewish sources show that the pork prohibition was a well known, highly publicized practice, and that other nations exploited it to oppress the Jews. The Talmud places this prohibition in the category of commandments that cannot be rationally deduced and for which the reasons are unclear, and which have been used by the nations of the world to vilify Jews.[23]

Engraved on the collective memory of the Jews is the consciousness that oppressors have throughout history used the pig to inflict pain and humiliation on them. The decrees issued by Antiochus Epiphanes compelled Jews to sacrifice pigs and eat their flesh: "to build illicit altars and illicit temples and idolatrous shrines, to sacrifice swine and ritually unfit animals."[24] A well-known account of these events is provided by Josephus Flavius: "And when the king had built an idol altar upon God's altar, he slew swine upon it, and so offered a sacrifice neither according to the law, nor the Jewish religious worship in that country. He also compelled them to forsake the worship which they paid their own God, and to adore those whom he took to be gods; and made them build temples, and raise idol altars in every city and village, and offer swine upon them every day."[25]

The ensuing Maccabean revolt is particularly well known due to its association with the Hanukkah festival that celebrates it. For centuries, stories of the self-sacrifice and devotion of those who refused to abide by these edicts have served as educational examples. The foremost legend is that of Hannah and her seven sons, who were martyred for their refusal to eat pork: "At that time seven brothers, too, with their mother were arrested, and the king tortured them with whips and thongs in an effort to force them to partake of pork contrary to the prohibitions of the Torah."[26] In a later book, Mary Douglas considered these experiences a turning point that bestowed upon the pig its special symbolic status in Jewish culture. Referring to the persecutions of Antiochus, she states: "So it was he, by his action, who forced into prominence the rule concerning pork as the critical symbol of group allegiance."[27]

The humiliation of Jews in connection with their refusal to eat pork is known also from the Roman era and after the spread of Christianity throughout Europe. The Jews' abstention from pork was a source of wonder to the Romans, since Greco-Roman societies were relatively free from taboos and regulations regarding food. Pork was also a Roman favorite, as widely reflected in Roman literature,[28] and Romans viewed the Jews' abstention from pork as a further instance of their troubling distinctiveness. In this context, Josephus Flavius remarks about the Roman attitude: "He accuses us for sacrificing animals, and for abstaining from swine's flesh."[29] The Roman historian Tacitus criticized Jewish practices and explained their abstention from pork by referring to a baseless story concerning a plague of leprosy that had afflicted the people of Israel. "Pigs are subject to leprosy, the foul plague with which they too were once infected; so they abstain from pork in memory of their misfortune."[30] Rabbi Isaac Herzog, in an article relating to the prohibition against pig-breeding and the "curse" on those who do so, also refers to the historical aspect: "We have found that ancient nations would always scorn Jews and mock them for refraining from the meat of that animal. When the Jewish delegation from Egypt led by the great philosopher Philo of Alexandria appeared before that foolish and evil Caesar, Gaius Caligula, he berated them in a manner at once clownish and stinging: "Jews, why do you not eat pork?" When the wicked Greeks, and with them their evil collaborators from our own camp, forced Jews to defile their souls with forbidden foods—they began with swine flesh!"[31]

Nor could Jewish collective memory disregard the fact that a wild boar, whose image resembled a pig, had been the insignia of the Tenth Roman Legion stationed in Jerusalem during the Bar-Kokhba revolt. In her historical novel *Memoirs of Hadrian,* Marguerite Yourcenar describes the Jews' sensitivity to the use of this emblem: "Jewish affairs were going from bad to worse. Construction was nearing completion in Jerusalem, in spite of the violent opposition of Zealot groups. A certain number of errors had been committed, not irreparable in themselves but immediately seized upon by fomenters of trouble for their own advantage. The Tenth Legion Fretensis has a wild boar for its emblem; when its standard was placed at the city gates, as is the custom, the populace, unused to painted or sculptured images . . . mistook that symbol for a swine, the meat of which is forbidden them, and read into that insignificant affair an affront to the customs of Israel."[32]

The significance of the Jews' loathing of pigs persisted in Christian Europe, where it assumed even greater significance, as Claudine Fabre-Vassas describes in *The Singular Beast,* dealing with the pig's special status in anti-Semitic tradition.[33] In the New Testament, pigs still appear in negative contexts. Jesus warns his believers: "Do not cast your pearls before swine" (Matthew 7:6). He also drives demons out of possessed men into a herd of swine (Matthew 8:28–34). During the period of early Christianity, however, the consumption of pork was already recommended as a form of proclaiming antagonism to Judaism.[34] Later, it also became an important aspect of agricultural economy and culture. According to Fabre-Vassas, "The pig incarnates a way of life, it is as much a sign of good domestic management as of Christian belonging; one never goes without the other."[35] The Jews, on the other hand, rejected the pig and again emerged as different and suspect. In the traditional carnivals of Christian Europe, the pig was a symbol of the carnival's pleasures, and the Jew was ridiculed as a joy-killer and as the enemy of the pervading spirit of levity associated with the event.[36]

In the Middle Ages, a myth prevalent in Europe stated that Jews refrained from eating pigs because they were themselves pigs and would be committing cannibalism had they eaten their flesh. The suspicion which followed was that Jews ate Christian children as a substitute for pork.[37] In addition, Jews were despised for the traits they were believed to share with pigs—carnality and diseases of the flesh.

The pictorial translation of the identification of Jews with pigs was the German *Judensau,* a depiction of a large sow nursing Jews.[38] A famous example was the painting on the bridge tower in Frankfurt, depicting a "typical" Jew licking a sow's behind. A reference to this degrading drawing appears in Goethe's work *Dichtung und Warheit* ("Images and Truth").[39] In the legal sphere, the similarity between Jews and pigs was expressed by the use of an upside hanging as a form of sentencing.[40] In addition, legal procedures in some regions of medieval Germany required Jews to stand on the fresh skin of a sow when taking an oath.[41]

In fifteenth-century Spain and Portugal, "New Christians" (Jews who had converted to Christianity under duress but who nonetheless retained secret ties with Judaism), were most strict about avoiding pork, both because it was ritually prohibited and because of its strong Christian associations.[42] Their abstention was naturally noticed, and the eating of pork was later used as a criterion for proving true allegiance to Christianity in general, and specifically at Inquisition trials.[43] Interestingly, hostile neighbors sometimes referred to these new converts as Marranos, a word believed to have a semantic tie to the Spanish word for pig.[44]

Anti-Semitic persecution was not confined to the Jews' abstention from pork, and was sometimes directed at other aspects of the dietary laws as with the 1930's decrees in Poland that prohibited ritual slaughter by Jews.[45] Generally, however, persecution based on the refusal to eat pork was far more common and is more deeply etched upon the Jewish collective memory.

Unswerving adherence to the taboo associated with pigs is also evident in the customs and folklore that were prevalent among traditional Eastern European Jews until the Second World War. Mottel, the protagonist of a famous work by Scholem Aleichem depicting life in a small village at the turn of the twentieth century, often speaks of pigs with hatred and revulsion.[46] In Zalman Shneur's *The People of Shklov,* a work devoted to Jewish life in the author's hometown in White Russia (or Belarus), two chapters deal with a pastime that was common among Jewish boys: hitting the pigs their Gentile neighbors had let loose outside.[47] Shneur writes: "Over many generations, Jews saw pigs as the concretization of the ultimate other, of all evil and impurity."[48] He then refers to the collective memory of Antiochus and Hadrian and explains: "Mother and father, may they be blessed, bear in their hearts the legacy of pig hatred, and they, the loyal sons, vent it in the public space."[49] When the

poet Uri Tsvi Greenberg accused God of forsaking the Jewish people during the Holocaust, he challenged God to make Gentiles his new chosen
people, and "to remember to bless their pigs, horses and poultry."[50]

Another recurring theme in both Jewish and non-Jewish literature is
a sense of guilt among those who broke the taboo. In *The Periodic Table,*
Primo Levi describes his father guiltily buying and eating ham: "My
father was l'ingegne ("the engineer"), with his pockets always bulging
with books and known to all the pork butchers because he checked with
his logarithmic ruler the multiplication for the prosciutto purchase. Not
that he purchased this last item with carefree heart: superstitious rather
than religious, he felt ill at ease at breaking the kashrut rules, but he liked
prosciutto so much that, faced by the temptation of a shop window, he
yielded every time, sighing, cursing under his breath, and watching me
out of the corner of his eye, as if he feared my judgment or hoped for my
complicity."[51]

In *Auntie Esther,* a novel by Arieh Eckstein about a Jewish orphan living in Poland on the eve of the Second World War, the child Arieh Leib is
faced with the temptation of pork on a day when he is extremely hungry:
"I remembered what my mother had said . . . If you eat pork you become
like a pig and then you start hitting the Jews." His dilemma is resolved by
a Gentile companion covering his head with a coat, intending to hide him
from God. He then adds: "I swallowed the sausage in such a hurry that
God had no time to see."[52] The dilemma resurfaces when the protagonist
and a group of hungry boys are given soup for lunch at a Polish government school. "Moishele did not want to eat soup and claimed that Jews
are forbidden to eat pork, but Benny said it was beef. I quickly agreed with
Benny." Although he is a child of a broken family that had forsaken the
traditional model of Jewish life, the incident evokes for the protagonist
the memory of his mother, who had warned him against eating pork.[53]

Contemporary American Jewish poet Allen Grossman refers to pigs as
the ultimate symbol of forgetting Jerusalem, thus associating them with
the betrayal of Jewish tradition:

> Pigs do not remember Jerusalem. I hunger
> I have a hunger, as deep as the sea,
> to forget Jerusalem. I commit my right
> hand (all its famous cunning) to oblivion.[54]

Awareness of the Jewish aversion to pigs resonates also in the writings of non-Jews. Robert Southey addresses his poem "The Pig" to "Jacob," trying to persuade him not to dislike it.[55] In his description of a restaurant in *Down and Out in Paris and London,* George Orwell notes: "In the corner by himself a Jew, muzzle down in the plate, was guiltily wolfing bacon."[56]

For many years, avoiding pork was also part of the mores of secular Israeli society, where many continued to abstain from it even when they failed to comply with other dietary prohibitions.[57] Berl Katsanelson, a secular Zionist leader of the Labor movement, persistently condemned pig-breeding and pork-consumption when invoking national ideals.[58] As early as 1934, he decried pork-trading in a political address, saying: "I am not afraid to say that I view some elements in our religious tradition as crucial national assets, and in no way do I regard this as a flaw in my socialist ideals . . . Thus, I can conceive that a nation whose liberation struggle in the Hasmonean era was linked to its refusal to eat pork, a nation that endured no little suffering during two thousand years because it did not submit to those trying to force it to do so, would honor this ancient practice by forbidding its sale within the precincts of the Jewish city."[59]

He reiterated this position with no less fervor and pathos a decade later in a feature entitled "How Far Does the Love of Israel Extend." In this article, which carried the meaningful subtitle "In the Wake of a Hanukkah Controversy," Katsanelson condemned some of his colleagues for attacking the publication of a circular against pig-breeders: "How will we be able to teach our children, sensibly but also passionately, about the devotion of old Elazar and about Hannah and her seven sons, if the very issue for which they gave their lives has no hold on our way of life? And how will we teach our children, with awe and admiration, about our young heroes, the cantonists,[60] who suffered hunger and blows and refrained from eating pork, if the whole matter is nothing more than an obsolete prejudice?"[61]

Katsanelson's stance on this matter was consistent with his attitude toward other issues of mixed religious and national character. In another well-known article, he formulates his attitude toward the Ninth of Av (the date in the Jewish calendar commemorating the destruction of the Temple in Jerusalem) as a day of national mourning, in response to a decision to run a summer camp on that date.[62] In her biography of Katsanelson, Anita Shapira describes his approach: "He did observe several Jewish practices, but without any connection to the 613 commandments. He strictly observed the Ninth of Av as a day of mourning—on national grounds. He carefully abstained from eating pork because Jews had died in the sanctification of God's name only to avoid eating it. He did not keep the dietary laws nor did he go to synagogue, even on the High Holidays."[63]

When the controversy over the legislation restricting the breeding and sale of pigs was at its height in the 1950s, Natan Alterman supported the restrictions. Alterman was a celebrated engagé poet associated with Mapai, then the ruling party, and was the writer of "The Seventh Column," an influential and widely read weekly press feature (in verse) on current events. In one of his columns, he described his reservations about overly zealous opposition to religious coercion on this matter:

> It seems that in the heart of every nation—and sevenfold in this one
> and in this land that was its cradle—
> Memories of revulsion etched in by sword and whip,
> are now engraved as an unconscious instinct.
> Even those unable to discern a cloven-hoofed one from
> one that is not, will sense this:
> When a Jewish nation in Israel makes the pig a sine qua non,
> its history shudders.
> Religious zealots and secularists then appear, as it were, to
> complement each other . . . Slightly odd perhaps, but hard to ignore.
> On one side religion, and on the other—a bit of ancient geography
> and a bit of long history . . .
> And the pig, right in the middle, is a little uncomfortable.[64]

This column was written in 1956. In another column, written in 1957, the poet urges a moderate approach to the religious-secular conflict in Israel, and again resorts to the example of pig prohibition: "Despite certain limitations, the secular public is presently living a full life, and even a natural freethinker may not miss the additional freedom of pig-breeding."[65]

The special attitude toward eating pork is also reflected in the once widespread custom of refraining from uttering the word "pork" even among those who did not abstain from it. Restaurants that offered pork dishes usually referred to them euphemistically as "white meat."[66] An attempt was also made to ignore, as far as possible, the very existence of pigs. A children's book by Erich Kastner originally entitled *The Pig at the Barber* (*Das Schwein Beim Friseur*), was translated into Hebrew as *The Goat at the Barber,*[67] changing also the original illustrations. Many years later, in the Israeli branch of Toys "R" Us, a children's animal farm set was sold to the public without any pigs, which the importer had removed.[68] Indeed, one of the lyric depictions of Israel by poet David Avidan reads: "A land whose cattle are sheep, whose sheep are cattle, and whose pigs are outlawed."[69]

When Rabbi Eliezer Shakh, acknowledged at the time as the spiritual leader of ultra-Orthodox Jews in Israel, embarked on a sweeping attack on the kibbutzim for forsaking tradition, he chose to emphasize that they were "rabbit and swine breeders": "I want to speak without fear. If today there are people living in kibbutzim who do not know what is the Day of Atonement, what is the Sabbath, what is a ritual bath, who have no idea about Judaism, who breed rabbits and swine—do they have any connection with their ancestors?!"[70]

In the early 1990s, the Tel Aviv Cameri Theater staged *Fleischer,* a play dealing with the struggle between Orthodox and secularists in Israeli society.[71] The protagonist is a man called Fleischer, the owner of a non-kosher butcher shop. Instead of "merely" nonkosher meat, Fleischer loves pork, which invariably emerges as the quintessential nonkosher food. In Scene Two, Fleischer tells Bertha, his wife: "Heat up some of the pork cutlets you made for lunch." In Scene Three, when Bertha learns that all the new residents in the nearby housing estate are Orthodox Jews, she says to her husband: "Now, you listen to me, we no longer sell ham," and later: "You can eat your ham at the back." In Scene Six, the couple's retarded son says: "I want my roll with ham and cheese." Yigal Tomarkin, a renowned sculptor known for his hard-line anti-religious views, created a work which presented a pig's head with Jewish ritual objects.[72]

Religious and cultural sources, as well as historical documents, seem to leave no doubt as to the significance of pig prohibition in Jewish civilization and culture, which has only intensified though the ages to attain mythological proportions. Although its religious aspect was always in the background, the prohibition has acquired an independent significance that is also evident in modern and secular Hebrew literature.

Due to its early origins, the prohibition is an inherent feature of their culture for Jews who have immigrated to Israel from various countries—Ashkenazi Jews (originating from European countries) and Mizrachi Jews (mainly from Arab countries in the Middle East). The Biblical and Talmudic prohibitions on pigs, as well as the Hanukkah festival lore, preceded the division of the Jewish people into the Ashkenazi and Mizrachi versions of tradition. Whereas European Jews were more exposed to persecutions associated with pigs, Mizrachi Jews lived among Muslims and were therefore socialized into a surrounding culture that abhorred pigs. When the public debate concerning the introduction of pig prohibitions into Israeli law began, support for it was indeed forthcoming from both Mizrachi and Ashkenazi politicians.

Relying on the deep roots of the pig symbol in Jewish culture, in both its religious and secular forms, the following discussion will trace the patterns and controversies marking the incorporation of pig prohibitions into Israeli law.

CHAPTER 3

Toward Independence

The British Mandate in the 1930s and 1940s

ISRAELI LAW RESTS on the foundations of the legal system instituted
during the British rule in Palestine between 1917 and 1948. The
establishment of the State of Israel, therefore, does not necessarily
mark a turning point in the periodization of Israeli law, because some
legal processes began during the Mandate and continued after the creation of the State.[1] Limiting the time frame to the period after the creation of Israel would be justified in the present context, since legislation
aimed at enforcing pig-related prohibitions began mainly after 1948.
Analysis of several earlier developments, however, may serve to shed light
on these later initiatives.

During the years of the British Mandate, attempts to develop a voluntary national legal system, independent of colonial state law, proved
unsuccessful.[2] The focus of the current discussion, therefore, is on the
pertaining British law, on which Jewish impact was minimal: "The issue
of religion and its place in the political system did not assume high operative significance in the period of the *Yishuv,* since the absence of sovereignty relieved Zionism and the organized *Yishuv* of the need to reach
decisions on most of the problems connected with the social role of religion ... The absence of a sovereign political framework meant, therefore,
that the ideological conflicts over the status of religion on the fundamental level were expressed only partially on the operative level."[3]

Some initiatives by the British authorities, such as the establishment
of the Chief Rabbinate,[4] did have an impact on the legal status of the
Jewish religion in Palestine. The scope of the issues covered by these

27

initiatives, however, was limited in comparison to the full regulation of
the relationship between state and religion in an independent state. Specifically concerning the "pig issue," the absence of legal initiatives reflected
the lack of any genuine interest in the matter on the part of the British
authorities, as well as the relatively negligible levels of pork consumption
among Jews due to cultural and historical reasons. Imposing religion-
based restrictions such as a ban on pork-trading would probably have
failed the legal test as well, because the provisions of the Mandate on Palestine guaranteed a series of liberties to all residents, including freedom of
religion and conscience. For instance, a Tel Aviv bylaw prohibiting the
opening of shops on the Sabbath was revoked in the 1920s[5] because it dis-
criminated between different communities by not applying to Muslims
or Christians. Pig-related legislation would have created a similar problem. To make such a distinction between members of different religions
on this count could have been invalidated as discriminatory, whereas a
general prohibition would have contravened the obligation to guarantee
freedom of religion and conscience.[6]

Despite the traditional aversion to pigs, data from the Mandate period
point to a gradual albeit modest increase in the consumption of nonkosher meat among the Jewish population, including pork. Records from
the official gazette of Palestine during the Mandate time attest to the
existence of pork-trading.[7] In addition, there are sources indicating that
some Jews in urban areas ate pork, even before the establishment of the
state. Haim Broide, who implemented the pig-related prohibitions enacted in the 1950s as the then-manager of the markets division of the Tel
Aviv municipal sanitation department, describes these changes in his
memoirs: "Already during the Mandate, several years before the violent
outbreaks of 1929 and in the early years of the Third Aliyah, the German
colony of Sarona was a pork supplier. Covertly, in wrapped packages, the
meat was carried through the streets of the city on a donkey and delivered to the homes of regular patrons. All was arranged clandestinely and
in disguise, because of the shame. R. Jonah Hochman of the Chief Rabbinate, together with other volunteers, led a campaign against the people of German Sarona. The war took various forms, and sometimes ended
with kerosene being poured on the meat, which was supplied to the city
in limited quantities."[8] Pork-trading later spread to city shops. Broide
identifies the man responsible for breaking through this line of defense:

"The first breach Jews made in this wall was the work of one Max Cohen, owner of a deli in Eliezer Ben-Yehuda Street, who brought in pork and sold it openly."[9] Correspondence with the Jewish Agency from 1938 reveals an initiative to move an industry of pig-hair products from Poland to Palestine. The Jewish Agency was asked to assist in getting immigration certificates to the Polish Jews involved with this initiative.[10]

In 1944, Tel Aviv council member David Tsvi Pinkas raised a motion concerning the transportation of pork within city limits. He was informed that the matter would be brought before the High Commissioner.[11] As Broide emphasizes in his memoirs, however, the struggle against pork-trading in Tel Aviv during the Mandate had no legal basis. Referring to the first shop that sold pork in Tel Aviv he writes: "Barring a law, and while under British rule, the Rabbinate only used pickets carrying placards against it."[12] The records of the Chief Rabbinate reveal that, in addition to the activities of local rabbinates against specific butcher shops, the Chief Rabbinate itself appealed to the public in this matter during the 1940s. In 1940, a public announcement by the Chief Rabbinate asked the public to denounce those who had begun to sell nonkosher meat in butcher shops, stores, restaurants, and kitchens, to regard them as enemies of the nation and to dissociate from them, which included not renting them property or doing business with them.[13] In 1944, the Chief Rabbinate published an announcement that specifically demanded to put a stop to pig-breeding in the land of Israel[14] that charged, "Cursed be a man who rears pigs."[15]

Besides these measures, which were only meaningful in the context of community life, the pig prohibition had some impact in the legal sphere even during the time of the British Mandate.

First, the Municipal Corporations Ordinance 1934[16] included a provision empowering municipalities to prohibit pig-raising within their area. Section 96(12) of the ordinance stated: "As regards animals: to regulate or prevent the keeping of swine . . ."[17] This provision was later explained as originating in the historical qualms about pigs, albeit without basing this interpretation on documentation.[18] Chaman Shelah has speculated that the British legislator wanted to avoid offending the feelings of both Jews and Muslims.[19] This explanation was also mentioned in decisions of the Israeli Supreme Court when it dealt with these provisions. Whereas Chief Justice Olshan emphasized that the power to impose restrictions on the raising of pigs was confined to the goal of preventing nuisance,[20] Justice Goitein was open to an interpretation that explained the source of this provision on religious grounds: "This provision may originate on religious or health grounds, or perhaps in the composition of the population in the Land of Israel, which was largely repulsed by swine and opposed its breeding and rearing."[21] Opting for one of these interpretations of the provision is not easy, when one takes into consideration that the British ruler which legislated the ordinance was aware of the common law approach to pigs as a source of nuisance,[22] and even of municipal bylaws that prohibited maintaining pigs near residential housing.[23]

Second, evidence indicates that Jewish organizations that purchased land in Palestine and leased it for settlement (such as the Jewish National Fund, known as the JNF), tried to impose restrictions on pig-breeding. This restriction needs to be understood in the broader context of the dispute about observance of religious commandments, and particularly the Sabbath, on lands purchased with funds donated by the entire Jewish people. Observance of the Sabbath was the main issue of contention discussed in this context, from a relatively early stage in the history of Jewish settlement in Palestine. The issue was discussed by the JNF board of directors in 1930, which decided that the demand for Sabbath observance (as well as exclusive recourse to Jewish labor) would be made part of the lease agreement.[24] Accordingly, as early as the 1930s, the standard JNF lease agreement had contained two express clauses regarding "the duty to observe the Sabbath and Jewish holidays" and the duty to ensure "Jewish labor."[25] Although the problem of pig-breeding arose later and was not reflected in the standard JNF lease, indirect evidence reveals attempts to prohibit the breeding of pigs and other forbidden animals for Jews on national lands.[26]

The early 1950s correspondence of Avraham Granot, chairman of the JNF board of directors, indicates the lease agreement with the settlers did not enable the JNF to intervene in cases that involved the breeding of pigs. The correspondence begins with a letter from the Rehovot Rabbinate concerning pig-breeding in Sdeh Akiva, signed by R. Schiber: "We are deeply shocked by this abomination of pig-breeding in Israel on national land and in farms established with national funds."[27] This letter was followed by two others signed by Joseph Burg and Yitzhak Raphael of the Mizrachi religious party.[28] Granot's answer was that "we were sorry to read your letter," but "according to the lease agreement between the JNF and the settlers on its land, the JNF can only intervene in cases of desecration of the Sabbath by agricultural work, construction work, and commercial and industrial activity. The National Fund, however, has no legal option of intervening in other cases."[29] Nevertheless, the JNF did write to the Sdeh Akiva group issuing a "request to cease this misconduct and prevent the great unpleasantness that may be caused to the Israeli public."[30] In a similar vein, Chief Sephardi Rabbi Yitzhak Nissim applied in 1956 to the Chairman of the JNF board insisting that it prohibit pig-breeding on its lands[31] and JNF activists in England complained about pig-breeding on JNF lands.[32]

Other lease agreements, however, contained explicit prohibitions. These are agreements drawn up in the early 1950s concerning lands belonging to PICA, the Palestine Jewish Colonization Association founded by Baron Edmund Rothschild, which were leased to settlers in Binyamina[33] and in Talmei-Elazar.[34] These leases include a religious provision that reads: "The settler undertakes that he and his family will not perform any work on the land on Sabbaths and Jewish holidays, and will not breed or rear animals forbidden by Jewish religion on this land."[35] These restrictions later formed the basis of a "legend" that I also heard when I began researching this subject, according to which farmers were breeding pigs on raised platforms because of the prohibition of pig-breeding on national land. This "legend," of unknown source, "grafts" the seventh year moratorium [*shmitah*] laws on the pig prohibition. According to the biblical laws of *shmitah,* the land of Israel should lie fallow on every seventh year.[36] One of the solutions adopted in order to enable agriculture during this time was to grow plants on platforms raised above the ground. The myth regarding pig-breeding described their growing on platforms detached from the ground in a similar manner.

Jewish leaders began negotiating questions on the status of religion in the State of Israel as soon as the international processes that eventually culminated in the creation of the state had matured, but the pig issue was not one of those debated in this context. The most representative document originating from this process was the letter that the Jewish Agency (which was controlled by the labor movement, known at the time as Mapai) sent in 1947 to the international organization of Agudat Israel, the hegemonic movement within the ultra-Orthodox. This letter, also known as the "Status Quo Document," included commitments to observe certain traditions in the future state, and centered on issues considered central from a religious perspective. It mentioned the recognition of the Jewish Sabbath as the official day of rest, the provision of kosher food in public institutions, abstention from non-religious law of marriage, and a commitment to ensure the autonomy of the ultra-Orthodox educational system.[37] The pig issue is not mentioned, and several explanations may be cited for this omission. First, negotiations preceding the creation of the state concentrated on the aspects most vital for the religious public. The ban on pork-trading is mainly of symbolic value for a religious way of life, as opposed to the vital importance of ensuring a steady supply of kosher food. Furthermore—and this is important for the understanding of later developments—abstention from pork was not regarded as a religious interest at the time, and enjoyed far wider support. In fact, until the food shortages at the time of the War of Independence, discussed in the next chapter, the scope of pork-trading was relatively negligible and therefore not an issue.

Only later, when the transition from a community governed by a British Mandate to an independent Jewish state after two thousand years of Diaspora life triggered a political dialogue on the character of this state, initiatives focusing on legal prohibitions on pigs began to attract extensive political energy.

CHAPTER 4

The Establishment of the State and the Politics of Nation-Building

INTENSIVE LEGAL CONCERN with pig-related prohibitions began only after the State of Israel was established in 1948. One reason was a significant increase in pork consumption ensuing from a scarcity of meat and food shortages in general. At this time, such food scarcity problems and the option of importing nonkosher meat as a potential solution were the subject of extensive political debates reflected mainly in the minutes of the Provisional State Council that operated before the elections to the First Knesset. On 12 August 1948, Council Member David Tsvi Pinkas from the Mizrachi asked the minister of commerce, industry, and supply whether the food controller had purchased nonkosher food. The minister answered that negotiations to that effect had been interrupted following a government order.[1] Council Member Nahum Nir-Rafalex then asked why the government was showing concerns for religious demands while starving the population. The minister replied that the government took into consideration not only the religious population, but also many others who valued religious tradition, and that every possible effort was being made to ensure basic supplies.[2] A lengthy discussion about meat imports took place in December 1948, following a complaint about the particular scarcity of kosher food.[3] Religious speakers reiterated during the discussion that pork itself and pig-breeding were the worst offenses in the policy allowing the import of nonkosher meat. Minister of Immigration and Health Moshe Shapira, representing the Mizrachi, defined the import of pork as "a national crime."[4]

Besides the general scarcity of food, a second factor affecting the concern with pig prohibitions was a new expectation that Israel's character as the state of the Jewish people would be reflected in its legal system and its public sphere.[5] An extreme example of the struggle over the character of the newly established state during the early 1950s was manifest in the operations of an Orthodox underground movement that attacked shops that sold pork and cars driven on the Sabbath.[6] The expectations that the legal system would convey the national traits of the newly established state reflected the development pattern of modern law as an aspect of the nation-state project.[7] According to Peter Fitzpatrick, "the story of modern law is integral to that of nation. In its identification with nation, law acquires location and an existential purchase compatible with its disparate dimensions—with its combining determination and responsiveness, and with its occupying a generality in-between the particular and the universal."[8]

The two elements were actually intertwined. Expectations of arrangements compatible with the Jewish nature of the state would probably not have focused on initiatives to adopt pig-related prohibitions had it not been for an increase in the supply of and demand for pork. Broide refers in his memoirs to the expanding pig-trade after the War of Independence:

> The War of Independence broke out. Butchers whose trade had been confined to ritually unfit meat became greedy. They bought up cowsheds and stables in the surrounding orchards, particularly in the towns of Beth-Dagan, Azur, Ramle, and Lod, and set up pigsties for raising pigs and slaughtering them on the spot. According to the figures in our possession, there were more than forty pigsties in the areas surrounding Tel Aviv, which supplied the city with hundreds of kilograms of pork and pork products every day. Starting from two or three nonkosher butchers, numbers climbed to dozens selling nonkosher meat and pork, besides factories producing pork products in large quantities for shops and restaurant, all working openly and undaunted.[9]

From the letters of Rabbi Herzog we learn that in 1952, when the food shortages were at their sharpest, the government of Israel had intended to purchase pork and other ritually prohibited food so as to meet the needs of the population. Minister Moshe Shapira, from the Mizrachi party, asked Rabbi Herzog what should be done about this: Would Halakhah allow its distribution to the non-Jewish population and could it be used as animal feed?[10]

The linkage between food scarcity and the growing demand for pork in Israel's early years was also noted by Deputy Minister of Religious Affairs Zerah Warhaftig: "This problem was almost non-existent during the Mandate, and was certainly not serious. With the meat shortages during the first few years of the state, however, the problem of the breeding and sale of pigs became more severe."[11]

This reality forced a confrontation with a phenomenon many found highly disturbing: pork-eating Jews, a prima facie oxymoron in Jewish culture. By analogy to Mary Douglas, who explains Jewish qualms about pigs on grounds of the pig being an exception in its class,[12] Jewish "pork-eaters" could also be viewed as an exceptional and inconceivable phenomenon.

The food-rationing regime enforced in the first few years of the state enabled registration for supplies of kosher or nonkosher meat, heightening the public's awareness of possible alternatives. In response to a question by MK Hanan Rubin concerning a meat shipment from Poland that had been "disqualified" by the Rabbinate, Minister of Supply and Rationing Dov Yosef replied that: "The said meat has been allocated to citizens listed as consumers of nonkosher meat. The citizens of the state, therefore, have not been denied the possibility of eating it."[13] In a different context, Mizrachi MK Yitzhak Raphael, who posed a question on "the number of butchers selling ritually unsuitable meat," pointed to the results of a registration for meat rations, whereby 93 percent were reported as requesting kosher meat.[14]

Another perspective on the evolvement of pig-related legal prohibitions concerns the extent to which the delineation of the areas in which they applied contributed to the delimitation of a "Jewish zone" in the new state. William Miller noted that norms of disgust "help define boundaries between us and them,"[15] and thereby establish communities. In practice, however, the role of these legal prohibitions in creating distinction between ethnic zones is unclear. On the one hand, after municipalities were empowered to prohibit the sale of pork and pork products within their limits, it was chiefly the all-Jewish or mainly Jewish municipalities that exercised these powers. On the other hand, the Arab Muslim population also traditionally refrains from pork so that Muslim villages are in fact pork-free zones, even more than Jewish municipalities. Moreover, when pig-breeding was prohibited throughout the country, the only areas excluded from the application of this prohibition were those populated by Christian Arabs,[16] so that restrictions on pig-breeding applied to Muslim-populated areas as well.

The various attempts to legislate the traditional pig prohibitions proposed and debated during the 1950s should be viewed against the background of the political and cultural characteristics of the period, when significant efforts were invested in the creation of national symbols and a national identity: "The creation of Israel and the tripling of its population in three years led state leaders to feel that the country must be completely integrated; that the value-belief-systems separating the various camps must be abolished and replaced by a unified symbol system uniting the entire Jewish population in support of the state and its institutions."[17]

The dominant ideology of this period, known as "statism," was developed and led by Prime Minister Ben-Gurion. This ideology made the state an ultimate value and, in many respects, acquired the role of a civil religion for Israel,[18] as argued by Liebman and Don-Yehiya.[19] Statism needed symbols to fulfill this mission, and the entire period was characterized by a constant search for symbols of the new collective identity. The central symbols inspired by the spirit of statism were the national flag and the state emblem, enacted by law.[20] Another symbol of statism that became prominent at the time was Independence Day, declared a national holiday by the Independence Day Law 1949. During the early years of the State, this date marked a major event on the national calendar that, for many, surpassed in importance even the traditional Jewish holidays.[21]

In this process of symbol selection and identity building, the role to be played by Jewish history and religious heritage posed a recurrently emerging dilemma. Culture, as defined by Geertz, is a "historically transmitted pattern of meaning embodied in symbols, a system of inherited conceptions expressed in symbolic forms by means of which men communicate, perpetuate and develop their knowledge about and attitudes toward life."[22] In these terms, Jewish culture had many symbols that could be incorporated into the new state, and the question was whether they should be welcomed or replaced.

The debate in this matter influenced the process of choosing the national flag. Specifically, the choice was between a blue and white flag in the colors of the Jewish prayer shawl and with a Star of David at the center, and a new flag with seven gold stars with no connection to traditional Jewish symbols. The course toward the eventual choice of the blue and white flag could serve to illustrate the tortuous decision-making process in the building of a national identity inspired by a religious history but detached from religion as such.[23]

Similarly, the debate concerning pig-breeding and pork consumption hinged on whether the traditional ban on pigs should enter the new pantheon of national state symbols or be excluded because of the religious connotation. The extreme version of statism championed a system of values and symbols generally detached from religious tradition[24] although, as reflected in the debate over the choice of flag, alternative views were also propounded.

Proposals to regulate a ban on pigs into Israeli law were a particularly "hard case" that can shed light on other controversies of the time. On the one hand, the ban on pigs was a quintessential instance of the religious Jewish Orthodoxy that socialist Zionism had opposed from its early Eastern European origins. Since its inception at the end of the nineteenth century and the beginning of its work in Palestine in the early twentieth century, socialist Zionism rejected any association with traditional Judaism, including such basic tenets such as observance of the Sabbath and dietary laws.[25] From this perspective, turning a central feature of the dietary laws into the law of the state appears incomprehensible, a view that was indeed vigorously upheld by the more radical socialist parties in the Knesset debates. On the other hand, the labor movement was also identified with the preservation of certain traits of tradition or of "Yiddishkeit" (customs associated with Jewish life in general).[26] The inclination to preserve certain traditions and customs while ignoring their religious background could justify support for the entrenched Jewish tradition banning pigs and pork consumption.

The potential for split views on the status of the traditional pig prohibition in the State of Israel was even greater due to a more nuanced distinction introduced by David Ben-Gurion, the ideologue of statism, who differentiated the heritage of biblical Jewish statehood from Jewish tradition as it developed in the Diaspora. Ben Gurion viewed the State of Israel as a direct continuation of the biblical polis, implicitly rejecting the culture developed during the long period of exile as represented by the Orthodox way of life. He valued and celebrated the Bible, while distancing himself from Talmudic and rabbinic culture.[27] In this context, the Jewish abstention from pork could not be granted a major role because it was a cultural trait developed in the Diaspora and therefore associated with it. Going back to the Bible also meant rejecting Diaspora sensitivities to persecutions associated with the pig prohibition. In the Knesset debates, Ben Gurion indeed expressed reservations about the importance ascribed to the pig prohibition and described it as a "later" development.[28]

From another perspective, however, the newly evolving traditions of Zionism could also be interpreted as supporting legislation introducing a pig ban on national grounds. The persecution of Jews over their abstention from pork was not only associated with humiliation but also related to memories of national pride. The pig prohibition was strongly linked to the battle for national independence during the Maccabean revolt against the Hellenistic conquerors and the resistance to the decree compelling pig sacrifices and desecration in the Temple in Jerusalem.[29] Although this historical association may not have sufficed for Ben-Gurion, who favored biblical tradition, it could inspire others to support a legal ban on pigs. The Hanukkah festival, celebrating victory over the Hellenistic rulers, had never been considered a particularly significant holiday from a strictly religious viewpoint. In the Zionist culture developed by secular segments of the movement in the pre-state era, however, it attained prominence because it was perceived as a celebration of Jewish courage and political independence.[30]

Although the campaign supporting the introduction of the pig prohibition into the Israeli legal system was dominated by religious politicians, their arguments touched mainly on the communal cultural level (without denying that they were probably inspired also by their religious beliefs, as well as by several declarations on this question published by the Chief Rabbinate during these years).[31] Indeed, prohibitions on pig-breeding and pork consumption have no greater religious significance than many other religious commandments that never made it to the political arena. Had mitigating sin been the concern at stake, focusing on the enforcement of dietary laws in general, for instance, would have served this purpose better. In addition, major bills seeking to apply pig prohibitions during the 1950s and early 1960s were also introduced by secular MKs from the right and the center of the political map (although not from the left). At the same time, although opponents of these motions argued in the name of freedom of conscience, they did acknowledge that these initiatives were also widely supported by non-religious elements in the population.

Ha-Modi'a, the daily newspaper of the ultra-Orthodox party Agudat Israel, published lively discussions on the political initiatives to ban pigs, clearly noting the symbolic importance of these initiatives from a national perspective instead of presenting them as merely a religious imperative. One article regarded the battle against pig-breeding in Israel as expressing a desire "to stamp one more Jewish symbol on the state of Israel."[32] Another article viewed the pig as "epitomizing the assault upon the eternity of the nation."[33] One column presented the argument in the form of a Jew's imaginary memories—forced to abandon his heritage in the Hungarian army, he relinquished his Jewish identity forever only after he began eating pork.[34] Yet another columnist cited the imaginary question of an innocent boy asking his father why they were serving ham sandwiches at a Hanukkah celebration, thereby pointing out that the ban is also relevant to Jewish holidays celebrated by the secular public.[35] Many of these reports emphasized the relatively broad support of secular Jews, both in the Knesset and outside it, for the political initiatives to ban pig-breeding,[36] an argument that was also echoed in articles published in *Ha-Tsofeh*, the daily newspaper of the National Religious Party.[37] Shlomo Lorenz, a Knesset member from Agudat Israel for nine consecutive terms (from the Second to the Tenth Knesset) and the first to initiate a bill in this matter, still argued fifty years later that he had chosen to promote this initiative because of its symbolic significance. He also attested that, for this reason, he had initially estimated that the initiative would enjoy wide support.[38]

Generally speaking, the prevalent perception concerning the symbolic and national significance of the pig prohibitions was also acknowledged by secular journalists, even when they resisted the idea of absorbing them into Israeli law. Meir Bareli, writing for *Davar,* the daily newspaper of Mapai, started his article "On the Question of Pig-breeding in Israel"[39] as follows: "I doubt that, on any other issue, the religious parties could have mobilized as much public sympathy for their cause as they have on the matter of pig-breeding." He then mentioned the two religious commandments that secular individuals in Israel tended to observe—the fast of Yom Kippur and the abstention from pork—and added: "Indeed, it is questionable whether the Torah views the eating of pork as an offense essentially different from the eating of any other unclean animal. Yet, in traditional Jewish existence, the pig remains the symbol of all unclean meat. Even non-religious Jews use the term "eating pork" to define an unbecoming act."

Bareli's concluded: "There is a public defined as non-religious concerning most of the issues at stake that, in the context of what is known in Israel as 'the pig problem,' is indistinguishable from the religious public." He was opposed to the proposed legislation for both democratic and pragmatic reasons (the cheap price of pork and the relative scarcity of meat in the country). He therefore sought to persuade the public at large to reject the proposed legislation despite its cultural preferences, although he did not deny that there was a secular tendency to support it. His article, then, was predicated on the assumption that the fault line in this debate was not between the religious and non-religious. Another writer objected to the strong pressure of the religious parties in what he called "the pig war," arguing that a more tolerant and conciliatory approach would have ensured them greater success because "the loathing of pork among many freethinkers is almost physiological and rests on deep, genetic psychological motives."[40] In the same *Davar* forum, poet Nathan Alterman not only recognized the historical and national significance of the pig prohibition but also supported the initiative to empower municipalities to restrict the breeding of pigs and the sale of pork, arguing that in this matter "religious zealots and secularists appear, as it were, to complement each other."[41] In the same spirit, another writer published a story about an encounter with a newcomer from Iraq, one of the many immigrants who came to Israel in its early years. Her article documented this man's shock when, for the first time, he was faced with Jews who ate and sold pork. She described him asking: "Are they Jews?" and "Is this the State of Israel?" She was at pains to define what exactly had led her to write this column and felt that, at least in part, it had been "a perceived civil duty to widen the resonance of this deep sound, which cries out in secret and seeks an attentive ear."[42]

Secular right-wing writers, who associated tradition with the national spirit, obviously expressed sympathy and support for legislative initiatives intended to incorporate pig prohibitions into the law.[43] Emphasizing the national significance of the pig prohibition, one of them denounced the tendency of some religious parties to be satisfied with less than an all-encompassing legal prohibition: "The pig problem is not only a Torah prohibition. This is an instance of a religious law that has become an inextricable part of the national culture . . . In the course of our long history, the pig became the symbol of evil, of all that is sordid and foul, the ultimate antithesis of Judaism and of its values."[44]

Israel Eldad, an ideologue of the Zionist right, sarcastically criticized his rivals on the left by writing that the Jewish Messiah was not expected to appear riding on the back of a pig. From his perspective, he said, "The State of Israel will be a Jewish state, or will not be a state at all."[45]

The vigorous effort to introduce pig prohibitions into the Israeli legal system should be understood as part of the nation-building project. The history of these initiatives during the 1950s and 1960s, which culminated in the enactment of two laws, will be the focus of the next chapter.

CHAPTER 5

Laying the Foundations

Legislation in the 1950s and 1960s

ATTEMPTS TO MAKE pig-related prohibitions part of the Israeli legal system used administrative measures based on existing laws, on the one hand, and specific legislative proposals on the other. Initially, whereas individual MKs tended to submit bills, the government preferred to rely on existing administrative powers. After administrative orders and secondary legislation were challenged and nullified by the Supreme Court, however, the government was willing to take the legislative route.

The characteristics of Israel's political system in its early years enabled intensive parliamentary activity focused on legislating pig prohibitions. The parliamentary system that Israel decided to adopt made a major contribution to this development. Elections to the Israeli parliament, the Knesset, are general and proportionate. The electoral threshold is low, enabling the participation of many parties representing specific interests and pressure groups.[1] Religious interests have always been protected in the Knesset by several religious parties representing various segments of the Israeli Orthodox society, and at the same time have also been resisted by parties upholding hard-line secular ideologies. The Labor movement (known as Mapai until the late 1960s) which was the hegemonic political force until the 1977 elections, was willing, to some extent, to go along with initiatives advanced by the religious parties on both pragmatic and national grounds. Labor tended to perceive at least some religious traditions as reflecting national culture, and even national pride.[2]

The legislative and administrative endeavor to ban pig-related economic activities was also affected by the Knesset's adherence to the principle of parliamentary sovereignty modeled on the British system. Accordingly, the legislature could move forward its initiatives without any limitations posed by a formal constitution or by the possibility of judicial review. During Israel's early years, the assumption was that a constitution would soon be drafted and ratified, but events took a different course. The Israeli Declaration of Independence states that the first elected parliament, which it defines as the "Elected Constituent Assembly," would vote on a constitution. Soon after, however, internal political debates regarding the content of the future constitution rendered it impossible to agree on a text that would gain broad-based support. The eventual compromise took the form of a resolution adopted by the First Knesset in 1950, stating that the future constitution would be enacted gradually, chapter by chapter, in the form of "Basic Laws." The process envisaged implied that controversies would be addressed piecemeal and, after reaching agreement, would be brought to the Knesset for enactment. This collection of Basic Laws would become the future Israeli constitution. In their absence, however, the Knesset could operate without constitutional restraints on the content of its laws, including laws that might be viewed as infringing upon certain personal liberties.[3]

Legislative initiatives concerning pig prohibitions began during the session of the Second Knesset with two bills seeking to forbid pig-raising. MK Shlomo Lorenz of Agudat Israel proposed the Pig-Raising Bill of 1953.[4] At the same time, a group of MKs from Agudat Israel, the Mizrachi, and Mapai proposed another bill—the Pig-Raising Prohibition in Israel Bill of 1953.[5] The MKs who proposed these bills advanced the same arguments which were later adduced to support the imposition of legal restrictions on the trade in pork—namely, claims bearing on the place of the pig in Jewish history. MK Lorenz, who was the first speaker, emphasized that his motion was not religiously inspired: "I put it to the Knesset that most Jews are revolted by pigs, which symbolize abomination and abhorrence to our people, evoking our oppression and the loss of our freedom."[6] MK Israel Yeshayahu Shar'abi of Mapai followed suit with an historical argument: "We cannot ignore that the pig has always been a symbol and a distinctive sign of Israel's enemies."[7] MK Yitzhak Raphael, from the Mizrachi, submitted a question protesting the publication of a report issued by the Israeli consulate in Vienna that stated in its economic section: "Since pig-breeding in Israel has registered dramatic growth, pork might be released from control, although other types of meat are still rationed." Foreign Minister Moshe Sharett answered briefly: "This publication has been brought to the Foreign Ministry's attention and the necessary comments have already been sent."[8]

Minister of Trade and Industry Peretz Bernstein presented to the Knesset the government's response to these bills on 8 July 1953. In his speech, the minister referred to an earlier decision to limit pig-breeding activities through the implementation of administrative measures, such as reducing food supplies to pig breeders and confining pig-breeding to a limited area.[9] In the debate that followed, the main speakers were MKs Benjamin Mintz and Shlomo Lorenz of Agudat Israel, who conveyed their displeasure with this response and reiterated their demand for the enactment of a law on this matter.[10] The Knesset decided "to refer the government proposal to the Interior Committee, including the bill on the prohibition against pig-breeding in Israel."[11] On 11 August 1953, the committee stated: "At this stage, the problem of pig-breeding in the State of Israel does not require the enactment of a special law."[12] The committee then added: "We have noted the government's decision on the restriction of pig-breeding in the country, as read by the minister of trade and industry at the Knesset's plenary session."[13] The committee further noted the request that Trade and Industry Minister Bernstein had made a few days earlier, "to give us the opportunity to implement the government's decisions as they stand. If it becomes apparent that pork-trading far exceeds the boundaries of the permitted breeding area, the government will seek additional means to prevent its transportation."[14]

The government took steps to implement the decision it had adopted by using powers legislated in control statutes that, quite obviously, had not been originally intended for the regulation of such issues. First, individual orders were issued to owners of pig farms under the Defense (Prevention of Profiteering) Regulations of 1944.[15] According to these orders, keeping pigs was contingent upon a receipt of a permit from the supervisory authority at the Ministry of Trade and Industry; obtaining this permit was dependent upon maintaining the animals in a defined area in the northern part of the country. In practice, this measure proved unsuccessful; recipients of the permit disregarded the orders and were prepared to stand trial for failure to comply, and even to pay the resultant fines. The authorities having no power to confiscate the merchandise, this measure had no practical effect.[16] Second, and as a further step, the Food Controller issued the Food Control (Pig-Raising) Order, 1954,[17] using his powers under the Food Control Ordinance of 1942.[18] This was a general order that banned pig-breeding unless authorized by special permits, which were granted only to breeders working in certain areas in the north populated mainly by Christians. Violation of this order could serve as a basis for confiscation.[19]

These measures notwithstanding, pig-breeding remained a matter of constant debate during a period characterized by great turmoil over religious matters. In 1953, Agudat Israel left the government over a controversy concerning compulsory national service for women who had been exempted from military service for religious reasons. MK Yitzhak Meir Levin from Agudat Israel criticized the Mizrachi and Ha-Po'el ha-Mizrahi for remaining in a coalition that had neglected to care for important religious matters and, among other things, blamed them for "surrendering" on the "pig issue."[20] Other MKs from Agudat Israel also criticized the government directly on these questions. In a motion to the agenda, MK Zalman Ben-Yaakov attacked the government for failing to act properly and demanded: "Let us measure up to the challenge of our historical identity, of our chosen status, of the purity and sanctity that make us unique, and uproot this abomination."[21]

At the same time, several local authorities began adopting initiatives intended to restrict pork-trading, following requests, questions, and complaints that had surfaced at the municipal level. Discussions began in Tel Aviv as early as 1948, and the issue was raised persistently at City Council. Minutes from an August 1948 meeting state: "As for the complaint of Mr. Pinkas about bringing pork into Tel Aviv with the consent of the national veterinary department, the mayor states that neither he nor other municipal officials have consented, explicitly or implicitly, to bring in pork for distribution."[22] Four years later, council member Rabbi Abramovicz complained about the serving of pork in Tel Aviv restaurants. In order to remove this shame from the city, he asked the mayor to demand, in the strongest of terms and from the council platform, that restaurant owners stop serving pork. The mayor responded by stating that he viewed "the serving of pork in restaurants as an offense, and promised to address a suitable request to the association of restaurant owners to desist from it."[23] A year later, Rabbi Abramovicz again raised the issue and pointed out that, according to a report he had received from the Chief Rabbinate, Tel Aviv-Jaffa had become "a center for pork distribution and pig-breeding." He called upon the city council to act rather than to wait for the Knesset "to uproot the bane" by forbidding pig-breeding and pork sales in the city. He was joined by Mr. Moshe Ikhilov, from Herut, and by Mr. Abraham Boyer, another representative of the religious public, who argued for the need "to expel pork vendors from the area around the synagogue in the Yad Eliyahu neighborhood." The mayor noted measures that the city had already adopted and promised "to find out from the city lawyer what could be done in order to uproot this bane from the city."[24] In Tiberias, the (secular) mayor of the city bought pork only to burn it publicly in the street.[25]

The municipalities also began resorting to administrative powers that had not been originally instated for this purpose. One tactic, discussed in the *Axel* case,[26] was to make business permits contingent upon abstention from pork sales. Another tactic, employed but never tested in the Supreme Court, was to put butchers on trial for selling pork without veterinary sanction after instructing the municipal veterinary staff not to authorize pork. This policy is evident in letters by Tel Aviv municipality officials. Adv. Tsvi Silbiger, municipal legal counsel, explains in a letter to the secretary of Haifa's religious council: "The legal basis for charges we bring concerning the sale of pork is Rule 8 of the Slaughterhouse Rules that forbids, among other things, displaying for sale meat that does not bear the official stamp of the municipal slaughterhouse."[27] Another letter, by Boyer, who was deputy mayor at the time, states: "The veterinary surgeon of the Tel Aviv municipal abattoir does not examine pork, and unexamined meat cannot be sold. As far as possible, unexamined meat is confiscated. Until not long ago, the practice was that Ramle's veterinary surgeon would examine the meat and stamp it with Ramle's municipal stamp . . . but Ramle's veterinary surgeon has also stopped stamping pork and pork distributors have found their way to Rishon Le-Zion's veterinary surgeon."[28]

At a later stage, the municipalities chose a more direct course of action and enacted bylaws expressly prohibiting pork sales within the city's precincts. Haim Broide notes in his memoirs that the enactment of the bylaw was prompted by Boyer, although Mayor Haim Lebanon also supported it: "The Tel Aviv-Jaffa municipality, at the initiative of Deputy Mayor Boyer and with the warm support of Mayor Lebanon, adopted a municipal bylaw on the pig issue, first among all local authorities."[29] This legislation was accompanied by intense public pressure intended to let the municipality know that the bylaw enjoyed wide support.[30] On 17 March 1954, Rabbi Shmuel Greenberg, chairman of the Tel Aviv-Jaffa Religious Council, sent a letter to Mr. Boyer: "We hereby express our deep appreciation to you for the enactment of the law banning swine in Tel Aviv, which marks the culmination of the entire public endeavor on this question, in which you had a decisive share. Through this deed, you have exalted the glory of the first Jewish city, in honor and splendor."[31] As noted, Tel Aviv was the first municipality to enact a bylaw, and others followed.

At the same time, Local Councils Order (A) 1950[32] was amended to include a provision enabling prohibitions on pig-breeding and pork sales within the precincts of the smaller municipalities, to which the Municipal Corporations Ordinance does not apply: "to regulate, restrict or prohibit the raising, keeping or sale of pigs, and the keeping or sale of pork or its products."[33] This prohibition replicated mandatory legislation concerning municipal corporations,[34] but its reach was even broader, extending to trade aspects and not only to pig-breeding. The validity of this amendment was never directly ruled on by the Supreme Court. Decisions dealing with other restrictions on pork and pigs clarify, however, that the court would not have considered this amendment a basis for religiously inspired limitations in the absence of express authorization in primary legislation to take religious considerations into account.[35]

The handling of the issue through administrative measures was brought to the attention of the Supreme Court relatively quickly, at first in relation to activities at the local level. The decisions by the court revealed a legislative lacuna, at least from the perspective of those supporting pig-related legal prohibitions. First, in *Axel*,[36] the court ruled against making a ban on pork sales part of business licenses. The decision relied on the view that an issue as fundamental as pig-related prohibitions, lacking any local uniqueness, required regulation at the national level: "In our opinion, this is a general, nationwide problem that is not specific to a particular place, and its solution is within the exclusive purview of the national legislator, unless the national legislator were to decide to transfer the power of decision on this matter to the local authorities."[37] The ruling did not deal with the validity of municipal bylaws imposing restrictions on the sale of pork because the bylaw in this matter, which the Netanyah municipality had enacted in the interim, had not so far been authorized by the minister of the interior.[38] The rationale of the judgment, however, clarified that it also applied to measures adopted by local authorities through the promulgation of bylaws.

Soon after, any hope that bylaws would prove capable of restricting pig-trading swiftly collapsed. After *Axel,* Adv. Silbiger prepared an opinion for the Mayor: "This ruling did not surprise me since my advice to you on several occasions, both orally and in writing, has been in the spirit of the recent decisions." He added, however, that the Tel Aviv bylaw in this matter might be considered valid because it did not ban pork sales altogether but rather allowed it in public markets, and could therefore be seen as a legitimate form of regulation and control.[39] Nevertheless, this bylaw was declared void in *Fridi,*[40] once again expressing the view that municipalities cannot regulate religious matters.[41] In both cases, Supreme Court decisions were drafted in formal legal language, without yielding to the potential emotional consequences that this issue kindled in the political arena. Referring to *Axel* in his memoirs, Justice Olshan wrote: "Leaders of the religious parties did not view this ruling favorably, although extreme care was taken to avoid stating a view as to whether enacting such a law would be desirable."[42]

In view of the Supreme Court rulings, the handling of the question shifted away from the municipal arena to the Knesset. At a session of the Tel Aviv municipal council, Rabbi Abramovicz asked the mayor "to address the Knesset from this podium concerning the enactment of a nationwide law to prohibit the sale of ritually unfit meat in Israel." The mayor answered: "The city council cannot take any further action in this regard, and the initiative in the solution of this problem is, therefore, in the hands of the Knesset."[43] Sure enough, and responding to the judicial rulings, the Knesset hastened to "fill the power vacuum," pressured by the moderate religious parties that were part of the government coalition—the Mizrachi and Ha-Po'el Ha-Mizrahi.[44] Since the legal rationale of the judicial precedents in this matter had relied on the local authorities' lack of powers to prohibit the sale of pork, the Knesset's immediate goal was to enact such powers. This practical goal was anchored in the coalition agreement that preceded the creation of the government after the November 1955 elections to the Third Knesset. The agreement included an explicit promise by then Prime Minister David Ben-Gurion to enact appropriate legislation aiming to solve the problem of authorization. A letter from Ben-Gurion to the Mizrachi leader Moshe Shapira, which accompanied the agreement, stated: "Local authorities will be authorized to restrict pig-breeding and pork sales within their area of jurisdiction. Were it to emerge that local authorities lack the necessary powers in this regard, a law will be enacted in the Knesset to empower them to restrict the breeding and sale of pigs. Ha-Po'el Ha-Mizrahi and the Mizrachi will be free to vote in the Knesset for a general or limited prohibition on pig-breeding in Israel if one of their members or one of the other MKs were to submit such a bill."[45]

At the same time, Agudat Israel renewed the initiative to enact a general law on pig-breeding (as distinct from the political compromise seeking to empower local authorities to ban pork trading and pig-breeding). The initiative came to the fore in the Pig-Raising Prohibition in Israel Bill of 1956.[46] When presenting his bill,[47] MK Mintz explained his persistence in demanding a general law: "Must all Jewish history, all the Jewish suffering of uncounted generations who sacrificed their lives when rejecting the pig abomination and were burnt at the stake of wicked nations, must all this exalted past of pain and glory be blotted out from our present reality in this country because of the intemperance of a small minority?"[48]

Ben-Gurion was fervently opposed to this initiative and confronted the historical arguments ostensibly supporting it. He pointed out that, until the end of the Hasmonean era, pig-breeding had not been forbidden. The prohibition was born, as noted, following the siege of Jerusalem during the rule of Aristobulus and Hyrkanus (mentioned in the Talmudic story about the pig that dug its hooves into the walls of Jerusalem).[49] Ben-Gurion argued that the views of younger people in this matter differed from the traditional attitude. The Knesset, therefore, should go no further than authorizing municipal authorities to enact bylaws on pig-breeding and pork trading.[50]

The Knesset, then, was presented with a bill supported by the majority coalition that confined the initiative to the empowerment of local authorities to ban pork trading and pig-breeding as they wish. Whereas the decisions of the Supreme Court had largely ignored the symbolic aspects of the matter and had focused on issues of formal authorization, the parliamentary debate over the bill was intensely passionate. The driving forces behind the legislation were, as noted, the Mizrachi and Ha-Po'el ha-Mizrahi, whose coalition partnership with Mapai had generated the bill. During the first reading,[51] Deputy Minister of Religious Affairs Zerah Warhaftig introduced the bill and reviewed the history of earlier efforts to impose restrictions on matters involving pigs, explaining that case law had exposed the need for legislation. Without criticizing the judiciary, he pointed out it had created a problem for which the Knesset had to find a solution. He also explained that the bill was designed to fill a legal vacuum that had just been discovered and was not a substitute for a more comprehensive regulation of the matter in the future, including a prohibition against pig-breeding.

The origin of this legislative initiative with the religious parties enabled its opponents to describe it as a case of surrender to religious demands. This is how Justice Olshan describes it in his memoirs:

> Neither the Knesset majority nor the government took a favorable view of religious coercion in the State, and certainly not when exercised through legislation . . . But the political regime, due to the antiquated electoral system, consistently forced the creation of coalition governments. In order to ensure their existence and ability to act, these governments had to follow a path of compromise and concessions to the religious parties. Various promises were given to these parties that, to be fulfilled, demanded recourse to administrative means even without legal power and in contravention of the principles of the rule of law . . . The main hindrance to the adoption of administrative measures to solve these conflicts was the Supreme Court, in its role as High Court of Justice. As a result, the government was occasionally forced to abandon the improper administrative path. Concerning pork, it had no choice but to enact a law in the Knesset empowering the municipalities and the local councils to enact bylaws concerning prohibitions and restrictions.[52]

The many nuances emerging in the parliamentary debate, however, reveal a more complex story. During the debate, the Knesset split apart into

several camps. Many speakers emphasized that their reservations about
pig-breeding rested on national grounds. The main opponents came from
the socialist left (Ahdut ha-Avodah/Po'alei Zion and Mapam, as distinct
from Mapai), the Communists (Maki), and the Progressive Party.

The national argument was most strongly emphasized in the speeches
of Esther Raziel-Naor and Menachem Begin, representing Herut, who
were actually critical of the bill for its incomplete nature and for renounc-
ing a priori the option of a broader prohibition. Raziel-Naor argued that
a sweeping prohibition against pigs was deeply entrenched in the national
consciousness common to all and not only in religious law:

> What is national consciousness if not the essence of the memories, the
> experiences, and the impressions that, bequeathed from generation to gen-
> eration, became the nation's collective patrimony? Can we say that all the
> stories on which we were raised and from which we drew strength to
> endure tribulations and war throughout our history were merely non-
> sense? Why did historians and storytellers seize on this abominable beast
> and turn it into a symbol? Why did they fail to say that when the Greeks
> entered the Temple and began sacrificing mice on the altar? After all, mice
> are also ritually unfit animals forbidden on religious grounds. And why
> did they say about the pig that when it dug its hooves and claws into the
> wall the entire country shook four hundred parasangs? Because eating
> pork was the symbol of alienation from the people and its denial.[53]

MK Menachem Begin emphasized that this question touched "the nation's
soul,"[54] and urged all to honor the traditions of the Jewish towns destroyed
in the Holocaust in the spirit of the commandment, "Honor thy father
and thy mother."[55] Shoshanna Parsitz of the General Zionists also argued:
"For the Jewish people, the problem of the pig is not only a religious
problem. It is *also* a religious problem, but not only a religious problem.
Because since the bitter and awful day when the pig defiled our Temple
and this impure animal began to serve as a symbol of our humiliation,
a symbol of the collapse of our independent existence and our political
sovereignty—from that date the pig ceased to be only a religious problem and became a symbol, a symbol of Jewish oppression."[56]

On these grounds, she supported expanding the proposed prohibition.
Speakers for Mapai accepted the national dimension of the problem, but

their approach favored compromise rather than maximalist positions. Mapai MK Israel Yeshayahu Shar'abi, who had backed the previous bills on pig-breeding, explained: "Can I help it if this creature symbolizes the efforts of our oppressors to wipe out the name of Israel, subvert our faith and uproot our Jewish, religious, and national consciousness?"[57] Yitzhak Meir Levin (Agudat Israel and Po'alei Agudat Israel) joined all the condemnations and denounced religious-Zionist parties for their conciliatory approach,[58] as did his fellow party member Kalman Kahana.[59] General Zionists Peretz Bernstein and Israel Rokah cautioned against the partial nature of the bill, particularly because the prohibitions would become a sham, since pig-breeding would still be allowed in many places.[60]

By contrast, left-wing parties opposed the bill altogether and refused to see the national aspect of the prohibition, pointing to the religious coercion entailed by even the relatively narrow prohibition enabling local authorities to issue bylaws on the matter. Yitzhak Ben-Aharon of Ahdut ha-Avodah/Po'alei Zion was unflinching in his rejection of "coercion." In his view: "Coercion and legislation by way of party haggling is more improper and more tainted than any pig."[61] Yaakov Riftin of Mapam made a similar point.[62] Reservations about the bill because of its perceived coercion are also evident in the remarks of Yizhar Harari, from the Progressive Party, although he was ready to compromise. In his view, "granting local authorities the power to impose restrictions is the 'final frontier' we are ready to reach in our compromise with those seeking legislation on these matters."[63] The Local Authorities (Special Enablement) Law of 1956 (hereinafter, Special Enablement Law), was finally enacted over persistent protests by MKs from Ahdut ha-Avodah/Po'alei Zion and Mapam, even during the second reading.[64] These protests, however, remained confined to a small minority. Reports in *Ha-Tsofeh* emphasized this fact in an attempt to focus attention on the consensus converging on the new legislation.[65]

According to Section 1 of this new law: "Notwithstanding the provisions of any other law, a local authority shall be competent to make a bylaw limiting or prohibiting the breeding and keeping of pigs and the sale of pork and pork products destined for food." The law did not directly prohibit pork consumption, which would have entailed broader infringement of personal liberties and required interference with activities in the private sphere. Instead, it banned various economic activities related to pig-breeding and pork trading, just as the Eighteenth Amendment to the U.S. Constitution prohibiting alcohol applied to "the manufacture, sale, or transportation of intoxicating liquors" (rather than to their consumption). Accordingly, many municipalities indeed hurried to enact new by-laws in this matter, as detailed in the next chapter.

The Special Enablement Law represented a significant step forward for those aspiring to make the anti-pig legacy part of Israeli law. Yet, the law still left pending the nationwide aspect of pig-breeding, epitomized in the symbolic aspiration to eradicate pigs from the land of Israel. As noted, the administrative regulation of this matter was ensured through an order issued according to the Food Control Ordinance of 1942, which limited pig-breeding to a restricted area. Here as well, however, administrative arrangements soon proved a poor substitute for legislation. An important ruling on this matter was issued in *Lazarovitz*, regarded to this day as a crucial Supreme Court precedent in the realm of administrative law.[66] The court held that the Food Control Ordinance did not provide authorization for religiously inspired regulation. The Food Controller, who had issued the order prohibiting pig-breeding, was indeed formally competent to impose restrictions on the breeding of animals. The court, however, held that this power could only be exercised to attain the objectives for which it had been granted and the Food Controller had certainly not been empowered to make such decisions on religious grounds. This Supreme Court ruling, like previous ones, nowhere alludes to value issues. It assumes that only legislation can impose restrictions based on religious grounds and functions only as a "traffic policeman," criticizing an administrative authority that acted without legislative authorization. In the words of Justice Berenson: "Nor is it the respondent's role to solve religious and national problems by resorting to administrative means made available to him for entirely different aims and goals."[67]

The result of the *Lazarovitz* decision was that pig-breeding, unlike pork-trading, could continue in various areas of the country for several more years due to the absence of specific legislation on this matter. Documents show that many kibbutzim[68] and private farmers[69] kept developing this agricultural branch. In the absence of state enforcement, some attempts were made to put economic pressure on pig-breeders based on their land leases and the distribution of their agricultural supplies. As noted, the Chief Sephardi Rabbi Yitzhak Nissim had demanded in 1956 of the JNF Board Chairman that pig-breeding be banned on farms built on its lands.[70] In 1958, the Chief Rabbinate warned Tnuva, the cooperative marketing most of the country's agricultural produce, that it would cancel the kashrut certificate of its entire milk supply unless it stopped using milk from farms that also engaged in pig-breeding.[71] In 1958, the Chief Rabbinate's Council again demanded that Tnuva should publish a circular stating it would not accept milk from farms that bred pigs.[72] This pressure seems to have had some impact.[73]

Eventually, the *Lazarovitz* ruling led to legislation, this time a nationwide law prohibiting pig-breeding. The possibility of proposing private bills restricting pig-breeding had already been mentioned in the 1955 coalition agreement, which led to the Special Enablement Law. The *Lazarovitz* decision, however, made this course of action more relevant. The possibility of further legislation was therefore indicated in the coalition agreement reached after the 1961 elections to the Fifth Knesset.[74] Concerning pig-breeding, the agreement stated: "In the Enablement Law on pig-breeding and pork sales, flaws that may be prejudicial to the terms of the 1955 coalition agreement will be rectified."

Debates surrounding this new attempt to promote legislation on pig-breeding resembled the controversy surrounding the Special Enablement Law of several years previously. In his memoirs, Justice Olshan described this initiative too as a case of religious coercion: "Not all municipalities and local councils consented to use the powers that had been vested in them. Those that did, or were forced to do so abiding by agreements made with representatives of the religious parties, usually failed to make their bylaws sufficiently stringent so as to preclude loopholes enabling appeals to the High Court. These appeals usually claimed that the bylaw's provisions had exceeded the powers vested in the council by the Enablement Law. As a result of numerous petitions and of the pressure of religious parties vying with each other in their extremism and zealotry, the government was forced to enact a Knesset law prohibiting pig-breeding in the country except for a few specific places, to the chagrin of progressive members of the public."[75]

Once again, however, Olshan's description represents a personal interpretation that does not fully account for the subtleties of the parliamentary debate. The new bill submitted on the matter of pig-breeding reflected the national consensus that was still prevalent concerning pig-breeding prohibitions, at least within part of the secular public.[76] The bill was signed not only by representatives of the religious parties, but also by such MKs as Israel Yeshayahu of Mapai and Esther Raziel-Naor of Herut who had expressed their views on this matter in the debates leading to the enactment of the Special Enablement Law.[77] Knesset debates on the new bill indeed replicated, in many respects, the range of approaches and the fervor that had accompanied the Special Enablement Law six years earlier. Moshe Unna, from the National Religious Party (NRP), who presented the bill during the first reading in the name of the Knesset's Committee on Constitution, Law and Justice,[78] reiterated its national rationale: "This law is unquestionably unique and probably without precedent in the world's statutes. Some view this as a reason for shame. I view this as a reason for pride, because this law in some ways conveys the uniqueness of the State of Israel as the preserver of this nation's special tradition, upholding the need for continuing ways of life endorsed by the Jewish people throughout its history."[79]

The speech of Herut leader Menachem Begin in this matter was particularly striking. He welcomed the bill as an initiative long due, and regretted even the few exceptions it had granted (and particularly the law's stipulation setting aside areas in which pig-breeding would be permitted).[80] By contrast, representatives from the left remained determined and relentless in their opposition to the law, invoking freedom of conscience and the prevention of coercion. Israel Bar-Yehuda of Ahdut ha-Avodah/ Po'alei Zion argued that laws respecting traditional practices could prove a slippery slope—why not Sabbath observance, for instance?[81]

The outcome of this parliamentary procedure was the enactment of the Pig-Raising Prohibition Law of 1962.[82] *Ha-Tsofeh* again emphasized the wide support mustered by this bill, submitted by representatives of several parties, including Mapai and Herut.[83] According to Section 1 of the law: "A person shall not raise, keep, or slaughter pigs."[84] Accordingly, the Special Enablement Law was amended so that it would no longer apply to raising and keeping pigs but rather only to pork-trading.[85] The sweeping prohibition excluded only a small number of municipalities, populated mainly by Christians, which were defined in a schedule to the law in accordance with Section 2(1),[86] and could be omitted from it upon request.[87] The regulations required for enforcing the new law followed soon after.[88]

In sum, the 1950s and 1960s may be described as a period of determined and significant legal activity aimed at absorbing pig prohibitions into Israeli law. The religious parties were the catalyst for various legal initiatives in this regard, but they were also supported by secular political forces. The enactment of laws in this matter followed pertinent Supreme Court rulings that insisted on clear statutory authorization for prohibitions on pig-breeding and pork-trading and considered administrative initiatives insufficient. A political coalition based on Mapai and the religious-Zionist parties, supported in this context also by Herut, was successful in enacting these prohibitions. The intensive enforcement of the new laws in their formative years will be the subject of the next chapter.

CHAPTER 6

Formative Battles of Enforcement

A N EVALUATION OF PREVAILING ATTITUDES toward the incorporation of pig-related prohibitions into Israeli law should address not only the legislation but also its actual enforcement. The Special Enablement Law and the Pig-Raising Prohibition Law were not merely declarative statements, and included mechanisms aimed at their effective enforcement. Enforcement initiatives, originating at both the municipal and national levels of government, attested to the relatively broad even if not consensual support enjoyed by these laws.

Following the enactment of the Special Enablement Law, Tel Aviv again blazed the trail and enacted a new bylaw designed to replace its original bylaw on the pork trade, which the High Court of Justice had nullified.[1] Preparations for the promulgation began immediately after the enactment of the Special Enablement Law.[2] Before voting on the new bylaw, members of the council engaged in a lengthy debate and explained their positions.[3] The range of opinions during the debate largely reflected the divisions in the Knesset plenum. Support for the bylaw came not only from the religious members in the city council (Boyer and Abramovicz) but also from representatives of secular factions, some of whom supported the law for its symbolic and historical value. Thus, for instance, M. Cohen indicated: "Throughout history, the pig has symbolized hatred for the people of Israel—during the period of the Marranos in Spain, the persecutions in Europe, and so forth. I think that Jewish morality and Jewish honor require us to consider and implement this law."[4] Other members of the council, however, were sharply critical of the religious coercion implied by the proposed bylaw, of the lack of any exemptions for Christians, and of the faulty priorities represented by the discussion of this question before other and more urgent social issues.[5]

The approval process for the bylaw by the Ministry of the Interior continued the debate that had accompanied the Knesset legislation.[6] As a rule, municipal bylaws require authorization by the minister of the interior in accordance with the Municipal Corporations Ordinance. Yet, some proponents of the bylaws enacted under the Special Enablement Law argued no such authorization was required in their regard, since these bylaws were enacted according to a separate and independent law and thus not subject to the general regulation of the Municipal Corporations Ordinance.[7] Silbiger, the municipal legal counsel, supported the stricter approach requiring that the new bylaw be submitted for authorization so as to remove any doubts in regard to its validity. In a letter to the deputy mayor, Silbiger explained: "At present, lawyers are seriously divided as to whether a bylaw of this type requires the endorsement of the minister of the interior. Yet, the very fact that doubts prevail concerning such a fundamental question justifies seeking this endorsement in order to preclude significant objections in this regard."[8] Deputy Mayor Boyer, who wanted to see swift progress with this bylaw, criticized Mayor Lebanon for sending it for authorization "when you know that the pig issue is controversial."[9] In response, Silbiger reiterated the rationale of his cautious approach: "I will only note that I was bound to ensure that, in a bylaw of this type, it was particularly important to ensure the widest possible legal validity."[10] Deputy Mayor Boyer pointed out that the authorization of the original bylaw invalidated by the Supreme Court had also been prolonged unnecessarily. He even wrote on this matter to Deputy Minister of Religious Affairs Zerah Warhaftig, protesting that two months had already elapsed since the new bylaw had been sent for authorization to the minister of the interior and had since been "lying in someone's drawer."[11]

Israel Bar-Yehuda, then the minister of the interior representing the Ahdut ha-Avodah party, returned the bylaw to the Tel Aviv municipality with many comments intended to limit its scope.[12] The reservations conveyed in his letter relate to definitions (narrowing the term "pig" to "domestic pig," confining the restriction on "consumption" in general to "human consumption," and further narrowing the restriction to exempt medical uses), as well as to the scope of the powers to enforce the bylaw.

The minister held that the bylaw should state that the confiscation of pork, as opposed to its attachment, would only be possible with a court decision and that no searches could be conducted on residential premises. Bar-Yehuda's demands were resented by the Tel Aviv municipality,[13] and Mayor Lebanon rejected most of them. In his response, however, the minister insisted on most of his original demands.[14] This conflict was a focus of political turmoil involving extensive parliamentary activity.[15] The matter was finally settled by means of a compromise mediated by Prime Minister Ben-Gurion.[16] This compromise involved, among other things, the reformulation of the confiscatory powers and the addition of a stipulation that inspectors could search private residences only if authorized by a search warrant issued under the Criminal Procedure (Arrest and Searches) Ordinance.[17] At the end of this process, the Tel Aviv bylaw was enacted,[18] and most municipal authorities subsequently enacted their own bylaws restricting pig-breeding and the sale of pork.[19]

As noted, the purpose of enacting bylaws was not only symbolic, and a campaign to implement them was immediately put into effect. The person responsible for enforcing the Tel Aviv bylaw was Haim Broide, who related in his memoirs:

> I was summoned by the municipality's executive and assigned the task of making provisions for the bylaw's enforcement. Ten workers from the sanitation department were recruited, and the mayor granted them the necessary legal powers required to implement the bylaw. The new unit of inspectors (including a pickup truck with a driver) went through an intensive course taught by Dr. A. Levitt, the municipal veterinary surgeon, to learn about the different cuts of meat. On 1 July 1957, equipped with knowledge and motivation, the inspectors' unit began its activities within the city. A list of businesses was prepared in which, according to our information, pork and pork products were being sold. Indeed, a month after the beginning of the inspections, pork disappeared from butchers' counters in shops and stores and went underground. The open sale of pork had ceased.[20]

At this stage, since the power to enact applicable bylaws could no longer be contested, opposition to the legal enforcement of pig-related prohibitions focused on questioning the scope of their application and implementation.

One matter of principle concerned the prohibition's relevance to non-Jews.[21] This issue was considered by the Supreme Court in its decision in the case of *Manshi v. Minister of the Interior and the Municipality of Tel Aviv–Jaffa*,[22] rendered in a matter involving a Christian who owned a butchery. In principle, however, the question was also pertinent to Christian buyers of pork. Among the group of Christian pork consumers, the diplomatic representatives residing in Tel Aviv were an important subgroup. One report on the early stages of the bylaw's implementation refers to an incident in which purchases made by clients from diplomatic missions were searched.[23] In *Manshi*, the petitioner objected to the application of the Tel-Aviv bylaw to the whole city without any distinctions, arguing that this broad application was unreasonable. Earlier, church leaders in Jaffa had appealed to the mayor on behalf of the petitioner to the effect that, as a Christian, he should be permitted to engage in pork-trading. The mayor rejected the request explaining that eating pork and breeding pigs, were not prohibited by the Christian religion but were not considered religious duties.[24] A petition in this matter was subsequently submitted but dismissed, since the shop in question was not located in an area that could be properly distinguished and exempted from the prohibition on grounds of its population's specific characteristics. Nevertheless, the option of invalidating a bylaw of this type by reason of its failure to exempt areas manifestly populated by non-Jews was acknowledged in Justice Berenson's separate opinion:

> The law's intention is, above all, to meet the national and religious needs of the observant Jewish population, for whom the pig is the symbol of impurity. The Knesset, however, did not see fit to issue its own legislation concerning the breeding and upkeep of pigs and the sale of pork and its products on a nationwide basis. It empowered the local authorities to impose such prohibitions or restrictions on a local basis, but enabled each local authority to exclude certain areas from the prohibited or restricted zones. Bearing in mind the purpose of the law and the way in which the legislature chose to implement it, I hold that if a local authority were to abstain from the use of this option in regard to a defined body of citizens living in a concentrated territorial location and interested in implementing this possibility for its own benefit, it would be acting contrary to the legislator's intention.[25]

Justice Berenson's remarks emphasize that the legislation had been motivated by Jewish concerns, although it was certainly compatible with Muslim traditions. Although his comments had no effect on the result in this case, they eventually proved significant, as discussed in chapter 8.

In Haifa, for instance, a city with a mixed population of Arabs and Jews, the local bylaw did distinguish between various city neighborhoods.[26] Even this bylaw, however, was subject to litigation, which concentrated on other matters. Thus, the Court was asked to consider the argument that an abattoir for pigs within city limits did not contradict the bylaw, because the pigs were kept in it only for a short period of time. The Court dismissed this petition as well, and held that the prohibition against keeping pigs in the city applied also to the abattoir, regardless of how long the animals were actually there.[27]

Another question of principle related to the scope of the powers to confiscate pork possessed contrary to the bylaw's stipulations. Was this an independent administrative power, or could it be exercised only when the possessor was convicted of a criminal offense for trading in the merchandise targeted for confiscation? The Supreme Court preferred a restrictive interpretation of these confiscatory powers, protecting individual rights and allowing their infringement only after proper judicial process, and so ruled in the case of *Lubin v. Municipality of Tel Aviv–Jaffa* (henceforth "HC *Lubin*").[28] Justice Silberg dissented and favored the wider interpretation of these confiscatory powers, bearing in mind the uniqueness of the empowering statute, which conveyed the traditional revulsion and abhorrence evoked by pigs. Justice Silberg opens HC *Lubin* with a reference to the Jewish attitude toward pigs: "Since time immemorial, Jews have viewed pigs as a symbol of abhorrence, abomination, and revulsion."[29] Likewise, in *Municipality of Tel Aviv–Jaffa v. Lubin* (henceforth "FH *Lubin*"), Justice Silberg referred to the "feelings of nausea and revulsion arising in the heart of a Jew—an 'ordinary' Jew and not necessarily a very Orthodox one—at the sight of pork chops displayed in shop windows or shop counters."[30]

Given these arguments, it is surprising to realize that several years later, in his decision in *Yizramax Ltd. v. State of Israel*,[31] Justice Silberg described pig-prohibition laws as an instance of the legal enforcement of religious doctrine, which he classified as traditional *mitzvot shimiy'ot* (ritual and ceremonial commandments that are not based on reason).[32]

In that decision, Justice Silberg made no allusion to the culturo-national significance of these prohibitions. The context appears to explain this change: in the *Yizramax* decision, Justice Silberg attempted to justify the legal regulation of the Sabbath rest, explaining that, contrary to pig prohibitions, it belonged to a category of religious rules that could also be justified in secular terms, that he classified as traditional *mitzvot sikhliyyot* (commandments that human beings would have discovered on rational grounds, even if they had not been divinely revealed).

An additional difficulty concerned searches for the purpose of seizing pork. As noted, in his comments on the wording of the Tel Aviv bylaw, the minister of the interior had sought to add a qualification concerning searches of private residences. The compromise reached in this matter was that inspectors would conduct such searches based on special authorization by the minister of police, in accordance with the Criminal Procedure (Arrest and Searches) Ordinance. Nevertheless, when the mayor asked Minister of Police Bekhor Sheetrit to appoint the inspectors as police officers according to the Criminal Procedure (Arrest and Searches) Ordinance, the request was denied based on the opinion of Attorney General Haim Cohn, who considered such appointments impossible. According to Cohn, the municipality could not empower the minister of police to appoint inspectors as police officers because "the minister of police's powers (namely, the powers of the government) are not vested in legislation enacted by local authorities, unless the legislature expressly empowers local authorities to act in this manner. These are simple and fundamental issues." At the end of his opinion, the attorney general added: "As for myself, I see no need for legislation in order to amend this situation: in my view, it would be best if searches of residential homes were only conducted in the letter and spirit of the provisions of section 17 of the Criminal Procedure (Arrest and Search) Ordinance, and the more stringently applied, the better."[33]

Beyond these fundamental issues, enforcement occasionally dealt with other challenges. In HC *Lubin,* the Supreme Court dismissed the argument that the law's prohibition applied only to pork, rather than to all products made from pigs.[34] Another argument adduced by several pork dealers was that the prohibition related only to the sale of pork within the city, as opposed to the mere possession of pork. Thus, an additional difficulty concerning confiscatory powers was that they could only be exercised in respect to pork sold in the city, as opposed to meat meant for sale outside it. In one case, a factory that manufactured pork products claimed it only sold them outside city limits. The petition was supported by an affidavit signed by one of the owners. Cross-examination, however, revealed that the firm had been involved in the sale of pork within city limits as well, although goods had only been sold to merchants who owned shops in other cities.[35] The issue emerged again in a case ruling that confiscatory powers could only be exercised when the local authority had proof that the meat was intended for sale within its area of jurisdiction, since the law did not prohibit the possession of pork as such.[36] Note that some of the merchandise confiscated in this case had been intended for the butcher shop of Joseph Lubin, who had been central in the litigation that resulted in the precedent-setting ruling on confiscatory powers.[37]

Likewise, a magistrates' court acquitted a person who had been charged with attacking inspectors, after the latter testified they "had come to check whether the accused 'was holding' pork in his restaurant." Judge Magori held in this case that, in the given circumstances, "from the point of view of the inspectors' intention when coming to the restaurant of the accused, they had done so without lawful authority." An additional reason for the acquittal was that the inspectors' letter of appointment had not been signed by the mayor.[38]

In some cases, owners of butcher shops even engaged in actual physical opposition: "Owners of 'the other thing' did not accept the new situation easily. There were serious cases of physical attacks by ruffians from among the pork sellers. Yet, the support of the police—who deserve praise here—deterred the aggressors. Moreover, the attitude of the vast majority of Tel Aviv's population toward the inspectors is worth noting, as manifest in calls of encouragement wherever the unit has acted in the city."[39] In general, however, the enforcement of the new bylaws was by then on course. City archives contain numerous reports of attacks on inspectors by shop owners. In these cases, details of the incidents were recorded and the inspectors gave witness statements to the police.[40]

The enactment of the Pig-Raising Prohibition Law was also followed by rigorous enforcement. After the law was passed, most of the kibbutzim liquidated their pig herds. Although the law included no compensation for pig-breeders whose businesses had suffered damages, the Ministry of

Finance did authorize a scheme indemnifying them for their losses.[41] At the same time, several private breeders decided to move their businesses to the restricted areas defined as the exception to the rule. Pig-breeding, then, was forced to concentrate rather than to disappear completely.

One noteworthy instance involved eight breeders who established a partnership in order to buy land in the Arab locality of Iblin in order to raise pigs. The partnership obtained a written declaration from the mayor of Iblin, who was interested in attracting economic investment, that the locality would not apply to the Ministry of the Interior for the purpose of omitting its name from the schedule to the law which mentions the areas in which the raising of pigs is legal.[42] This declaration was intended to assure the partnership that pig-breeding would be legal in Iblin in the future as well, although it remained questionable whether such a promise could be fulfilled if local circumstances and preferences were to change.

In general, the law was followed by several initiatives that were meant to hamper pig-breeding even in the restricted areas where it had been allowed. First, the letter of the law was interpreted in strict terms, making it impossible to transport pigs from a legal farm to a legal abattoir if the road from one to the other passed through an area where the keeping of pigs was prohibited. This interpretation was based on a precedent that established that a municipal bylaw forbidding the keeping of pigs applied also to keeping them for slaughter, even for a brief period.[43] In practice, applying the law in this manner resulted in the seizure of vehicles transporting legally bred pigs to legally established abattoirs.[44] Justice Halevi explained: "The purpose of the law prohibiting the breeding, keeping, and slaughter of pigs in most of the country is to prevent pigs— which, as it were, should be 'neither seen nor found'—from 'gaining a foothold,' as the Hebrew idiom goes. This notion rests on the deep aversion, common to most people in this country and dating back to ancient times, for this symbol of impurity and anti-Jewish hatred. For this reason and with this purpose, limitations were made to apply not only to its breeding areas, but also to its keeping and slaughter, confining it to the localities enumerated in the schedule (every one of these localities can decide to delete its name from the list in the schedule)."[45]

Second, the general policy of establishing only one abattoir in each municipality created great difficulties for pig-breeders, who were concentrated in a few municipalities. In one case, the court dismissed a petition against this policy of single abattoirs. The petitioners were the pig-breeders who had moved their business to Iblin when the Pig-Raising Prohibition Law was enacted. The condition of the roads hindered their access to the only permitted abattoir located in the municipality, whereas transportation to another abattoir nearby was technically illegal because the route to it passed through an area where keeping pigs was illegal. The court dismissed the petition nonetheless, on the grounds that strict sanitary supervision in abattoirs was imperative and made easier when each locality concentrated its activities.[46] In practice, according to regulations bearing on the veterinary aspects of animal slaughter, only three abattoirs for pigs were legally authorized, and two of them were in the north where most pigs were bred.[47] Furthermore, the Ministry of the Interior allowed the municipal authorities in pig-breeding areas to impose relatively high local taxes on the breeders.[48]

These initiatives supplemented other administrative measures that had burdened pig-breeding even before the enactment of the new law, such as the enforcement of emergency regulations limiting the use of bread and flour for feeding animals in a way that placed additional restrictions on uses of food for breeding pigs,[49] and the insistence on municipal ownership of abattoirs, which led to the closing of private pig abattoirs.[50]

In another context, the Pig-Raising Prohibition Law had casted its shadow on the litigation concerning the change in status of the municipality of Kafr Yasif from a type A local council to a type B local council (for the purposes of local government law).[51] This change of status would have enabled the appointment of two more members to the local council, both of whom supported the removal of Kafr Yasif from the list of towns allowing pig-breeding. According to the petitioners, the minister of the interior's decision to change the status of Kafr Yasif reflected his desire to expand the application of pig-related prohibitions. The petitioners' argument relied on a report to this effect that had appeared in *Ha-Tsofeh*, the daily published by the NRP (the National Religious Party), which was the minister's party. But the Court rejected this assertion as unsupported by fact.

A frontal attack against the validity of the law as enacted was attempted in the case of *Bazul v. Minister of the Interior*.[52] The petitioners argued that, despite a provision in the law requiring that maps delimiting the districts to be exempted from the pig-breeding prohibition be submitted to the offices of the district commissioners prior to the law's enactment, this had in fact not been done. Their claim was that the law was therefore based on an incorrect factual determination. This challenge to the provisions of the law instigated a serious discussion at the Supreme Court regarding the Knesset's sovereignty, and the petition was ultimately dismissed on this basis. In Justice Berenson's words: "I think that all would agree that the courts cannot pass judgment on the legislators' qualities."[53] This ruling is unique insofar as its concern was probably the sole instance in which the challengers of pig-related legislation were Muslims opposed to the setting-up of an enclosure for pigs in their village. Rather than the prohibition itself, however, the petitioners were challenging one of the exceptions stated in the schedule—the village of Raineh in which they resided. One of the additional arguments presented in the petition was that licensing the building of a pig enclosure would offend the sensibilities and way of life of the area's Muslim residents. The Supreme Court dismissed this argument by reiterating prior precedents establishing that planning authorities can only take planning and sanitation considerations into account.[54]

The *Bazul* decision, which approved the constitutional principle of parliamentary sovereignty, indirectly strengthened the Pig-Raising Prohibition Law and the Special Enablement Law by sanctioning the legislature as the final instance in Israel's political system. Arguments that these laws curtailed liberties, therefore, were deemed irrelevant once the legislative process had been concluded. In any event, and as this chapter has shown, the two laws imposing pig-related prohibitions enjoyed relatively broad popular support in the 1950s and 1960s and, accordingly, were seriously enforced in the years following their enactment.

CHAPTER 7

From Status Quo
to Political Conflict

The 1970s and 1980s

A FTER A PERIOD OF INTENSIVE LITIGATION over pig-related prohibitions during the 1950s and 1960s, interest in the issue waned. During the 1970s, not a single case dealing with pig prohibitions
reached the Supreme Court. What was behind this quiescence? The explanation is complex.

One hypothesis would be that pork consumption was not normative
in Israel during a time of adequate food supplies, as opposed to the scarcity that had characterized the 1950s, and restricting the availability of
pork was thus no cause for bother. Yet, this explanation for the relative
dormancy of this issue at the time is only partial. No less significant
might be the relative tolerance toward infringements of the statutory pig
prohibitions. It is common knowledge, for instance, that all nonkosher
butcher shops in the large cities sold and still sell meat products manufactured at kibbutz Mizra, despite Mizra's open admission that their
goods contain pork.

The deterrent effect of enforcing the municipal bylaws on these butcheries was relatively minor, as evidenced by their long-standing activities.
Indictments were issued, but shop owners learned to contend with them
as perhaps irksome, but not unbearable. Adv. Gabi Priel, who currently
heads the civil law section of the Tel Aviv municipality legal department,
recollected her work as a young prosecutor for the municipality in
the 1970s, when she dealt with many indictments against the owners of
butcher shops that sold pork. This was part of her routine, and appar-
ently also of that of the shop owners concerned. Legal proceedings would

usually end with a fine. Priel remembered that most indictments dealt with the seizure of relatively small quantities, since butchers tended to keep the display of pork products to a minimum, and were probably storing the bulk of such products in a "safe place."[1]

The chairman of the Tel Aviv religious council at the time, Pinhas Sheinman, warned Mayor Yehoshua Rabinowitz against the "pig bane that has recently spread in our city" when "pork is transported in open vehicles traveling daily from the Carmel market to local shops, for sale as meat or for the manufacture of sausages."[2] The "Pigs and Pork Bylaw" folders of the legal department at Tel-Aviv municipality for 1957–1988 show extensive dealings on this matter dating from the 1950s and the beginning of the 1960s, but no correspondence whatsoever for the years 1966 to 1978. The single document from the latter period is a page of guidelines and explanations on "powers regarding the control of pork" prepared by Adv. Sherry of the legal department, accompanied by a handwritten note saying, "Personally delivered to Israel Grabinsky, assistant to the mayor, 20.2.75."

Penalties for offenses legislated in both the Special Enablement Law and the Pig-Raising Prohibition Law were limited to fines.[3] Worth noting in this context is a ruling issued in a civil action undertaken to evict a butchery owner in the city of Petah Tikva from premises where she enjoyed a protected-tenant status.[4] The indictment claimed that the defendant had conducted illegal activities on the premises by selling pork from the Mizra plant, infringing the municipal bylaw. We learn from the judgment that the defendant had been convicted of selling pork on two previous occasions in 1978.[5] The ruling was issued in 1992, and notes no further enforcement measures against the shop, which evidently kept selling pork throughout this period, even though it was situated in the same building as the offices of the Petah Tikvah Chief Rabbinate.[6]

A temporary lull also prevailed regarding pig-breeding, which continued unabated in areas that had been excluded from the application of the Pig Raising Prohibition Law. Thus, for instance, the successful meat plant at kibbutz Mizra relied on the purchase of pork from districts where pig-breeding was permitted. Note also the skillful use of other exceptions included in the law, such as the one allowing pig-breeding in "scientific and research institutions" (in addition to "public zoological gardens").[7] The most prominent instance was the creation of an "Institute for Livestock

Science and Research" at Kibbutz Lahav. According to the kibbutz, the institute maintained pigs for research purposes. When the authorities began to exercise their powers of confiscation and slaughter, a petition was submitted to the High Court of Justice arguing that the law did not apply to research institutes. The dispute hinged on the definition of the criteria for recognizing an organization as a research institute, and the Court ultimately held that the petitioner had succeeded in establishing its status as a scholarly institution.[8] In practice, indirect evidence suggests that Kibbutz Lahav had overstepped the narrow boundaries of research. Dov Rosen, a senior official responsible for implementing the law at the Ministry of the Interior, wrote on this matter to Justice Berenson after his retirement from the bench. In his letter, Rosen criticized the Court's ruling by referring to the scope of the pig-breeding program at Kibbutz Lahav, which was expanded even further over the years, and pointing out that the "Institute for Livestock Science and Research" was incorporated only close to the time at which the law came into effect.[9] All the parties involved, however, seem to have found it convenient to accept the existence of exceptions, as long as these did not exceed certain limits— the status quo at its best.

A comparison with the national prohibition on alcohol in the United States could shed light on the contribution of restricted scope and mild enforcement to the endurance of the Israeli pig prohibitions. Pig prohibitions were enacted in Israel against a background of relatively small demand and, from the start, were limited to economic sanctions. By contrast, the 18th Amendment prohibition on alcohol in the U.S. went against accepted social practice and a significant demand for liquor[10] and resulted in many arrests.[11] These differences shed light on Prohibition's "short, stormy and unhappy life."[12]

In the broader context of religion and state relationships, the quiescence in the context of pig legislation was part of a general decrease in the struggles and controversies surrounding religious issues during the same period. Religious-Zionist circles, which had always been the standard-bearers of religious legislation intended to shape and influence the public arena, now invested most of their energy and efforts in the settling of the territories occupied during the Six-Day War in 1967. The settling of ancestral lands substantially replaced traditional concerns about the role of religion in the State of Israel, a process that Dan Horowitz and Moshe

Lissak describe as follows: "In the Religious-Zionist camp, the stress has shifted from a desire to use the party's political leverage to strengthen the status of religion in Israel, to an approach that sees the Halakhah as a source of policy guidelines for central national issues not directly concerned with matters of religion and state. Thus, certain Religious Zion ist groups led by Gush Emunim justify their struggle for preserving the state's hold on Greater Israel and for settlement across the Green Line by resorting to ideological arguments based on their interpretation of the Halakhah. This can be termed a transition from the 'politicization of religion' to a 'religiosization of politics,' also involving a 'theologization' of ideology.'"[13]

Indeed, as argued in previous chapters, legislation on pork-trading and pig-breeding did not rest solely on religious grounds but was also borne on the wings of nationalism. Religious parties, however, were highly instrumental in initiating it and in lobbying support for it among secular politicians. The shift of emphasis in religious politics is therefore relevant to the understanding of the relative silence surrounding the enforcement of pig-related legislation during the 1970s. A decade after extensive legal efforts had been devoted to the introduction of pig prohibitions into Israeli law, the entire issue had become almost irrelevant in both legal and political terms. Not for long, however.

The issue of pig-breeding resurfaced in Israel in the 1980s, with the renewal of the historical conflict over the ethos of Israeli society. After the 1977 elections, and for the first time since the establishment of the state, the right-wing Likud party formed a government after joining forces with the religious parties. The hegemony that the Labor movement (under various names and guises) had preserved throughout Zionist history collapsed, resulting in social processes led by political forces usually described as right-wing and traditional.[14] The 1980s were characterized by a surge of religiously inspired laws and policies, as well as by a confrontation between religious and secular politics. Pressed by the religious parties within the ruling coalition, the government ordered in 1982 that the national airline El-Al should not fly on the Sabbath and Jewish holidays.[15] In roughly the mid-1980s, several Sabbath battles were fought over the opening of movie theaters on the eve of the Sabbath in municipalities with significant religious populations such as Petah Tikvah[16] and Jerusalem.[17] The conflict surrounding the operation of the Heikhal cinema in Petah-Tikvah was particularly fierce.[18] These Sabbath battles led to the enactment of an amendment to the Municipal Corporations Ordinance, which authorized municipalities to enact bylaws prohibiting the operation of businesses on the Sabbath.[19] The renewed efforts to eradicate pigs should be considered within this context.

Given the dismal failure so far of all efforts to eliminate the pork trade, bills intended to widen pig-related prohibitions were placed on the Knesset agenda as early as the beginning of the 1980s. These bills were submitted with the understanding that the municipal enforcement of pig prohibitions had not proved a significant deterrent.

Documents in the Tel Aviv municipality archives reveal increasing discomfort among representatives of religious parties in the face of what they regarded as tepid enforcement of the pig prohibitions. In 1978, the chairman of the municipal committee for religious services, Dr. David Rosen-Zvi, wrote to the municipal legal counsel, Adv. Talmor, cautioning him, "There is no justification for delaying the filing of legal proceedings in matters dealing with the municipal bylaw for the eradication of pigs and, accordingly, suspending the filing of such proceedings is not possible."[20] The legal counsel adopted a conciliatory approach in his reply: "I never had any intention of reducing the trial days allocated to cases linked to the pig-eradication bylaw." Counsel went further: "The problem is not with detracting from what exists, but with the demand to add trial days to these proceedings, given the present backlog regarding these cases. Trial days available for this issue appear to be insufficient. The prosecution was therefore of the opinion that filing additional proceedings was pointless as long as so many old cases have not yet been brought for adjudication, and no date has been set for trial."[21]

Soon afterwards, an urgent letter was addressed to Mayor Shlomo Lahat by deputy mayors Adv. Haim Basok and Rabbi Abramovicz representing the NRP, and by Dr. Rosen-Zvi, the above-mentioned chairman of the committee for religious services. In this letter, they write that the municipal legal counsel had informed them he "had received instructions to cease filing legal proceedings on the municipal bylaw on pig eradication."[22] Basok presented the mayor with a number of proposals for improving enforcement in this area, including one to expand the scope of the bylaw and one to amend the national prohibition law.[23] In another letter, he suggested putting offences under this bylaw into a category allowing offenders to opt for paying a fine instead of going to trial. Basok explained that the effectiveness of bylaws lay in the speed of their implementation and that rapid enforcement was more easily achieved through fines.[24]

Lack of enforcement, however, cannot explain by itself the new legislative initiatives in this area during the 1980s. These initiatives may be better understood as reflecting the empowerment of the religious parties during that period, together with their expanded political activities.[25] This period also saw the enactment of, for instance, the Festival of Matzot (Prohibition of Leaven) Law of 1986, which focused on another prohibition whose significance is mainly religious and symbolic.[26] This law, however, was far more moderate than the bill aimed at a complete ban on pig-breeding and marketing. It was concerned with a time-restricted prohibition (the seven days of Passover), and was limited to the public domain in localities with a Jewish majority.[27] In the broader context of this period, the enactment of the Foundations of Law Act of 1980 should also be noted. This law ordained that pending legal questions that could not be settled by statute, case law, or analogy, should be decided by reliance on "the principles of freedom, justice, equity, and peace of Israel's heritage." This choice of inspirational sources for Israeli law is of no practical significance in the vast majority of cases which are usually regulated by statutes or settled by case law, but its symbolic value is unquestionable.

The statutory forerunners of pig-related prohibitions were two identical bills proposed by religious MKs from Agudat Israel and the NRP, which sought to impose an absolute ban on pork-trading. The bills accepted the existence of an "enclave" in the north, which had already been acknowledged in the original Pig-Raising Prohibition Law, but sought to prevent a situation whereby this district served as a springboard for the marketing of pork to the entire country.[28] The religious representatives justified these motions as a necessary supplement to the extant law, which had failed to achieve its objective.

The Knesset debates around the new bills revealed irreconcilable differences between religious and secular MKs. Religious MKs pointed out that the existing legislation had not achieved its goals. Although their new initiatives were aimed at broadening existing prohibitions, they insisted that their intention was to preserve the basic "core" of past legislation, namely, that pork should not be easily accessible in Israel. By contrast, secular MKs argued that the new legislative initiatives in this matter represented a never-ending crusade to broaden enforcement of religious norms through state law.

Although religious speakers resorted to national and historic explanations, this time they failed to convince the other side. MK Yehuda Meir Abramovicz from Agudat Israel cited a reader's letter to *Davar* (the Labor party daily newspaper) supporting his initiative and relying on Berl Katsanelson's well-known position.[29] MK Yehuda Ben-Meir from the NRP quoted a childhood anecdote of a former Mapai MK, who had learned from his father to avoid places that "smelled of pigs" because "wherever there are pigs, Jews are beaten."[30] These exhortations no longer resonated among secular MKs, who viewed these bills as part of a wider surge of religious legislation. MK Mordechai Virshubski of Shinui, who represented the secular "side" in the debate, was strongly opposed to any expansion of existing prohibitions, given the radical nature of the new proposals and the dangerous precedent they implied for the enforcement of other religious prohibitions, such as driving on the Sabbath.[31] In his remarks, he drew a distinction between the legitimacy of an arrangement seeking to refrain from "offending people's sensibilities" and "laws that would establish a halakhic life style."[32] He viewed pig legislation, then, as a religious rather than a national matter, and said that it should be confined to ensure that religious feelings would not be offended. A vote at the conclusion of the debate referred the bills to the Knesset's House Committee, which was to decide on the parliamentary committee that would proceed with the preparation of the bills for enactment. There they languished for a number of years, but the matter did not vanish from the new agenda of religious legislation, as will be clarified below.

Interest in the issue intensified in 1985 following a new bill seeking to expand extant pig-related prohibitions,[33] this time initiated by a group of MKs from the NRP, Shas and the Likud. This bill also aimed to replace the compromise embodied in the Special Enablement Law (leaving pork-trading to the discretion of each local authority) with a nationwide prohibition on pork sales. The debate on the new pork bill exposes even more visibly the shift in the approach of secular MKs to any legislation in this matter. In contrast to the qualified willingness of many MKs to approach pig prohibitions as a national symbol in the 1950s, the division between secular and religious representatives was now very obvious. The bill was submitted by MK Avraham Shapira of Agudat Israel, who was then known as "the country's CEO" due to his pivotal role in political life and his contribution to keeping the government coalition together. Like his predecessors, Shapira tried to justify the bill by claiming it was a national rather than a religious law.[34] MK Menachem Hacohen, of the Religious Worker movement affiliated with the Labor party, also focused on national-cultural facets in the legislation of pig prohibitions in a debate on a similar bill submitted at the time.[35]

By contrast, note that the minister of the interior, Rabbi Yitzhak Peretz from Shas, supported the bill by stressing its religious value. Shas was a new religious party that had emerged as a significant political force in the 1980s and called for a "return to the roots." Rabbi Peretz quoted at length from traditional sources and even crossed over into religious preaching: "My dear friends and brothers, honorable Knesset members, let us abandon for the moment the dispute between us and let us all unite with the values of Israel, with the Torah of Israel, with the heroes of Israel. Let all of us, without exception, bear this banner, the banner forbidding the breeding and marketing of pigs in the Land of Israel. We shall then provide a wonderful educational example to the young generation in the Land of Israel as to what are the people of Israel, what is the Torah of Israel, and what are the values of Israel."[36]

This selection of Knesset speeches highlights the renewed vigor of religious politics at the time and the internal competition between the various religious parties, each seeking to emphasize its own contribution.

Unlike the 1950s, however, the Knesset's secular majority no longer welcomed such exhortations, and the opposition was not confined to distinctively left-wing parties. During the bill's first reading,[37] almost all the secular speakers sharply opposed all attempts to broaden extant statutory prohibitions, judging them to be a form of religious coercion and an illegitimate break with past compromises. The inclination to view these prohibitions as a legitimate expression of a national symbol had almost vanished. Secular MKs also recoiled from the zeal displayed by the religious parties to expand their achievements in the area. Not surprisingly, MKs from left-wing parties, such as Yosef Sarid (Citizens' Rights Movement), Mordechai Virshubski (Shinui), and Eliezer Granot (Mapam), fiercely rejected any legislation on this matter. But even Yitzhak Artsi and Shevah Weiss (Labor), who were aware of the sensitivity of the issue, were deterred by the bill's extremism. For similar reasons, the Association for Civil Rights in Israel published its opposition to the bill, claiming that its prohibitions were too far-reaching as it aimed to target all inhabitants indiscriminately, and focused not only on publicly performed acts.[38] The bill passed the first reading[39] and was referred to the Knesset's Economics Committee for further discussion.[40] There, however, the hearings came to a standstill. When a new Knesset was elected in 1988, legislative proceedings on the bill were left on the shelf. Generally, legislative proceedings on bills from a previous Knesset are continued only if the government so desires, in which case it notifies the new Knesset about its decision. In this case, the government did not exercise this option. MK Menahem Porush from Agudat Israel criticized the government for not continuing the proceedings on a bill that, in his view, had mustered wide support,[41] but his objection had no political impact.

The pig issue returned yet again to the political agenda in 1990, during a period marked by intense competition between the Likud and Labor parties for the support of the religious parties in order to form a coalition. In these circumstances, a new bill on this issue was initiated by Orthodox MKs.[42] The bill passed the preliminary reading and was referred to the Interior Committee after a roll-call vote in the plenum. Records reveal that many Likud MKs supported the proposal as an expression of their partnership with the religious parties, whereas the majority of Labor MKs were absent from the plenum and thereby supported the proposal indirectly, choosing political compromise.[43] Progress on this bill was one of the demands in the coalition negotiations towards the creation of a government led by the Likud later that year. The main coalition agreement between the Likud and the other coalition partners, mainly religious parties,[44] stipulated the preservation of the religious status quo and government support for bills on religious matters, including the "Pig Law."[45] This demand was reiterated in an additional agreement signed with Agudat Israel, which joined the coalition only later.[46] The agreement included the following proviso: "The enactment of the law prohibiting the marketing of pigs, which is on the agenda of the Knesset's Interior Committee, will be completed, in a version to be agreed."[47]

These agreements gave new impetus to the debate over the bill. They also fanned public resentment against a perceived slide towards religious coercion, and the media of the time reflects bitter controversy. Some writers concentrated on the extreme interference with civil liberties involved in legislation affecting decisions about what types of food should be available.[48] In this context, degrading comparisons were drawn with the Muslim republics of Iran and Saudi-Arabia.[49] Another article argued that the banning of "unclean" animals was the ultimate distinguishing trait of a primitive society.[50] Yet another comparison was made to the former Soviet Union. It held that that despite the extreme restriction of civil liberties in the USSR, the state had refrained from any involvement in the consumption of specific types of food.[51] Dan Margalit, a prominent columnist, emphasized the adverse effect of the proposed legislation and argued that secular Jews would refrain from abiding by tradition all the more if coerced to do so by law. By way of example, he mentioned the example of the Day of Atonement, which almost everyone respects by refraining from driving because this custom has not been coerced.[52] Referring to the northern area where pigs are bred, another journalist used the term "white line" to describe an imaginary border dividing it from the rest of the country (choosing "white" after the popular euphemism for pork as "white meat," and the phrase "white line" in contrast to the "green line" commonly used to describe the border between Israel and the occupied territories).[53] A further argument touched on the infringement of the liberties of Israel's Christian community and, in this regard, the Knesset's Interior Committee invited the Vatican's cultural attaché in Israel to speak.[54]

Another objection that, for the first time, became one of the leading arguments was that of the potential damages to pig-breeders who had developed a thriving industry over the years. By 1990, the bill could no longer be discussed at the abstract level of principles and MKs were required to consider its potential implications for investments in this sector and for its long-term development. Proceedings at the Knesset's Interior Committee, therefore, focused largely on the economic aspect of the law, following the pig-breeders' demands that compensation for the infringement of their property rights be included in the framework of the proposed legislation.[55] No wonder that the kibbutzim whose economy was based on the pork industry (Lahav and Mizra) led the public opposition to the bill[56] together with the daily *Al ha-Mishmar,* published by their movement.[57]

The opposition was not entirely successful in its attempt to bring these legislative proceedings to a stop. Agudat Israel's threat to quit the coalition government influenced the Knesset's Interior Committee to support the bill and even to take it a step further in a vote based on a small majority (10 to 9).[58] Yet, the opposition eventually succeeded in halting this initiative, which was not enacted into law until the end of that Knesset's term.

The legislative initiatives of the 1980s, intended to "notch up a degree" the moderate prohibitions of the 1950s and 1960s, ultimately failed to reach their aims. The only (and last) amendment to the Pig-Raising Prohibition Law was the removal of the town of Raineh from the list of places that, according to the law's schedule, were allowed to breed pigs, and even this change was carried out by an administrative order rather than by legislation.[59]

By the end of the 1980s, the Tel Aviv municipality initiated an order declaring offences against its bylaw on the pork trade an offense for which fines were optional.[60] Prima facie, this order could be viewed as a contribution to the bylaw's enforcement, which thereby became less dependent on setting a date for court proceedings.[61] In practice, however, the measure was an additional nail in the bylaw's coffin, since offences against it now carried less criminal connotations. Soon afterwards, the unit in charge of enforcing the bylaw was indeed disbanded.[62]

The 1980s, then, instilled new energy and motivation into the debate over the pig-related Israeli legislation, but had no practical effect on its scope. The new bills submitted during this period, seeking to expand existing legal prohibitions on pig-breeding and pork sales, were driven solely by religious motives. Not only were they not successful but they also served to emphasize even further the old-new battle over the status of religion in Israeli law. The secular public had neither tolerance nor respect for these bills, viewing them as obvious instances of religious coercion, and large segments within this public had by then abandoned any deep attachment to the age-old pig prohibition. At this time (in 1983), the Labor daily *Davar* began to publish a satirical section entitled "The Other Thing" (*Davar Aher*). This phrase is used as a euphemism for pigs in traditional texts, and the newspaper's choice of title suggests complete detachment from any associated sensitivities.[63]

In any event, the controversy around the proposed amendments during the 1980s was confined mainly to politicians and to the industry. "Ordinary Israelis" were not directly affected by the bills, which were never enacted. The battle was mainly over hegemony. This situation would change drastically in the years to follow, when legal prohibitions in this matter became relevant to the daily reality of many Israelis.

CHAPTER 8

The Renewed Challenge

The 1990s and Onwards

T HE RESURGENCE OF THE PIG CRISIS in Israeli law during the 1990s
can be attributed to developments in three main areas: the legal,
social, and political.

The chief development in the legal arena, described as a "constitutional
revolution,"[1] was the enactment of two new Basic Laws of 1992 aimed
at securing the constitutional status of human rights—Basic Law: Freedom of Occupation[2] and Basic Law: Human Dignity and Liberty. For
the first time since the establishment of the state of Israel, the Knesset
had enacted basic laws on human rights rather than basic laws merely
concerned with structural aspects of the regime. Soon after, the new Basic
Laws were interpreted as empowering the judiciary to overrule legislation that restricted the rights and freedoms guaranteed by the Basic Laws.[3]
Prohibiting pork sales or pig-breeding could easily be viewed as an instance of such a restriction, one that curtailed several freedoms. Pig prohibitions, therefore, were potential targets for petitions prompted by the
new Basic Laws. True, the two Basic Laws did not expressly protect freedom of religion. Attempts to ensure this freedom through a Basic Law
could not have mobilized sufficient political support due to the power
of the religious parties. These parties understood that full recognition of
this liberty could threaten the validity of religiously inspired extant legislation, including the implementation of religious law on matters of
marriage and divorce. The new Basic Laws included, however, other relevant provisions that potentially threatened the future of pig prohibitions in Israeli law, such as the constitutional guarantee of freedom of

occupation. Indeed, the new Basic Law: Freedom of Occupation, which had seemed politically neutral when originally enacted, was soon seen to be directly relevant to restrictions on pork trade and hence controversial. As shown below, pig prohibitions have since been challenged largely on grounds of freedom of occupation rather than by recourse to the arguments concerning freedom of religion and opposition to religious coercion that had characterized the 1950s debates.

The new Basic Laws, then, did have an impact on the implementation of pig-related legislation, even if their application with regard to prior legislation was limited. Basic Law: Freedom of Occupation secured existing legislation from judicial review for several years, and Basic Law: Human Dignity and Liberty permanently protected from judicial review all laws that had been in force prior to its enactment. But Supreme Court rulings soon acknowledged the indirect impact these had on existing legislation as well, as far as the interpretation of these laws and the application of the administrative powers they granted were concerned.[4]

In the period immediately following the adoption of the Basic Laws, a general controversy over recourse to religious considerations in decisions on food imports was at the forefront, and not the specific issue of pig legislation. The context was a plan to privatize the import of meat, a task traditionally performed by the government. The government decided to delay the privatization of meat imports until the enactment of a law prohibiting the import of nonkosher meat (not merely pork) but the Supreme Court held that this decision was unlawful in the absence of empowering legislation to this effect. The decision by the Court noted, however, that such legislation would probably not be in compliance with the requirements of the Basic Law: Freedom of Occupation.[5] This Basic Law was then amended to incorporate an "override clause" in the model of the Canadian Charter of Rights and Freedoms, which enables provisional legislation that does not meet constitutional standards. Furthermore, the amendment made an exception that enabled an unprovisional overriding legislation in this matter. Accordingly, the Import of Frozen Meat Law, 1994, was enacted, to expressly prohibit the import of nonkosher meat (not only pork). This law is now called the Meat and Meat Products Law, 1994, and it was recognized by the Supreme Court as meeting constitutional standards.[6]

Eventually, however, pig-related prohibitions reverted to their central place in the public arena. The challenge that the new Basic Laws posed to these prohibitions is especially complicated, since their declared purpose is to "establish in a Basic Law the values of the State of Israel as a Jewish and democratic state."[7] In this context, as in others, this constitutional formulation provokes questions and tensions. How should "Jewish" and "democratic" be reconciled? Pig prohibitions might be expected in a Jewish state, but is this also the case when democratic values are considered? Do democratic values necessarily contradict the enforcement of national symbolic norms that have become an integral part of state law? Do democratic values require rejecting only sweeping prohibitions on the consumption of pork that have never existed in Israeli law, or do they negate prohibitions on pig-breeding and trading that entail lesser privacy violations as well?

In the social realm, the 1990s saw a large wave of immigration from the former Soviet Union. About a million people arrived in Israel during this decade, amounting to approximately a sixth of the country's overall population. The new immigrants came to Israel as Jews, taking advantage of the Law of Return, 1951, which was enacted in order to secure a safe place for all Jews in their own homeland after the Holocaust. Culturally and religiously, however, and after some seventy years of a communist regime wary of religion and nationalism in general and of their Jewish manifestations in particular, these immigrants were detached from Jewish traditions. In addition, many Jews in the former Soviet Union had married non-Jews. Accordingly, the new immigrants, some of them not even Jews according to halakhic criteria, showed little of the usual revulsion evoked by pigs. Pork was part of their diet, and their demand for it gave new momentum to the pork trade. In an interview given in 1995, Chief Rabbi Bakshi-Doron expressed his concern about the potential effects of the new, non-traditional immigration on the secularization of Israel, and gave as an example the dramatic rise in the number of stores selling pork.[8] In a book devoted to developments in religious society in Israel,[9] the columnist Yair Sheleg also attributed the revival of the pig debate to the new wave of immigration from the former USSR.[10]

Another factor affecting the demand for pork was the spread among the more affluent segments of Israeli society of a sophisticated gourmet culture with a strong international orientation. This development had an impact on restaurant menus, which began to offer more pork dishes.[11]

Most of the patrons at the more expensive restaurants that offer these menu items are established Israelis rather than immigrants from the former USSR, who usually cannot afford to dine in them. In this sense, then, the demand for pork was influenced not only by the new immigration. Although the wider market for this kind of meat at butcher shops was indeed confined mostly to immigrants, with shops selling pork opening mainly in the areas where they lived, it was also sold in gourmet butcheries serving Israeli born secularists.[12]

In the political sphere and due to a change in the electoral system, the 1990s were marked by flourishing sectarianism. The change was introduced in a new version of the Basic Law: The Government, also enacted in 1992. According to this law, voters elected the prime minister in separate and direct elections in addition to voting for a party, unlike the traditional system of parliamentary elections that grants the office to the leader of the party supported by a parliamentary majority. Although the split-vote system was intended to take effect only in the elections that would follow four years later, its repercussions were nonetheless felt in the 1992 elections.

Voters increasingly used the split-vote system to support small parties that represented their group interests. This system of elections proved just as problematic as the one it had been meant to improve. It was changed once again in 2001, when a new-old version of Basic Law: The Government was enacted, abolishing direct elections for the prime minister and reverting to the conventional parliamentary system. At any rate, while in force, the split system had led to voting patterns that increased competition between the religious parties, including where symbolic issues such as pig-related prohibitions were concerned. They also intensified opposition to these attempts in such parties as Israel be-Aliyah, which drew its constituents mainly from former Soviet immigrants, and Shinui, an ultra-secularist party that made the struggle against religious coercion its motto.

The influence of the new immigrants' consumer culture on the pork trade and its concomitant confrontations surfaced during the 1990s in different municipalities.[13] For their part, the religious parties vied with each other in their condemnation of this culture. As early as 1992, MK Shlomo Benizri queried the minister of industry and commerce concerning the wide availability of pork in many shops throughout the country, including Jewish areas.[14] The minister acknowledged this but said that, according to the Supreme Court decision on this matter, he was not empowered to deny private traders import licenses for nonkosher meat. In 1993, MK Menahem Porush of Yahadut ha-Torah (formerly Agudat Israel) submitted a motion aimed at the expanding pork sales.[15] "We should hide in shame when faced with a list of about 130 shops that sell pork," he said.[16] He then took issue with the municipalities for failing to use their power to close these shops.[17] The bill was referred to the Knesset's Interior Committee for further debate.[18] Also that year, the minister of police, Moshe Shahal, was specifically asked in the Knesset about the large number of shops selling nonkosher meat in the city of Ashdod—a city that had attracted many immigrants from the former USSR in the 1990s.[19] In his response, Shahal said that fourteen or so shops were indeed selling nonkosher meat in Ashdod, and that he assumed that this was due to "the large concentration of new immigrants in the city."[20] His ministry, however, did not have the authority to act on the matter in the absence of a general law prohibiting the sale of nonkosher products, except for the specific laws concerning pork. This ignored the fact that most goods sold in the new nonkosher butcher shops were pork-based and were therefore subject to legal prohibitions, including a municipal bylaw in this regard in force in Ashdod.

In 1997, MK David Tal of Shas posed a further question on this matter, explicitly linking two issues: non-Jewish immigrants and the sale of pork, this time relying on a report of the Orthodox newspaper Day to Day, identified with his party.[21] The respondent this time was Deputy Minister for Religious Affairs Yigal Bibi of the NRP, who agreed with Tal and pointed out that "opening up shops to sell pork and registering non-Jews as Jews are, sadly, common and well-known occurrences, and the law has proved impotent in regard to both." As for the pig question, Deputy Minister Bibi explained that the Special Enablement Law had indeed been enacted to meet this problem: "The Enablement Law, however, has lost any legal significance after the enactment of Basic Law: Human Dignity and Liberty and Basic Law: Freedom of Occupation, which deprive the Enablement Law of its power. Finding now a solution within the framework of the bylaws is a questionable if not impossible proposition, despite the Enablement Law. This issue too must be resolved within the context of the Knesset legislation."[22]

In 1998, MK David Azoulay of Shas again raised the issue of the sale of nonkosher meat in cities with large immigrant concentrations. The response by Minister of the Interior Eli Suissa (also of Shas) referred to the powers granted to the local authorities to promulgate bylaws on this issue in accordance with the Special Enablement Law.[23] This parliamentary activity illustrates not only the competition between representatives of the various religious parties, but also the renewed relevance of the dispute over pig prohibitions.

From a legal point of view, changing reality gave rise to two constitutional questions. The first concerned the legality of the restrictions stipulated in extant municipal bylaws in light of the constitutional duty to respect freedom of occupation, which also includes the principle of proportionality. This principle requires that any infringement of this freedom should not exceed necessity. The second concerned the need for new bylaws in municipalities that still lacked them, wherever a flourishing pork trade emphasized the absence of legal regulation in this matter.

In places where bylaws already existed, there was concern about the scope of the prohibitions. An approach inspired by freedom of occupation would, prima facie, support distinctions between districts, as did the bylaw promulgated many years previously in Haifa, a mixed city. As noted above, the Supreme Court had already referred to the need for such a distinction in *Manshi*, although the argument in this regard did not influence the result in the specific circumstances of the case.[24] Following the "constitutional revolution," the distinction argument was raised in two test cases heard before magistrates' courts involving butchers who had sold pork in their shops in contravention of municipal bylaws. The Netanyah Magistrate's Court issued the first of these two rulings in 1996 in the *Rubinstein* decision,[25] which dealt with the legality of the Netanyah bylaw on pork trading. Judge Groves approached the matter from a constitutional perspective, referring to the new Basic Laws and especially to Basic Law: Freedom of Occupation: "The State of Israel is a Jewish and democratic state, and a law aiming to safeguard the rights of observant Jews and avoid harming their sensibilities is certainly compatible with the values of the State."[26] Yet, he thought that an absolute and all-encompassing restriction equally enforced in all areas of the city does not meet the constitutional requirement of proportionality. He argued that an absolute restriction on the sale of pork could, at most, be imposed in areas of the city with a religious majority: "The purpose and objectives of the law could certainly be attained by implementing an absolute prohibition, for example, in areas populated mainly by religious residents, or in areas where there are institutions or a concentration of businesses and shops serving a primarily religious population. Areas can be discerned where the religious public determines the mode and forms of everyday life."[27]

After this ruling, which addressed the pig-related prohibitions from a constitutional perspective, the attorney general held a discussion on whether to appeal. Participants at this discussion included senior officers from the Ministry of Justice, among them Uzi Fogelman, then the director of the ministry's High Court of Justice department, and Deputy Attorney General Meni Mazuz,[28] who opposed appeal on the grounds that the outcome was correct, even without reference to the Basic Laws. The attorney general summed up with the request that municipalities re-examine their bylaws "with due attention to the required scope [proportionality], in light of the needs and distribution of the population." He added, "Before bringing charges for infringement of bylaws enacted under the Enablement Law, prosecutors will examine the reasonableness of the restrictions imposed under Section 2 of the law. In all cases, the needs and circumstances of the specific local authority will be taken into account."[29] Following this basic guideline, no authorization was granted for any further bylaws including sweeping prohibitions banning the sale of pork and pork products throughout a city. A new policy was also introduced, refraining from bringing charges for the breach of extant bylaws involving disproportionate prohibitions.

In line with this new policy, the Ministry of Justice opposed a proposal for a new bylaw in Acre banning the sale of pork altogether within the city limits. The new bylaw was intended to replace an earlier one from the 1950s, which had confined the prohibition against pork sales only to areas outside the public market (in practice, the market within the old city of Acre).[30] Deputy Attorney General Mazuz issued another and more general letter of guidelines to the Ministry of the Interior's legal counsel. The ministry was asked "to inform local authorities, through a circular issued by the ministry's director general or otherwise, that before promulgating bylaws prohibiting the sale of pork or its products, they must examine whether this prohibition is required in view of information about the locality's population, its needs and its customs, and to consider whether a partial restriction, limited to defined areas, would not suffice." Local authorities were also required to supply demographic and other data when applying for the ministry's authorization of the bylaw.[31] As for indictments, a letter was sent to all prosecutors in local authorities, updating them on these guidelines: "Before bringing indictments on this issue under local bylaws, prosecutors will examine the reasonableness of the restrictions imposed in the bylaw, in accordance with the specific needs and circumstances of the local authority under consideration."[32]

Parallel to these developments, which had largely been triggered by the ruling of the Netanyah Magistrate's Court in *Rubinstein,* a contrary judgment was issued by the Ashkelon Magistrate's Court in *Shmukler.*[33] This ruling, issued in 1998, dealt with offences against a municipal bylaw prohibiting pork sale in Ashkelon, a city that had absorbed a large number of immigrants.[34] In this case as well, the defendant contended that the bylaw should be considered invalid since it contradicted Basic Law: Freedom of Occupation and Basic Law: Human Dignity and Liberty, and that religious feelings could be protected by a less comprehensive prohibition. Judge Yitzhak, however, rejected these arguments and emphasized the national aspect of the prohibition: "Why, then, has the pig been 'picked on'? The reason is obviously not religious-halakhic. The reason is historical national. The pig became a symbol of abomination in the course of Jewish history, of the hatred of Edom, a symbol against the nations of the world that endangered the very existence of the Jewish people throughout history. The pig is an animal that possesses the external sign of ritual purity—a cloven hoof—but not the internal sign. It does not chew the cud. Externally, the pig looks pure, but it is actually not so. The pig, therefore, represents outside without inside, the symbol of hypocrisy and evil."[35]

Based on this analysis, Judge Yitzhak held that, since the new Basic Laws acknowledged the values of the State of Israel as a "Jewish and democratic State," the status of pig-related prohibitions in the Jewish national heritage could be taken into consideration when judicial review was exercised. The argument by the defense that the bylaw was very damaging in a city where a third of the population was made up of immigrants from the former Soviet Union was rejected because it had not been proved in the course of the hearing.[36] Elsewhere, the judge remarked on the immigrant population by saying, "Social values entrenched in the nation's heritage should not be undermined because of social fluctuations of one type or another, such as the immigration wave from the CIS. This immigration is welcome. The melting pot of the people of Israel absorbing new immigrants into the land of Israel functions as an ongoing process, and requires a long term perspective before we proceed to abrogate or modify a value that is not only religious but also national."[37]

This ruling attracted much public attention and was hailed by religious MKs in parliamentary debates.[38] It was appealed,[39] but the appeal was dismissed at the Beer-Sheba District Court which decided this matter in a panel of three judges. The decision in the appeal further defined the distinction between perceptions of pig-related prohibitions as symbolic or as purely religious interest.[40] Writing for the majority, Judge Pilpel essentially confirmed the magistrate's court ruling and emphasized the national aspect of the pig prohibition. In a dissenting opinion, Judge Laron stressed the religious aspect of the prohibition and clarified that the Basic Laws now required assigning greater weight to civil liberties.

Judge Hendel, also for the majority, sharpened the controversy with a direct reference to the symbolic aspect of the prohibition. He wrote: "The desire of society to define itself through a symbol rooted in religious law is an act of crucial importance beyond the details of a specific law. This matter should not be trivialized. The purpose determines the proportionality and reasonableness of the decision."[41] Still further, he wrote: "In terms of a perception that views the pig as a symbol, the claim that the municipality must first consider refraining from imposing an all-embracing prohibition is not persuasive. When the purpose is to minimize injury to a person wishing to sell or purchase pork, refraining from imposing any prohibition whatsoever must be considered first."[42]

In practice, the impact of the earlier Magistrate Court decision in *Rubinstein* was greater because it was followed by the attorney general's guidelines. These guidelines created direct and indirect pressure to update existing bylaws on pork trade. This was evident, for instance, in the correspondence relating to the enforcement of the bylaw in Carmiel, another city with a significant immigrant population. Amnon De-Hartog, head of the section of legal advice and legislation in the Ministry of Justice, wrote to the Carmiel municipality legal counsel[43] asking him "to refrain for the time being from issuing indictments under this bylaw, until it is re-examined by the municipal council."[44] The letter makes extensive reference to demographic changes in Carmiel that resulted in new immigrants comprising 35.5 percent of the town's population. According to the letter, municipalities that had enacted sweeping pig bylaws in their books faced a hard decision: either replace the general prohibition with a more limited one, or forego enforcement under the policy of not issuing indictments for the infringement of bylaws considered too far-reaching. One exception was the institution of criminal proceedings against several shop owners in the municipality of Petah Tikvah based on a general bylaw applying to the entire city, before the municipal prosecutors were informed of the new policy adopted by the Ministry of Justice. After the city council refrained from reconsidering the bylaw for over two years, the local prosecutor decided to continue the proceedings. His argument was that the city of Petah Tikvah had religious characteristics, and that the shops in question were all located in the center of the city and in residential areas rather than in the industrial zone. Eventually, the district attorney's office quashed the indictments on other grounds: flaws in the reports on meat inspections. The Petah Tikvah Magistrate's Court was notified of this decision, ratified the dropping of the indictments, and stopped the court proceedings.[45]

The new Ministry of Justice policy was also reflected in the comments of Haim Ramon, the minister of the interior at the time, on a bill initiated by MK Amnon Rubinstein seeking to speed up the process of publishing bylaws.[46] According to Ramon: "Following petitions to the High Court of Justice, the Supreme Court has held that the prohibition of pork sales throughout a city area is unlawful in the vast majority of cases. Accordingly, when a municipal bylaw that prohibits pork sales throughout a city reaches the Ministry of the Interior, it is not validated, not because of the minister's ideology but because the bylaw is tainted by illegality." Note that Ramon's description of the legal situation was not completely accurate. At the time, case law was not yet available from the Supreme Court regarding the restriction of pork sales to specific districts within the local authority. This restriction was based solely on the guidelines issued by the Ministry of Justice.

In practice, the policy of the Ministry of Justice spurred de facto changes, as manifest in the establishment of new businesses failing to comply with municipal bylaws. Disregarding a bylaw was cheaper and more effective than filing a petition to the Supreme Court against it. Indeed, such petitions to the Supreme Court were quite rare before some municipalities began to enact updated bylaws in this area at a later stage. Initiating a clash with the municipality when enforcement procedures are ultimately stalled was indeed pointless.

Another reason for not petitioning against existing bylaws could have been that enforcement by means of indictments and fines had failed to block pork trading in any substantial way. The goal of stopping pork trading is effectively attainable only if the prohibition in the municipal bylaw serves as grounds for refusing business licenses to shops that engage in such trade. As noted, a refusal to grant business licenses to butcher shops that sold pork was grounds for the historical litigation that resulted in the Special Enablement Law—the *Axel* and *Fridi* rulings.[47] Yet, in cases that have reached the courts in recent years, municipalities have chosen to bring charges against butchers for violating the bylaws' provisions on pork trade instead of taking administrative steps concerning the licensing of their shops. An exception was a case wherein the Ramat Gan municipality decided not to grant a business license to a butcher shop linked to the Mizra network, which had opened up at a new shopping mall. This refusal led to the filing of a test-case petition arguing that "the bylaw had no powers to close the business simply because it sold pork."[48] According to the petitioners, the municipality could, at most, place offenders on trial and confiscate the prohibited meat in accordance with the municipal bylaw, but could not use the bylaw as grounds for refusing to grant a business license.

The petition did admit that the municipal bylaw was promulgated under the Special Enablement Law, which had been enacted in order to dismiss the claim that municipalities were not authorized to take religious considerations into account for licensing purposes. It argued, however, that the bylaw as it stood could not make pork sales grounds for license refusal. The petition also included other claims, adduced previously, concerning the bylaw's lack of validity in light of the new Basic Laws, as well as arguments bearing on its selective enforcement, given that another Mizra branch was located "close to the business licensing department of the Ramat Gan municipality."[49] After the petition was filed, counsel for the municipality announced that "within ten days, the petitioner would be informed of the respondent's decision as to whether it would be granted a business license, including reference to the question of whether the license could be granted in light of provisions in the Ramat-Gan (Pigs and Pork) Bylaw, 1958."[50] The municipality may have entertained doubts regarding the validity of the bylaw, given that it prohibited pork trading throughout the city, or was unable to justify its selective enforcement. In any event, it showed no readiness to engage in a legal struggle.

Controversies regarding pork-trading prohibitions in the municipal arena eventually reached the Supreme Court when several municipalities, usually after enacting new bylaws on this matter, began to invest further resources in enforcement. This tended to involve cities and towns with relatively large populations of immigrants, which influenced the local trade in pork.

The problem surfaced at first in municipalities that had no bylaws concerning pig prohibitions, when demographic changes suddenly highlighted their absence. This was the background for developments in Beth Shemesh, which had no prior municipal bylaw on pork trading. The immigrant population that settled there prompted the opening of several businesses that met the demand for pork. At the same time, the development of the Ramat Beth Shemesh Orthodox neighborhood led to the influx of an Orthodox population. A clash between these two groups was not long in coming, and hinged on pig prohibitions. Shas launched a public offensive in Beth Shemesh against shops selling pork and began a struggle for the promulgation of a municipal bylaw prohibiting it. A large demonstration on 21 November 1999 against the opening of shops selling pork turned into an outpouring of angry criticism targeting immigrants from the former Soviet Union.[51] The "anti-Russian" character of the demonstration was condemned at a Knesset debate devoted to the issue.[52] The debate focused on attitudes to the immigrants and on claims questioning their Jewishness, but also dealt with pig-related prohibitions. Referring to claims raised by secular MKs about "looking into other people's plates," Shas minister Shlomo Benizri stated: "I am not against the sale of pork. In other words, I would not want pigs in Israel, but since we are speaking of reciprocity, then why not? Eat pork. We do not look into other people's plates. But as a Jew, when I walk in my neighborhood and shops there sell pork, it hurts me to my soul; it harms my way of life. I say to you: listen, you can sell pork, but let's do it in the city outskirts, in the industrial area."[53] The obvious question when reading this passage is whether these remarks suggest that the issue of the pig as a symbol has undergone reconsideration.

Following these disputes, the Beth Shemesh city council voted to promulgate a municipal bylaw that would set limitations on the sale of pork in the city.[54] The bylaw imposed restrictions on the breeding and keeping of pigs, and on the sale of pork and its products throughout the city of Beth Shemesh, except for industrial areas. Minister of the Interior Natan Sharansky, from the immigrants' party Israel be-Aliyah, refused to authorize the bylaw and delayed its publication due to its expected impact on the city's immigrant population. Only later, after Haim Ramon became the new minister of the interior, did he authorize the new bylaw. At this stage, MK Marina Solodkin, also from Israel be-Aliyah, submitted a petition to the High Court of Justice[55] emphasizing the harm to the immigrant population that makes up about one fifth of Beth Shemesh inhabitants.[56] Soon afterwards, Shinui and several Beth-Shemesh shop owners, all immigrants from the former Soviet Union, submitted an additional petition in the same matter.[57] In order to hear the petitions before the new bylaw was enforced, the Court not only issued an order nisi but was also willing to give an interim order preventing the application of the bylaw until the end of the litigation in this matter.[58]

As noted, municipalities that did have bylaws prohibiting pork trading also faced problems because these bylaws had to be reviewed and updated. In Carmiel, which had been the target of a specific instruction to defer indictments, the municipality initiated a procedure to replace its old bylaw with a new one based on a distinction between various city districts. Although the language of the new bylaw adopted by the city council rested prima facie on this distinction, the Carmiel (Pork) Bylaw, 2001 actually preserved the prohibition in most of the municipal area. It stipulated that the prohibition against the sale of pork and pork products would continue to apply throughout the city, except for the industrial area and two specified commercial centers. Consequently, MK Marina Solodkin of Israel be-Aliyah submitted another petition to the Supreme Court together with some shop owners.[59] The petition stated that the new bylaw lacked proportionality, arguing it should have restricted the prohibition to religious neighborhoods or to areas adjacent to synagogues.[60] An order nisi and an interim order were granted here as well.[61]

Another petition related to the enforcement of the Tiberias bylaw prohibiting pork trade. This petition followed a city council decision not to
change the old 1958 bylaw, which applied to the entire municipal area
without exception.[62] The Court later issued an interim order against the
enforcement of this bylaw as well, after the newly elected mayor from
Shas intensified enforcement efforts.[63]

The revival of the pig dispute in the municipal arena influenced Knesset debates as well as old compromises. On several occasions, Likud MK
Israel Katz attacked former Minister of Agriculture Haim Oron, a member of kibbutz Lahav, over the kibbutz's involvement in pig-breeding.
Thus, for instance, in a Knesset debate dealing with another matter (transporting a generator of the electricity company on the Sabbath), MK Katz
decided to link the issues of Sabbath prohibitions and pig prohibitions,
saying: "At this very moment we see the behavior of the minister of agriculture, a minister in the government of Israel, who criminally breaches
the law and raises pigs in his kibbutz in blatant contravention of the law,
brutally tramples the law and distributes those pigs in all development
towns, and in cities and towns in the south and throughout the country."[64] A few months later, MK Katz posed a question on this matter to
the minister of religious affairs, Yitzhak Cohen from Shas. The question
concerned pig-breeding activities in kibbutz Lahav, which Katz considered to be commercial. The minister's response was that the information
cited in the question was correct and constituted a flagrant violation of
the law. He further added that he would assist the MK posing the question in bringing a complaint on this matter to the authorities responsible
for enforcing the law. MK Katz, adherent of the earlier Herut tradition,
added: "The prohibition against pig-breeding for consumption by Jews
in Israel, which is anchored in the law, is an ethical issue of the first
order."[65]

Attitudes toward activities in kibbutz Lahav depended on the speaker's
political identification. In response to a different question on the sale
of ritually prohibited meat as beef, the minister of agriculture, Shalom
Simhon from the Labor party, rejected the contention that members of
this kibbutz were engaged in the illegal breeding of pigs for commercial purposes. Concerning the comments of MK Nissim Ze'ev of Shas,
whereby "the former minister of agriculture [Haim Oron] was one of
the largest pig breeders and importers, the State of Israel's chief supplier,"

Simhon clarified: "First, I would like to use this opportunity to speak on behalf of the former minister of agriculture. He is not connected either to your question or to your answer, nor is he a pig-importer or a pig-breeder, as is well known. Pig-breeding is permitted in two regions in Israel. One place, which is primarily a laboratory, is the place you mentioned, and you insinuated that the former minister of agriculture permitted pork consumption or took advantage of this to do other things as well."[66]

In 1999, the Beer-Sheba Magistrate's Court issued a ruling acquitting kibbutz Lahav and its economic controller of operating a business without a license, following charges that they were breeding pigs for commercial purposes and operating a slaughterhouse. The prosecution claimed in court that about 8,000 pigs were slaughtered every year in the kibbutz, and this scope of activity could not be reconciled with the operation of a research institute. These contentions, however, were not sufficiently proved, and the defendants were acquitted after "the plaintiff failed to meet the burden of proof standards required for a criminal conviction."[67]

From the other end of the political spectrum, MK Yehudit Na'ot of Shinui submitted a motion criticizing the minister of the interior for making a religious goal such as the closure of shops trading in pork a priority of his ministry, in preference to more important issues such as the proper functioning of municipalities.[68] MK Na'ot's comments immediately attracted hecklers from the religious parties. MK Shaul Yahalom from the NRP reiterated the national argument: "Some matters are connected to the identity of a people. Aren't you interested . . . in something that distinguishes us, that singles out our country as a Jewish country, as a Jewish people?"[69] He then referred his listeners to Berl Katsanalson's well-publicized remarks on the matter.[70] Speaking for Shas, ministers Yitzhak Cohen and Eli Yishai—whose statements had been the target of Na'ot's criticism—followed the same line of argument. Cohen cited the rabbinic statement about the pig that had dug in its claws in the wall of Jerusalem, ironically referring to the possibility that the Supreme Court would reverse the ruling of the Ashkelon Magistrate's Court in *Shmukler,* "accepting the viewpoint of the 'knights' of Enlightenment in Israel."[71] Yishai made reference to the proceedings pending before the High Court of Justice on Beth Shemesh and commented: "I very much hope that the High Court of Justice will not interfere and will leave it to the legislature, and I very much hope that members of this House will understand the importance of preserving the status quo."[72] Casting a shadow over the entire debate was the "civil revolution" that Prime Minister Ehud Barak (Labor party) had proclaimed several months previously. Shas' representatives claimed that Barak's loss to Likud's Ariel Sharon in the subsequent prime ministerial elections reflected the failure of this initiative and its anti-religious spirit.[73]

Shinui's campaign against religious coercion had served as a catalyst for a renewed reference to symbols, among them the pig. Thus, for instance, in a debate related to an entirely different matter, MK Meir Porush of Yahadut ha-Torah raised the issue of a newspaper report on the activities of MK Yosef Paritsky of Shinui that included, among others, references to shops that sell pork.[74] In the course of a heated Knesset debate on a general ban on the import of ritually prohibited meat, Shinui leader MK Yosef Lapid argued: "To forbid a secular person to eat pork is exactly the same as compelling a religious person to eat pork . . . because democracy is a faith and a religion no less sacred than the Jewish religion."[75]

In the elections to the 16th Knesset in early 2003, Shinui became a significant political force after winning fifteen seats (out of 120) and became the senior coalition partner of the ruling Likud party. Avraham Poraz, the new minister of the interior from Shinui, declared soon afterward that he would allow the sale of pork and pork products in city centers and not only in industrial areas, contrary to his predecessor from Shas. He wrote to the attorney general and requested that his view be laid before the High Court of Justice in the proceedings still in progress at the time regarding the municipal bylaws of several cities.[76] A supplementary announcement to the Court in this regard was indeed submitted by the attorney representing the state in these cases. On previous occasions, when Eli Yishai from Shas had served as minister of the interior, the court was also notified that the minister's view differed from the official position of the Ministry of Justice that had been submitted to the Court. The Ministry of Justice stated that municipal bylaws prohibiting pork sales should be limited to certain areas, whereas Yishai held that, in a Jewish state, this prohibition should be one of general application. When the new minister from Shinui was appointed, the court was notified that, contrary to the view of the Ministry of Justice, the current minister of the interior holds that no bylaws prohibiting the sale of pork should be enacted at all.[77]

Given the raging controversies and the need for a doctrinal ruling, the Court decided to broaden the original panel of three justices dealing with all petitions in this matter to nine.[78] The enlarged panel heard the cases, and press reports on the oral proceedings again pointed to the highly charged emotions surrounding this issue. One newspaper columnist used as the title for a piece a quote from Justice Mishael Cheshin in court: "Where do you want pork to be sold, in the fields?"[79] This question, understood as reflecting prior hostility to the controversial prohibition, led MK Meir Porush from Yahadut ha-Torah to refer to Justice Cheshin in a Knesset debate as "The Pig Justice Mishael Cheshin."[80] After oral arguments had ended, an organization describing itself as involved in the promotion of Jewish values and traditions asked to join the proceedings as amicus curiae.[81] This request represented strong support for municipal bylaws prohibiting pork trade, as it was based on explanations and documentation affirming the national significance of the pig prohibition, including four written opinions by scholars and rabbis. Although these arguments centered on the national significance of the pig prohibition, the opinions forming grounds for the request had all been written by religious individuals.[82]

More than three years after the petitions were submitted, the Court's nine-member panel issued an unanimous decision. This decision, rendered in the so-called *Solodkin* case,[83] sought to find a middle ground between the conflicting views. Its success in achieving this goal, however, is an open question.

The decision, written by Chief Justice Barak, begins by outlining the purpose of the Special Enablement Law as understood by the court: to protect the sensitivities of Jews who perceived the pig as a symbol of ritual impurity and of persecutions suffered by the Jewish people, to protect individual liberties by setting limitations on the administrative power to regulate pork trade, and to make possible nuanced regulation of this matter according to the local characteristics of each community.[84] Based on this theoretical framework, the decision illustrates its application to a hypothetical municipality that includes three neighborhoods: one in which most residents would be offended by the sale of pork, one in which most residents are interested in purchasing pork, and one with a population divided on this issue. The decision emphasizes that the Special Enablement Law does not mandate one rule for the entire municipal area and includes the option of limiting the bylaw's scope to specific sections within its jurisdiction.[85]

The ruling then proceeds to outline a model analysis for each of these hypothetical neighborhoods. In the first neighborhood, populated by a vast majority opposed to the idea of pork sales, a ban on pork trading would be considered proportionate and therefore legal. The decision recognizes that the prohibition would infringe the liberties of minority residents interested in purchasing pork in this neighborhood as well as those of butchers interested in selling it. It argues that this infringement would be justified, however, considering the weight that should be given to the feelings of the majority, and assuming that pork could indeed be purchased nearby.[86] By contrast, in the second hypothetical neighborhood, where a significant majority opposes limitations on the sale of pork, applying a bylaw prohibiting the sale of pork would be disproportionate and therefore illegal.[87] On this basis, the decision then proceeds to evaluate the third hypothetical neighborhood, where a mixed population lives in an area that cannot be divided into smaller and relatively homogenous sections. According to the Court, decisions on this count may vary. The decision does recognize the possibility that applying a municipal bylaw prohibiting pork sale might be legal in such neighborhoods but only on condition that pork is made reasonably accessible, be it at the neighborhood's outskirts or in a nearby area.[88]

After setting the standard for reviewing bylaws prohibiting pork sales, the ruling ends without operative conclusions concerning the actual bylaws attacked by the petitioners. It emphasizes that each municipality first needs to re-evaluate its decisions on this matter according to the standards set by the court.[89] The result is that, for all practical purposes, legal controversies regarding the bylaws on pork prohibitions are not over. They will restart at the municipal level first, and will probably return later to the judicial arena as well.[90] The *Solodkin* decision did not deal with criminal proceedings still pending against shop owners for the infringement of existing bylaws against pork trading. Soon after this ruling, however, the state agreed to the acquittal of several butchers charged in the *Shmukler* case, in the appeal on the judgment of the District Court that had found them guilty of breaching a broad bylaw against pork trading enforced in Ashkelon.[91]

The *Solodkin* decision which sought a compromise reflected an awareness of the charged emotions surrounding these petitions. It was intended to be perceived as neutral and minimalist in the scope of its normative intervention. It did not decide any of the actual petitions. It cited traditional and historical sources to prove the Court's awareness of the religious and national sensibilities associated with pigs, but also emphasized the importance of functioning within a legal regime that gives weight to considerations of liberty. The decision granted broad discretion to municipalities in this matter as long as they followed the Court's normative guidelines, thus lowering expectations for judicial intervention. Largely, the ruling endorsed the policy that the Ministry of Justice was already enforcing as regards the duty to tailor pork prohibitions to the characteristics of each municipality.[92] Experts commenting on the decision have tended to view it as not granting a "victory" to any of the parties[93] and even as ratifying existing principles.[94]

Although the decision represented an attempt to refrain from normative judgment, at a deeper level it reflects a secular worldview completely alien to the symbolism of the pig prohibition in Jewish culture. The decision mentions that the Special Enablement Law had been intended to protect the feelings of Jews who might find pork-trading offensive because they saw the pig prohibition as having national and religious significance. The Court itself, however, displayed no understanding or sympathy for those who had chosen to translate this historical sensitivity into a legal prohibition of pork. In other words, it clearly refrained from supporting this choice as a positive value. According to the Court, adopting a bylaw prohibiting the sale of pork was justified only when a significant majority of a neighborhood's residents felt offended by the absence of such a regulation. The Court was willing to accommodate these feelings but did not share them. In fact, the Court could have written an identical decision on a hypothetical petition about a hypothetical bylaw against the sale of pork in an Arab municipality divided between Muslims and Christians on this question. The Court would have decided this case with the same emphasis on the offense to Muslims with religious reservations regarding pigs. Obviously, the potential of the *Solodkin* case to protect the feelings of Muslim Arabs who live in Israel should be appreciated. At the same time, this ruling tells us that the Court did not find it important or appropriate to consider the argument that a bylaw against pork-trading might be justified not only for the purpose of avoiding potential offense to citizens but also for expressing the state's Jewish character.[95]

Another tacit though significant element in the decision is the total dismissal of the possibility of applying pork prohibitions to an entire municipality if evidence emerges that various sections within it have different preferences in this matter. This decision necessarily precludes the possibility of a total prohibition on pork sales in most municipalities, except for several generally homogenous areas populated by a significant majority of Orthodox Jews. These localities, however, were never the locus of controversy concerning bylaws banning pork sales. Nobody wants to sell pork in them. True, the Special Enablement Law had been written to recognize from the outset the possibility of limiting bylaws on pork trade to specific areas. In practice, however, Jewish municipalities had never done this and the option was exercised only in mixed cities that were also populated by Christian Arabs. The shift from a model of a prohibition covering the entire municipality to a model of limited prohibitions applied according to preferences identified at the neighborhood level is a new development significantly restricting the bylaws' effect at the national level. The Special Enablement Law had indeed conveyed skepticism regarding the national significance of the pig prohibition when it ordered a municipally based regulation of the matter. The emphasis on a neighborhood-based regulation, however, decreases the national significance of the prohibition even further.

Hence, although the Court sought a compromise in the *Solodkin* decision and abstained from ruling for or against the pig-prohibition bylaws, its stand in this matter is obviously far removed from traditional sensibilities. Implicitly, its decision rejected the idea that the pig prohibition should be cherished as a characteristic of Jewish culture as a whole, and was only willing to consider it as a particular sensitivity of certain Jewish individuals or communities. More than its practical consequences, the secular overtones discernible in the *Solodkin* decision may shed light on some of the reactions it evoked in the political system. Shinui leaders Avraham Poraz (at the time the minister of interior) and Yosef Lapid, described the decision as an important achievement in the battle against religious coercion, whereas the ultra-Orthodox parties perceived it as another judicial blow to Israel's Jewish identity. Shas leader and former minister of the interior, MK Eli Yishai, described the decision as "a jewel in a swine's snout,"[96] and MK Meir Porush from Yahadut ha-Torah compared Minister Poraz to the ancient Greek leader Antiochus, who had ordered Jews to eat pork.

Other politicians reacted to the decision in more moderate terms, emphasizing its pragmatic merits. MKs Shaul Yahalom and Yitzhak Levi from the NRP described the decision as balanced, and welcomed the fact it had not completely overruled the possibility of bylaws prohibiting pork trade. MK Solodkin, the driving force behind two of the petitions, emphasized that she refrained from eating pork as a private person, but considered the decision important due to the protection it afforded to newcomers from the former USSR.[97]

Even from a pragmatic perspective, evaluating the ruling in *Solodkin* is not simple because of the significant bureaucratic and economic burdens it imposes on any future initiative to enact bylaws on pork-trading. The ruling states that the criteria for adopting a bylaw banning pork-trading and deciding on its scope should be formulated after careful evaluation of each community's characteristics, level of social agreement, and prevailing degree of tolerance.[98] It does not clarify, however, how should these evaluations be made and whether a local referendum might be needed for this purpose. The lack of clarity on this matter on the one hand, and the possibility that a referendum or a similar process might be needed on the other, could deter future initiatives to enact bylaws on pork trade. Indeed, Mayor Zohar Oved of Tiberias declared his support for the Court's ruling and his willingness to conduct a referendum on this matter, hoping it would prove that the majority of residents in his city were indeed opposed to the sale of pork.[99] By contrast, however, Mayor Tsvi Tsilker of Ashdod criticized the decision as being impossible to implement.[100] A press comment indicated that the decision to send the pig issue for resolution at the community level would generate controversies among neighbors.[101]

From the perspective of those supporting bylaws prohibiting pork trade, the difficulties entailed in the promulgation of new bylaws in this matter now face an additional obstacle, namely, that the Court would consider unreasonable any enforcement of existing bylaws without prior evaluation of their scope. Indeed, the immediate effect of the *Solodkin* ruling was to give the green light to pork-trading in the municipalities involved in the petitions, at least for the time being. The Court ordered that the bylaws being enforced in these municipalities should be suspended (thus continuing the effect of the interim orders issued during the proceedings). These municipalities were advised to engage in decision-making processes according to the guidelines set by the Court.

At present, pork is available for sale in Israel almost everywhere or, more accurately, wherever demand for it exists. In addition, whereas pork had previously been sold mainly in small neighborhood butcheries, a variety of pork products is now also available in the big supermarkets of the new nonkosher food chain Tiv Ta'am. Israeli food chains have refrained from selling nonkosher food (as well as from opening their business on the Sabbath) in order to qualify for the kashrut certificates that enable them to sell to observant Jews. Tiv Ta'am and other growing chains catering to the so-called "Russian" market in Israel do not bother to obtain these certificates. In fact, they appeal also to other customers by offering other, nonkosher products, including pork. Tiv Ta'am has opened new mega-stores and thus exposed new potential customers to pork. The fact that its branches are open on the Sabbath is an additional drawing card of this network, which offers nonkosher food to new customers who would not have visited its stores had other food chains also been open at the time. Tiv Ta'am stores, then, give the pork trade high visibility. For this reason, religious representatives in Petah Tikvah objected to the opening of a new Tiv Ta'am location in the city,[102] despite a previous history of pork sales in small stores.[103]

The increasing demand for pork[104] has also affected the pig-breeding business, which flourishes despite the limitations imposed by the Pig-Raising Prohibition Law. The scope of this market is reflected in decisions on the veterinary aspects of its regulation. The explanatory notes accompanying the decision to open a new and modern abattoir in Ma'aliyeh (replacing the old one in Nazareth) state: "During the last five years, the number of pigs slaughtered in Israel has increased significantly, from 96,520 in 1995 to 128,285 in 1999."[105] Additional data on the size of this industry was revealed at a Knesset hearing, when the head of veterinary services Oded Nir reported to the Knesset's Economics Committee: "The growth in the consumption of pork in Israel has been huge, and this sector is expanding all the time . . . According to my figures, there are about 40,000 sows for breeding in Israel."[106] The hearing concerned the addition of pigs to the list of animals that, in order to prevent the spread of animal diseases, require a veterinary permit in order to be transported. A question raised during the debates was whether the regulation of such transportation was justified when, prima facie, it had been deemed illegal in Supreme Court precedents on the application of the Pig-Raising Prohibition Law.[107] The Ministry of Justice dismissed this legal opposition based on the view that Basic Law: Freedom of Occupation should be understood as overruling previous interpretations that had also applied the prohibition on pig-keeping to their transport.[108] The result was the approval of a new regulation regarding the transportation of pigs.[109]

Ironically, the current prosperity of pig-breeding is also greatly indebted to the monopolistic control of this business by pig breeders concentrated in a few municipalities. Their monopoly is an outcome of the Pig-Raising Prohibition Law (restricting pig-breeding only to these areas) and the ban on the import of ritually prohibited meat (protecting pig breeders from competing imports).[110] The great interest of these breeders in preserving the advantages accruing from their monopolistic status is evident from a petition to the Supreme Court submitted by a partnership of pig breeders from the northern municipality of Iblin against a competing pig-breeding commercial center operating at Kibbutz Lahav.[111] Kibbutz Lahav, as noted, breeds pigs under the auspices of a research institute established according to the exception for scientific research centers stated in the Pig-Raising Prohibition Law. The Supreme Court has already ruled that this institute was indeed covered by the law.[112] The new petition against pig-breeding in Kibbutz Lahav challenged current practice on grounds that it far exceeded research activities. According to data cited in the petition, 18,723 pigs were slaughtered in Kibbutz Lahav in 2003.

The economic scope of pig-breeding activities in northern Christian municipalities is sometimes beyond their ability to supervise it. A ruling of the Haifa district court imposed heavy sanctions on pig breeders prosecuted by the Ministry of the Environment for polluting a nearby river.[113] Several days later, the Supreme Court declined to allow a petition of appeal against another decision of the Haifa District Court, which had approved a regulatory decision of the head of veterinary services to limit the number of pigs slaughtered daily in the (only) abattoir in Iblin to 250, due to its unsanitary conditions.[114]

These problems notwithstanding, municipalities with pig-breeding farms in their area tend to consider them profitable assets and secure income sources. These are prosperous farms, which pay high municipal taxes and have no viable relocation option. A new decision by the Israeli Supreme Court tells the story of this dynamic as developed in Iblin, where the municipality tried to retain control of the only abattoir within its precincts, which had served as a source of considerable revenue.[115] The local pig-breeders filed a petition challenging the decision of the municipality to administer the local abattoir even though it was privately owned by them. In addition, although the abattoir did not meet the needs of the local industry in terms of veterinary inspection, size, and prices, the municipality had made the building of a new abattoir—even with private investment—contingent upon its being operated by the municipality. On another level, since the Iblin municipality had faced a new reality of declining revenues due to the opening of the new abattoir in Ma'aliyeh and the new regulation that legalized the transportation of pigs, it applied to the minister of the interior for approval of an increase in the property taxes imposed on pig-breeding farms. After this request was dismissed, the municipality of Iblin decided to amend the local bylaw on the operation of its abattoir by adding a special municipal charge for pig-breeding within its territory (calculated on the basis of the number pigs bred in Iblin no matter where they were slaughtered).[116] The municipality meant that this fee would compensate it for the costs involved in pig-breeding within its jurisdiction, costs that had previously been covered by the fees paid to the Iblin abattoir and now had to be covered separately for the pigs slaughtered in Ma'aliyeh. Since the minister of the interior refused to approve this amendment to the bylaw, the municipality petitioned the Supreme Court. To justify this new fee, the petition mentioned both the municipal expenses incurred for environmental damages and the fact that most of Iblin's residents are Muslims, who find pigs objectionable.[117] Eventually, the Supreme Court decided to accept the petition by the breeders in the matter of the abattoir, holding that the policy of the municipality in this matter had violated freedom of occupation in a disproportionate manner. At the same time, the Court dismissed the Iblin municipality petition, explaining that a bylaw on abattoirs cannot regulate also issues related to pig-breeding. Interestingly, the decision dealt with these matters without referring even once to the sensitivities attached to the issue of pig-breeding. A reader from the outside would get the impression that this is a normal trade in Israel. In fact, currently, this may be indeed the case.

In sum, pig-breeding and pork trading have gained a foothold in Israel at the beginning of the third millennium. At present, special laws on these matters are still a unique characteristic of the Israeli legal system, but their actual impact has significantly diminished.

CHAPTER 9

National Symbol or Religious Concern?

D ISPUTES SURROUNDING THE LEGAL IMPLICATIONS of pig-related prohibitions in Israel reveal a continuing erosion of the symbolic status of these prohibitions in the perception of the Jewish public in Israel. They tell the story of a tradition in a phase of change.[1] In the 1950s, this symbol required almost no explanation for the vast majority of the secular Jewish population. Although some political elements, invoking fundamental principles of liberty and resistance to religious coercion, were vigorously opposed to pig prohibitions even then, the national dimension of these prohibitions was self-evident. Recognizing the national significance of pig-related prohibitions during the 1950s was consistent with the tendency prevalent at the time to incorporate Jewish symbols as well into the emerging Israeli nationalism. Describing this process, Jonathan Shapira writes: "On the issue of religion, the Mapai leadership headed by David Ben-Gurion gradually opted for the path accepting the religious principle as a central component in the definition of Jewish nationalism."[2] Shapira deals at length with the introduction of traditional and religious Jewish elements into the secular educational system, and with the gradual penetration of a rhetoric based on religious-nationalist language and images into politics. In this context, he also comments briefly on the enactment of the Pig-Raising Prohibition Law and its support by Mapai members.[3] With the passage of time, however, the symbolism of pig prohibitions has waned among secularists, despite the attempts of religious politicians to preserve it.

Current social outlooks on pork consumption in Israel must be examined empirically.[4] This examination, however, should address not only the data on pork consumption but also the broader cultural context of, for instance, attitudes toward this subject in the educational system, if there are any. Do children today still tremble upon hearing the story of Hannah and her seven sons? Can we still discern reluctance to call pork by its name? Although no comprehensive data is available, there are several indications that breaking this taboo has now become far more frequent. The many shops selling pork and the many restaurants offering pork in their menus will attest to this. A recently published textbook on civics widely used in Israeli public schools mentions the prohibition on pig-breeding in a chapter on "the religious schism" as an instance of religious legislation that the secular public views as controversial.[5] This contributes to the writing of a new narrative that associates pig prohibitions exclusively with religion and religious views. Recent reports in the Israeli news media may suggest that the symbolic status of the pig prohibition has at least to some extent waned among some segments of the religious public as well. These reports describe an initiative to use pigs to protect Jewish settlements in the occupied territories against terrorist attacks. An organization called "The Hebrew Battalion" asked rabbis for special approval to use pigs, whose sense of smell is more developed than that of dogs, to sniff out bombs. According to the reports, approval was granted based on the religious principle that saving lives overrides ordinary religious prohibitions.[6] There is room to wonder whether this initiative could ever have been possible in a cultural atmosphere in which the pig prohibition is also a powerful national symbol. Indeed, columnist and novelist Meir Shalev writes that this initiative casts aside "Jewish sensibilities that had regarded the pig as the foulest of all creatures."[7]

Knesset records attest that, at present, any willingness to support pig-related prohibitions is confined primarily to the religious parties. No remnant of it can be found, for instance, in the Labor Party, Mapai's successor. Another expression of the exclusive identification of these prohibitions with the religious public appears in an article by Menachem Mautner dealing with the relationships between various groups in Israeli society. Mautner analyzes the conflicts between religious and secular Jews and, in this context, uses the following example: "On the assumption that religious Jews find pig-breeding in Israel extremely offensive, and given that the harm inflicted on secular Jews by refraining from breeding pigs in Israel is relatively small, nothing precludes prohibiting pig-breeding in Israel's Jewish towns. In a similar spirit, importing pork into Israel could also be prevented." This analysis rests on a perception that identifies pig prohibitions exclusively with the religious public.[8]

An attempt to expand pig prohibitions during the 1980s proved unsuccessful. In fact, a rearguard action is now being fought to preserve existing gains. The period since the beginning of the 1990s can be described as one of unprecedented attack on established legal precedents prohibiting, or at least limiting, commercial activities related to pork. Growing segments of Israeli society no longer consider these arrangements legitimate or comprehensible. The scope of the "pig economy" in Israel has also expanded significantly.

New constitutional developments stemming from the enactment of the Basic Laws on human rights have enabled the translation of changing social mores into measures carrying actual legal impact. Since the beginning of the 1990s, most of the discussion concerning pig prohibitions has hinged on the balance between freedom of occupation and religious sentiments. The desire to integrate traditional pig prohibitions into law on the basis of their national-cultural value is no longer a majority aspiration. The secular public does not perceive its national identity as including the pig taboo, and prohibitions regarding the raising of pigs and the selling of pork have become identified only with religious sensibilities. The religious public tends to view this sensibility as a national interest, but the decision as to what constitutes a national symbol is made by the majority and the present majority no longer regards pig prohibitions as constitutive of its Jewish identity.

The Arab public has been almost entirely absent from the bitter political controversies surrounding pig-related prohibitions in Israel's Jewish society. The debate has been consistently viewed as an internal Jewish matter, as a struggle to define Israel's Jewish character. This can be explained on various levels. First, the Arab public is not a full partner to public life in Israel, despite the formal rights of Israeli Arabs to vote and take part in the political process. In addition, the Arab public is troubled by the definition of Israel as a Jewish state and does not take part in the development of norms inspired by Jewish principles. For its part, the Jewish public does not regard the state's Arab citizens as full partners for the

purpose of defining national characteristics. Second, the Arab public
has not been able to speak in one voice on the matter of pig legislation.
Muslim Arabs abstain from pork and consider it an abomination, while
Christian Arabs tend to consume it and also make large profits from the
pig-breeding industry concentrated in their areas of settlement. The interests of the Christian Arab population were indeed considered when decisions were made on the scope of laws and bylaws on this issue. Those
interests, however, were protected mainly by church representatives or
even by Jewish politicians rather than by Arab MKs. Third, bylaws on
the pork trade are enacted by municipalities and not by central state
authorities. Since most Israeli municipalities are populated by either Jews
or Arabs separately and only few cities are "mixed," opportunities for
Jewish-Arab interaction on this matter have been limited. In practice,
most bylaws on pork trading have been enacted in municipalities without an Arab population.

The cultural transformation of Israel's Jewish population seems to be
the primary reason for the scaling-back of pig prohibitions in Israeli
law, although several additional processes may also have influenced this
development. For instance, Israeli Jews may possibly find pork consumption just as repellent as historically, but may no longer be willing to give
legal expression to this revulsion. According to this alternative explanation, what has changed, rather than the symbolic status of the prohibition,
is the willingness to protect symbols and national culture by resorting to
coercive legal rules. Indeed, recent Supreme Court rulings do not ascribe
substantial weight to the protection of culture and language values when
these clash with individual rights. In *Kastenbaum*,[9] for instance, the Court
prevented the application of the rules of a Jewish burial society against
foreign-language inscriptions on tombstones (as opposed to Hebrew ones
only). In a majority opinion, Justices Shamgar and Barak declared void
contract provisions that had adopted these rules because they violated
human dignity and caused offense to families forced to abide by them.
The national rationale of sanctifying the Hebrew language, to which Justice Elon had pointed as the historical source of the prohibition in the
cemetery under litigation,[10] was not deemed to carry sufficient weight to
tilt the balance.

An additional element that could partially explain the disappearance
of public consensus around the pig prohibitions is the change in Israel's

political culture. In the past, when Mapai was a hegemonic party, it advo-
cated compromises with the religious public and political life was generally characterized as "consensual." By contrast, current Israeli politics
is based on competition between rival forces, and the religious issues
become part of this competition.[11]

  Understanding the competing perceptions surrounding pig-related
prohibitions is significant not only for cultural reasons, but also for practical legal purposes. If these prohibitions protect only religious interests,
the doctrine of proportionality would lead to applying them only in religious neighborhoods. If, however, they protect a national symbol, the
symbolic purpose can only be achieved through a relatively broad application. The symbolic impact is expected to be negligible if pork is forbidden on one street but available on the next.[12] The *Solodkin*[13] decision
may seem to be at odds with this analysis. The decision referred to the
national (and not only religious) significance of pig-related prohibitions,
but still held that bylaws prohibiting pork trading should be applied in
a limited manner. Indeed, a close reading of the decision reveals that it
did not endorse the national significance of pig prohibitions, referring
instead to the persistence of this view among some Jewish groups. The
decision would probably have chosen a different balance had the Court
itself regarded these prohibitions as a national symbol rather than merely
acknowledging that some Jewish groups perceive them in this way.

  Recognizing the status of pig prohibitions as a national symbol, then,
is expected to go hand in hand with a relatively broad application of them
throughout the whole municipal area, or at least its central zone. The
power of the symbol is reflected in the scope of its application. Accordingly, the Day of Remembrance for IDF Fallen Soldiers[14] and Holocaust
Remembrance Day,[15] for instance, are widely protected symbols drawing no territorial distinctions. The scope of the prohibition professes to
define a community. If pig-related prohibitions express national symbolism, their application should cover large segments of the area populated
by the national community.

  This argument, regarding the reduced symbolic power of prohibitions that are denied general application, could appear to contradict the
concept of "red-light" districts in which the general prohibition of prostitution does not apply. Even when prostitution is tolerated within limited zones, the very need for separation between legal and illegal zones,

together with the restriction of prostitution to a limited area, carry a clear symbolic message: this activity is wrong.[16] Why, then, could not a similar separation work for pig prohibitions? The original Pig-Raising Prohibition Law actually succeeded in transmitting this message, although it tolerated specified zones in which pig-breeding remained legal. The difference between these examples lies in the way the norm is articulated. When prostitution is generally illegal but still tolerated in discrete and limited zones, or when pig-breeding is generally prohibited although allowed in limited areas, the message of public revulsion does come across. By contrast, when these activities are generally allowed, albeit restricted geographically due to special sensibilities the legislature chooses to respect, the message of general public revulsion almost disappears. Returning to the example of the Israeli bylaws prohibiting pork sales, a significant symbolic difference prevails between the option of prohibiting pork only in religious areas, and the option of prohibiting pork but tolerating its sale in discrete industrial areas, far from city centers. Only the latter would carry a message similar to that of red-light districts. A general prohibition on the sale of pork would obviously signal even greater support for this taboo, inasmuch as denying the possibility of red-light districts signals stronger opposition to prostitution.[17]

So far, the new interpretation of the pig prohibitions as designed to protect religious sensibilities has indeed led to changes in their application. The *Rubinstein* decision[18] considered the prohibitions irrelevant to the secular public, a perception certainly far removed from the original legislative intention of both the Special Enablement Law and the Pig-Raising Prohibition Law. By contrast, the conflicting *Shmukler* decisions offered a conceptual alternative,[19] representing a continued perception of the pig prohibition as a national symbol. In *Solodkin*, the Supreme Court tried to formulate a compromise, acknowledging the national meaning of the pig prohibition and yet limiting its application according to the preferences of residents in each neighborhood. In fact, however, this decision strengthens the message of limiting the prohibition's national meaning. According to the Court, a municipality must acknowledge that pork-trading will be offensive to some Jews' national (rather than merely religious) feelings. This line of argument implies the Court does not assume a wide consensus is still prevalent on this matter. The national significance of the prohibition is described as only one possible view held by some Jews rather than as a dominating view.

Limiting the purpose of pig legislation to the protection of sensibilities heralds its dramatic curtailment. Sensibilities are not exclusive to people who regard pigs and pork as repulsive. If the legal system is willing to make room for such feelings, it is also obligated to take into consideration the feelings of others, including the secularists' objections to "religious coercion." In these circumstances, the application of the pig prohibition is doomed to be very limited.[20]

Another way to approach this issue rests on the distinction proposed by Avi Sagi between an "identity discourse" involving an encounter between the parties' identities, and a "rights discourse" based on claims and demands.[21] Sagi illustrated this distinction with a reference to the controversy over the placing of limits on Sabbath driving in religious areas. He argued that the Supreme Court interpreted secular opposition to these limitations as based on the right to freedom of movement,[22] whereas this opposition should also be understood as conveying the aspirations of the non-religious public to protect its secular identity. "For many secularists, protecting their right to freedom of movement is an indirect way of protecting their secular identity by resorting to he language of rights," he wrote.[23] The distinction between these two types of discourse is also useful in the context of pig- related legislation. Originally, this legislation had relied on an "identity discourse," in which opposing parties found a way to enact symbolic legislation by resorting to a common cultural denominator. By contrast, the present discussion of pig-related prohibitions has assumed the character of a "rights discourse," focusing on the conflict between the right to personal freedom (particularly the freedom of occupation) on the one hand, and the interests of the religious public on the other.

From another perspective, the public dispute concerning pig-related prohibitions reflects—even today—an identity discourse. Religious Jewish society in Israel defines its identity through its adherence to the traditional characteristics of Jewish society. For secularists, however, rejecting the compelling nature of traditional prohibitions is part of the definition of their new identity, which is based on an "adversary" approach to anything associated with religious coercion. In this sense, secular Jews in Israel also view the pig prohibition as symbolic, but in reverse: as standing for their opposition to what they perceive as religious coercion. In the same spirit, Minister of the Interior Avraham Poraz from Shinui declared a new policy during the Passover of 2003, stating that his ministry would not be enforcing the Festival of Matzot (Prohibition of Leaven) Law, 1986. This step was also imbued with symbolic significance, celebrating freedom from religious coercion.[24] Even Emuna Elon, a religious columnist, described this law as redundant and harmful when she said, "This law was enacted under the pressure of religious parties, and relates to the prohibition of leaven on Passover as if it were an interest of the religious parties. Passover is a national holiday . . . and should not appear as a monopoly of the religious public." She also added that the tradition of circumcising Jewish boys had probably survived in Israel only because no law had been enacted to endorse it.[25] These words acknowledge that secular resentment of religious laws mainly conveys resistance to coercion rather than opposition to a religious lifestyle or to religious tradition per se.

The shift of positions on the application of pig-related prohibitions reflects the fragmentation process now affecting Israeli Jewish society. In the 1950s, efforts focused on uniting the citizens of the newly established state around national symbols. At present, politics of identity lead to the consolidation of separate identities in each of the various communities of Israel's multicultural society, while emphasizing the differences that set them apart. Tracing the changes in secular-religious relationships throughout Israel's history, Yair Sheleg, a religious columnist, points out that the present stage is one of "segregation and separation."[26] This process is exemplified in the growing tendency of the various communities toward voluntary separation. It has become common for religious Jews to prefer segregated neighborhoods attuned to their religious preferences regarding dress codes, education, abstention from driving on the Sabbath and festivals, and so forth. The *Solodkin* ruling, which relegated decisions regarding prohibitions on pork-trading to the neighborhood level, both reflects and encourages this process. After this precedent, religious people will be even more strongly motivated to live among neighbors who share their cultural choices.

The pattern of the debate on pig-related issues is now being replicated where the traditional mourning day on the Ninth of Av is concerned.

According to the Jewish calendar, this day commemorates the destruction of the Temple in Jerusalem and has historically symbolized the loss of national sovereignty. Various municipalities had bylaws banning the operation of entertainment venues, restaurants, and cafes on the eve of this day. After the enactment of Basic Law: Freedom of Occupation, the Knesset ensured the validity of these bylaws by enacting an authorizing law in this matter.[27] Despite this law, however, the legal counsel of the Tel Aviv municipality, Ahaz Ben-Ari, advised the mayor in 2001 that he could allow restaurants and cafes to remain open on this date by adopting an extremely narrow interpretation, according to which these were not "entertainment venues" in the strict sense of the term (as compared with cinemas and theaters). The Tel Aviv municipality adopted this lenient interpretation gladly, in line with its self-assumed role as the capital of Israel's secular ideals, in contrast with Jerusalem, the official capital of history and tradition. The Knesset then passed an amendment to the Prohibition of Opening Entertainment Centers on the Ninth of Av (Special Enablement) Law, 1997, adding an explicit provision regarding its application also to restaurants.[28] In this context as well, the Tel Aviv municipality did not see the national dimension of tradition (this time the Ninth of Av mourning) and preferred to oppose it as another example of religious coercion.

Two facts highlighting the extent of the social change depicted here are worth noting. First, only fifty years ago Tel Aviv served as a model for legislating pig-related prohibitions in its bylaws. Second, in the past, the Ninth of Av had certainly been perceived as a meaningful date from a national perspective as well. Berl Katsanelson, the leading ideologue of the labor movement, also held strong views on the meaning of this day of mourning as a national symbol.[29]

The same pattern recurs in the so-called "Sabbath wars" concerned with the opening of shopping centers and the conduct of other commercial activities on Saturdays. Cherishing the seventh day of the week as a special day of rest is one of the most definitive aspects of Jewish tradition. Although its origin is obviously religious and based on biblical law, it was also honored by secularists because of its contribution to the preservation of the Jewish community and the social significance of ensuring a weekly day of rest to all. Ahad Ha'am, founder of cultural Zionism, is famous for saying, "The Sabbath has preserved the people of Israel even more than the people of Israel have preserved the Sabbath."[30] Socialist Zionism could support the legal enforcement of a day of rest on the Sabbath due to its social advantages, although controversy surrounding the public characteristics to be assumed by this day dates back to the early days of the Zionist movement. Jewish tradition specifies the prohibitions on labor on this day in great detail, and some of them clash with modern non-religious understandings of "rest," such as bans on driving and public entertainment. Unlike these early controversies, the current "Sabbath wars" involve a more sweeping secular negation of the Sabbath as a day of rest. In the past, secularists had concentrated on struggles for allowing public transportation and entertainment venues to operate, with the main controversies in the 1980s focusing on movie theaters showing films on Friday night, the traditional Sabbath eve.[31] In contrast, throughout the 1990s, hard-line secularists almost unconditionally supported the movement to broaden commercial activities on the Sabbath. This trend again demonstrates that present-day secularism has detached itself from any identification with the traditional symbols of Jewish culture, which it considers relevant only to religious Jews. Although the secular public never regarded religious rules as relevant to its own way of passing the weekly day of rest, it used to share a perception that the Sabbath should be preserved as a different sort of day.

Admittedly, the current controversy over commercial activities on the Sabbath can be understood in relation to other developments as well, such as the decline of socialism, the rise of capitalism, and the pressures of the global economy. The vast economic significance of commercial activities on the Sabbath makes this a far more complex case than the relatively narrow pig prohibitions discussed in this book. These additional factors, however, do not negate the feature that Sabbath controversies share with the debate surrounding the pig prohibitions: the growing reluctance of Israel's secular public to identify with traditional customs that were once regarded as part of Jewish national culture and are now perceived by this public as strictly religious and hence irrelevant.

Yet another connection links pork-trading and the opening of stores on the Sabbath. One of the conditions a food store must meet in order to obtain a kashrut certificate is to be closed on the Sabbath. Therefore, businesses catering to observant clients and wishing to retain a kashrut certificate have an additional reason to observe Sabbath laws. By contrast, stores selling nonkosher food (including pork) lack this additional incentive to remain closed on the Sabbath. Pork and non-observance of the Sabbath thus go hand in hand in many instances.[32]

Although significant changes can be traced in the attitudes to pig-related legislation over time, it should be noted that the incorporation of pig prohibitions into Israeli law based on their status as a national symbol was controversial even in the 1950s. Prime Minister Ben-Gurion, the architect of Israeli statehood, preferred the municipal regulation of the pork trade to a nationwide prohibition, and conveyed his unwillingness to view pig prohibitions as a symbol of Israeli nationhood.[33] On these very grounds, the statutory amendment enabling the promulgation of municipal bylaws on the closure of businesses on the Sabbath should be regarded as a problematic victory from the perspective of the religious parties.[34] Although this amendment did achieve practical results, the delegation of Sabbath regulation to the municipal level implies that the Sabbath is a local issue rather than a national, cultural matter.[35] Skepticism regarding the national aspects of pig-related prohibitions is also implicit in Supreme Court decisions from of the 1950s. These decisions usually are presented in a formal and detached style that does not make use of national terminology. Justice Berenson even defined these prohibitions explicitly as an interest of the religious public.[36] The seeds of skepticism, then, were sown from the start.

Despite the doubts and qualms, however, in the past at least part of the secular public was willing to acknowledge the national dimension of pig-related prohibitions. This willingness was the dominant factor in the enactment of the Pig-Raising Prohibition Law in the early 1960s, which established a nationwide arrangement regarding pig-breeding. In contrast, by the 1990s the image of the pig prohibition as a national symbol had dimmed in the prevalent social perception and, consequently, in Israel's legal structures.

The ongoing public and legal debate on pig-related legislation over the years has been characterized by a growing tendency to distance the popular sensibilities of Israeli Jews concerning pig prohibitions from those of Diaspora Jews.[37] The pig prohibition assumed symbolic meaning mainly in the Diaspora, or at least in contexts of national humiliation and subjugation. In the early years of the state, most of Israel's public leaders were not native-born and still carried memories (and possibly scars) of life in the Diaspora, and perhaps of affronts associated with pigs. As time goes by, this association is fading and resistance to pig prohibitions grows. An interesting and as yet unanswered question concerns the attitudes of Diaspora Jews to this Israeli controversy. I assume that many of them, certainly more than their Israeli brethren, continue to place the pig prohibition in a broader Jewish cultural and historical context because they still live among non-Jews. Avoiding pork used to be a symbol of national pride for Jews, who knew that their neighbors were also conscious of the power of this symbol. Anti-Semitic experiences in the Diaspora, as noted, enhanced the power of this symbol beyond the religious significance of the original prohibition. This need not imply, however, that Diaspora Jews would be interested in a legal regime that takes away from them the decision to avoid pork.

The story of the relatively discrete issue of pig prohibitions mirrors far deeper and more significant changes in the historical compromises that have dominated religion and state relationships in Israel. For decades, Israeli political life was described as following the model of accommodation or consociational democracy as defined by Arend Lijphart,[38] namely, as one based on cooperation, negotiation, and compromise.[39] Working within this paradigm, many legal arrangements reflected pragmatic compromises rather than doctrinal decisions. Representative examples were the exemptions from military service granted to yeshivah students and religious women, the wide autonomy granted to the religious school system, and the closure of public transportation on the Sabbath (although the use of private cars and taxi services was allowed). Another compromise applied religious law to the area of marriage and divorce, while registering civil marriages conducted abroad and also granting almost all the civil and economic rights enjoyed by married couples to unmarried partners. A prominent instance of this political culture of compromise was the decision not to draw up a written constitution. Given this background, pig-related legislation that rested on a compromise between religious and secularists was fully understandable.

This political culture of compromise, however, no longer exists. Cohen and Susser suggest that Israeli public life has shifted to crisis politics,[40] in an era of bitter conflict between right and left and without any political party enjoying hegemonic status. More controversies are brought to the courts and, against the background of a so-called constitutional

revolution, the courts tend to rule on them. No room is left for compromise.[41] Thus, the Supreme Court overruled the longstanding administrative exemption of yeshivah students from service,[42] prompting legislation
in this matter.[43] Other Supreme Court decisions have dealt with the enforcement of the legal provisions on a core curriculum (including math-
ematics, history and other subjects) in ultra-Orthodox schools that had
so far failed to implement it.[44]

With the growing confrontation between religious and secularists, tracing a significant "traditional" public in Israel—comprising people reluc-
tant to define themselves as secular while adhering to religious norms
only partially—is becoming more difficult. In the past, this public was
the "bridge" that contributed to compromises in religious-secular controversies. Menachem Begin, the leader of the Herut movement and the
Likud party, who supported the legislation on pig prohibitions, was a
representative example of this segment of the population. At present,
however, people increasingly identify themselves as either secularists or
religious. Avoiding nonkosher meat, especially pork, without necessarily observing all the minor details of Jewish dietary law, was considered
a "traditional" norm. The public adhering to this norm without describing itself as religious is shrinking.

Secular Jews in Israel are increasingly detached from more and more
dimensions of Jewish tradition that only a few decades ago had been
part of the life experience and education of even committed secularists.
A type of "universal" secularism appears to be developing. This secularism is influenced mainly by Western values and individualism and
inclines toward "militant" politics,[45] leaving hardly any room for partic-
ularized laws that reflect tradition like pig-related legislation. In fact, this
kind of secularism largely defines itself by its rejection of traditional
norms. For devoted secularists, consuming pork and opposing any restrictive norms in the name of traditional Judaism is symbolically significant. They view pig-related legislation as a symbol of Israel's association
with fundamentalist Muslim countries, and opposition to it as a source
of hope for Israel's full integration into the Western world. Secularists of
this type hailed the *Solodkin* decision. Journalist Yaron London, although
committed to a secular way of life, condemned this rejoicing, charging
that it was often accompanied by ignorance of Jewish history. London
noted that many of those who celebrated the new Court decision would

most likely oppose judicial precedents recognizing the legality of slaughtering dogs for eating (without displaying a similar openness to freedom of occupation in this regard), or the desecration of the national flag in areas populated by non-Zionists (again, showing no tolerance for Arabs or ultra-Orthodox Jews).[46]

Aviezer Ravitzky, the well-known researcher of Jewish thought, pointed out that both the religious and secular camps are currently less willing to search for a middle ground because they realize that by now their rivals are here to stay. "I would claim that the original political and social agreement was based on a mistaken assumption common to both sides. Each assumed, for reasons of its own, that the rival camp represented an ephemeral historical phenomenon. Secular, religious, and ultra-Orthodox all adhered to the belief that the 'other' was fated to decline in strength and numbers, and eventually to disappear. . . . And while they may not have thought their forecasts would be realized in the immediate future, all were sufficiently confident in the conviction that any agreement was bound to be temporary, that it assumed the status of a tactical compromise rather than a fundamental reconciliation," he wrote.[47]

Both the religious and secular now understand that this perception of the "other" is no longer realistic and they therefore fight harder, hindering compromise: "If it was easy in the past to display tolerance and solidarity towards those, who, one imagined, would soon be trading their colors for our own, today we are being asked to tolerate individuals and groups who seem determined and even likely to preserve their own identities. This demands a level of acknowledgement and acceptance not previously required," Ravitzky argued.[48]

The result is that even fundamental compromises considered virtually unassailable or unbreakable, such as the application of religious law to matters of marriage and divorce, are now under attack. Because only children born to Jewish mothers are considered Jews according to Halakhah and because patrilinear descent is unacceptable to traditional interpretations of religious law, many immigrants from the former Soviet Union cannot marry in Israel and proposals to recognize a civil alternative to religious marriages now garner wider support. For many years, marriage and divorce laws were considered the ultimate symbol of preserving the ideal of a single Jewish nation. This is now being contested, with a clear tendency to prioritize personal liberties over symbols. Although pig-related legislation has an advantage over the extant marriage and divorce laws in that it does not constitute a substantial impediment to personal autonomy, in the current atmosphere of a growing divide between religious and secular Jews many view even relatively slight sacrifices as unsupportable.

The question dangling over all these controversies is: what should be the role of cultural and historical factors in the legal system of a state that defines itself as both "Jewish and democratic?" The verdict is still pending.

Pig-Related Legislation in Israel

The English version of the laws included in this appendix is the official translation by the Israeli Ministry of Justice published at the time of their enactment.

LOCAL AUTHORITIES (SPECIAL ENABLEMENT) LAW, 1956
(as originally enacted on 26 November 1956, 11 LSI 16)

Prohibition of the raising and keeping of pigs and the sale of pork and pork products	1. Notwithstanding the provisions of any other law, a local authority shall be competent to make a bylaw limiting or prohibiting the raising and keeping of pigs and the sale of pork and pork products destined for food.
Application of the prohibition	2. A local authority may impose a limitation or prohibition as provided in section 1 on the whole of its area of jurisdiction or on a particular part thereof; but in the latter case it shall apply to the whole population of such area or part.
Auxiliary powers	3. Where a local authority imposes a limitation or prohibition as provided in section 2, it may, in the bylaw, lay down provisions as to the inspection, attachment and confiscation of pigs, or of pork or edible pork products destined for sale, to which the limitation or restriction applies.

Penalties

4. A person who contravenes a bylaw made under this law is liable to the same penalty as a person who contravenes a bylaw made under the Municipal Corporations Ordinance, or under the Local Councils Ordinance, 1941, as the case may be.

Saving of powers

5. This law shall add to, and not derogate from, the powers vested in a local authority by any other law.

Validation of bylaw

6. A bylaw made by a local authority and published in *Reshumot* before the coming into force of this Law and which would have been validly made had this Law been in force at the time shall be deemed to have been validly made; but a person shall not be prosecuted for an offence against a bylaw as aforesaid committed before the coming into force of this Law.

PIG-RAISING PROHIBITION LAW, 1962
(as originally enacted on 23 July 1962, 16 LSI 93)

Prohibition

1. A person shall not raise, keep or slaughter pigs.

Inapplicability of prohibition

2. The provisions of section 1 shall not apply–
   (1) in the areas of the localities specified in the Schedule to this Law;
   (2) to the raising, keeping and slaughtering of pigs in scientific and research institutions and in public zoological gardens.

Penalty

3. A person contravening the provisions of section 1 shall be liable to a fine of 10,000 pounds.

Responsibility of owners of premises

4. The owner of any structure or other premises who lets the same or renews the lease thereof or authorizes the use thereof or renews the authorization of such use, knowing that the structure or premises is or are used or will be

used for the raising, keeping or slaughter of
pigs, shall be liable to a penalty of 5,000
pounds.

Entry, search and
seizure

5. A police officer, or a person empowered in
that behalf in writing by the Minister of Police,
may–
   (1) enter any place of which he has reasonable
   grounds for assuming that pigs are being
   raised, kept or slaughtered therein in contravention of the provisions of this Law,
   and carry out a search therein;
   (2) seize pigs of which he has reasonable
   grounds for assuming that they are being
   raised, kept or slaughtered in contravention
   of the provisions of this Law, and pigs in
   respect of which a person has been convicted of an offence under this Law.
The provisions of sections 19 to 21 of the
Criminal Procedure (Arrest and Searches)
Ordinance shall apply *mutatis mutandis* to a
search and seizure under this Law, and for
the purposes of section 21 of that Ordinance,
"the occupant of any place" shall include the
possessor of a pig which has been seized.

Confiscation and
destruction

6. Pigs seized under section 5(2) shall be
confiscated and destroyed in the manner
prescribed by regulations. The confiscation
and destruction shall not be dependent upon
proceedings under section 7 or any other legal
proceedings.

Rights of owners and
possessors

7. The owners and possessors of pigs seized
under section 5(2) may, within two weeks from
the day of the seizure, apply to the Magistrate's
Court in whose area of jurisdiction the pigs
were seized, and if it is not proved that there
were reasonable grounds for seizing the pigs or
if it is proved that no offence under this Law
had been committed in respect thereof, the
Court may order the payment of the value
thereof to the applicant or to another person

entitled thereto, as the Court may think fit. An order under this section shall be appealable in like manner as a judgment of a Magistrate's Court in a civil case.

Definition

8. In this Law, "slaughter" means any killing for the purpose of eating.

Implementation and regulations

9. The Minister of the Interior is charged with the implementation of this Law and may make regulations for such implementation; The Minister of Justice may make regulations concerning procedure in connection with applications under section 7.

Amendment of Enablement Law

10. From the day of the coming into force of this Law, the words "the raising and keeping of pigs" in section 1 of the Local Authorities (Special Enablement) Law, 1956, shall be deleted, and the provisions in bylaws under that Law relating to the raising and keeping of pigs shall, from that day, be deemed to have been deleted.

Deletion from Schedule

11. The Minister of the Interior shall, by order, delete the name of any locality from the Schedule to this Law if that locality is a local authority and the council of the local authority has decided to request the deletion of the name.

Commencement

12. This Law shall come into force upon the passage of one year from the day of its adoption by the Knesset.

SCHEDULE
(section 2(1))

Iblin
Kafr Yasif
Ma'liyeh
Nazareth
Rama

The area of the local authority

Gush Chalav	The area marked for the purposes of this Law on
(Jish)	a map signed by the Minister of the Interior and
Eilabun	the copies of which have been deposited at the
Fasuta	District Commissioner's Offices of the districts in
Raineh	which these localities are situated

The Israeli Political Spectrum

Change and instability are prominent characteristics of Israel's political system, with parties joining alliances and then splitting off and re-emerging in new guises (cross-references between them will be indicated below by an asterisk). The two dominant forces throughout the period considered in this work have been the Labor movement (represented by several parties), which constituted the hegemonic political force until 1977, and the Likud bloc, which has since controlled Israeli politics except for two periods during which Labor returned to power under the leadership of Yitzhak Rabin (1992–1995) and Ehud Barak (1999–2001). A third important political force considered in the context of this book is represented by the religious parties.

The description below includes parties whose views were or are relevant to the subject matter of the book.

AGUDAT ISRAEL (The Fellowship of Israel)

Ultra-Orthodox political party founded in 1912 in Poland and established in Palestine in 1919. Although the party participates in Israeli politics, it upholds a strictly non-Zionist platform, rejecting the notion of a Jewish state that does not abide by Halakhah. The party is led by a Council of Torah Sages, whose approval is required for all decisions by its political representatives.

AHDUT HA-AVODAH (Unity of Labor)

A Zionist socialist party founded in 1919. In the 1920s it was the largest party within the Labor movement. In 1930, it united with *Ha-Po'el ha-Tsa'ir to form *Mapai. In 1944, a faction of internal opposition within Mapai broke off from the party and went back to this name. In 1965, Ahdut ha-Avodah forged an alignment with Mapai, and they eventually merged in 1968 to form the Israeli *Labor party.

CITIZENS' RIGHTS MOVEMENT (CRM)

Established in 1973 by Shulamit Aloni, who left the Labor Party. CRM (known as Ratz in its Hebrew acronym) champions separation of religion and state and compromise in the Israeli-Palestinian conflict. In 1992, it united with *Mapam and *Shinui to form *Meretz.

DEGEL HA-TORAH (The Flag of Torah)

Ultra-Orthodox party, established in 1988 as an Ashkenazi counterpart to *Shas after its spiritual leader, Rabbi Eliezer Shakh, broke away from *Agudat Israel.

GENERAL ZIONISTS

A centrist party of the bourgeoisie, joined the *Progressive Party in 1961 and created the Liberal Party. The merger was dissolved in 1965, when the *General Zionists formed a political alliance with *Herut and in 1973 created a new joint party, the *Likud.

HA-PO'EL HA-MIZRAHI (Spiritual Center Worker)

Religious workers' movement created in Palestine in 1922 by a socialist oriented faction of the *Mizrachi, which it joined in 1956 to form the *National Religious Party.

HA-PO'EL HA-TSA'IR (The Young Worker)

A Zionist socialist party founded in Palestine in 1905. Established the first kibbutz and counted celebrated *Yishuv* figures among its members and supporters. Joined *Ahdut ha-Avodah in 1930 to establish *Mapai.

Herut (Freedom)

Right-wing party founded by members of the IZL underground movement that had fought against the British Mandate in Palestine after its dissolution as a military organization in 1948. The party, led by the last IZL commander Menachem Begin, was a sequel to the pre-state Revisionist movement. Joined the *General Zionists in 1965 to create Gahal (acronym of Gush Herut Liberalim—Bloc of Herut and the Liberals), and later became the mainstay of the *Likud.

Israel be-Aliyah (Israel for Aliyah/ Israel on the Ascent)

Founded in the wake of massive immigration from the former Soviet Union, which is the party's main constituency. The questionable halakhic status of part of its supporters, as well as their secular background, has occasionally brought it into open conflict with religious parties.

Kach

A religious party with a strong anti-Arab platform established by Rabbi Meir Kahana, modeled on the Jewish Defense League he had established in the United States. Currently outlawed.

Labor Party

Founded in 1968, joining together *Mapai, *Ahdut ha-Avodah, and a small splinter party (Rafi) established by David Ben-Gurion. In its various forms, the Labor party was the hegemonic political force in Palestine and Israel until 1977, when the *Likud won the elections. Over the years, the party toned down its overt socialist slant to become the dominant left-of-center political movement in Israel.

Likud (Alliance)

Founded in 1973 through an alliance of *Herut, the *Liberal Party and three other small factions with a nationalist orientation. The Likud won the 1977 elections and became the dominant party on the Israeli political scene.

LIBERAL PARTY

Established in 1961 through the merger of the *General Zionists and the *Progressive Party. Joined *Herut in 1965 to create an alliance and was eventually absorbed into the *Likud.

MAKI (*Miflagah Komunistit Isra'eli t*—Israeli Communist Party)

A communist party established in Palestine in 1921. Currently represented in the Knesset by Hadash.

MAPAI (*Mifleget Po'alei Eretz Israel*—The Party of Workers in the Land of Israel)

Founded in 1930 through the merger of *Ahdut ha-Avodah and *Ha-Po'el ha-Tsa'ir. The party's ideology was a mixture of Zionism and pragmatic socialism, and its founders included David Ben-Gurion and Berl Katsanelson. It immediately became the hegemonic political force in the *Yishuv* and the Labor movement, and remained so until 1977, with its nominees holding key government positions as well as heading most local authorities. In 1968, it joined other factions to found the Israeli *Labor party.

MAPAM (*Mifleget Po'alim Me'uhedet*—United Workers Party)

Left-wing, Labor-Zionist party. Founded in 1948 through the merger of *Ahdut ha-Avodah/Po'alei Zion and Ha-Shomer ha-Tsa'ir (The Young Watchman), a youth movement and political faction since 1946. The party supported class struggle, state ownership, planned economy, and separation of state and religion. In 1992, it joined the *Citizens' Rights Movement and *Shinui to form *Meretz.

MERETZ

*Mapam, *Citizens' Rights Movement, and *Shinui joined in 1992 to create Meretz, a new party championing a left-wing platform that supports civil and minority rights and individual liberties. Later, part of Shinui left this alliance and ran for elections independently.

MIZRACHI (Acronym of Spiritual Center)

Founded in Vilna in 1902 as an Orthodox Zionist party, proclaiming the Torah as the spiritual center of Zionism. Its first Palestine branch was established in 1918. Joined *Ha-Po'el ha-Mizrahi in 1956 to form the *National Religious Party.

NATIONAL RELIGIOUS PARTY (NRP, or Mafdal in its Hebrew acronym)

A Zionist Orthodox party founded in 1956 through the merger of the *Mizrachi and *Ha-Po'el ha-Mizrahi. Unlike other religious Orthodox factions, the NRP is an avowedly Zionist party that began its political course as a natural ally of the Labor movement and was a member of all Labor-led government coalitions until 1977. Since the 1970s, however, it has progressively moved to the right in its support of a Greater Israel ideology and accordingly shifted its support to the *Likud.

PO'ALEI AGUDAT ISRAEL

Ultra-Orthodox party founded in Poland in 1922 and established in Palestine in 1933, calling for the application of the Torah's social principles in daily life. Affiliated with *Agudat Israel in various ways throughout its history (although it also ran as a separate list). It later merged with Agudat Israel to form *Yahadut ha-Torah.

PROGRESSIVE PARTY

Established in 1948 as a centrist liberal party, representing mainly immigrants from Central European countries and liberal trends within other factions. Favored a welfare state and opposed religious coercion. Merged with the *General Zionists in 1961 to form the Liberal Party. Broke from this merger in 1965 to create the Independent Liberal Party, after the General Zionists agreed to an alliance with *Herut.

SHAS (Sephardi Torah Guardians)

An ethnic religious party, supported mainly by Jews of Sephardic extraction. Led by Rabbi Ovadiah Yosef, it left Agudat Israel in 1984 to protest the discrimination of Orthodox Sephardi Jews. Although it is non-Zionist in its professed ideology, many of its supporters are only traditional (rather than Orthodox) Jews.

Shinui

Founded in 1974 by Amnon Rubinstein in protest against the leadership failure of the Labor government in the October 1973 War. In 1992, it joined the *Citizens' Rights Movement and *Mapam to form *Meretz. In 1999, a group from within the Shinui faction of Meretz left to run alone on a centrist platform with a militant secularist ideology opposed to religious coercion.

Yahadut ha-Torah (Torah Judaism)

Ultra-Orthodox party founded through the merger between *Agudat Israel and *Po'alei Agudat Israel.

Notes

ABBREVIATIONS

CA   Civil Appeal
Cr. A.   Criminal Appeal
DK   Divrei ha-Knesset [Knesset Minutes]
HC   High Court
KT   Kovets Takkanot [Regulations Compendium]
PD   Piskei Din [Court Decisions]
PG   Palestine Gazette
PLR   Palestine Law Reports
TAMA   Tel-Aviv Municipality Archive

PREFACE

1. The most prominent cases in this regard are HC 98, 105/54, *Lazarovitz v. Food Controller,* 10 PD 40 (a precedent confining the exercise of power solely to achieve the purpose for which that power was granted); HC 194/54, *Axel v. the Mayor, Councilors and Residents of Netanya,* 8 PD 1524, and HC 72/55, *Fridi v. Municipality of Tel Aviv,* 10 PD 734 (significant rulings bearing on the local authorities' lack of power to regulate religious matters); HC 8/63, *Bazul v. Minister of the Interior,* 19 (1) PD 337 (a leading ruling concerning the sovereignty of the legislature).

2. *Lazarovitz* has actually been reported as one of the one hundred most cited precedents of the Israeli Supreme Court. See: Yoram Shachar, Miron Gross, and Chanan Goldshmidt, "100 Leading Precedents of the Supreme Court: Quantitative Analysis," *Mishpat Umimshal* 7 (2004): 243, 251.

3. Kenneth M. Murchison, *Federal Criminal Law Doctrines: The Forgotten Influence of National Prohibition* (Durham, N.C.: Duke University Press, 1994).

4. See A. W. Brian Simpson, *Leading Cases in the Common Law* (New York: Oxford University Press, 1995), 45.

1. Religious Symbols and Culture in Israeli Law

1. The text of these two laws, as they were originally enacted, appears in appendix 1.

2. John Stuart Mill, *On Liberty,* ed. Stefan Collini (Cambridge and New York: Cambridge University Press, 1989), 85.

3. On this issue, see chapter 2.

4. The prohibition on *eating* pork, however, is the one expressly mentioned in the Bible, whereas other prohibitions were decided upon at later times. Some secular critics found it ironic that the earlier and hence the most binding religious prohibition was not made into law, in contrast to later prohibitions. See: Haim H. Cohn, "The Jewishness of the State of Israel," *Alpayim: A Multidisciplinary Publication for Contemporary Thought and Literature* 16 (1998): 9, 17–18 [in Hebrew].

5. On this question, see: Danny Statman, "Offending Religious Feelings" [in Hebrew], in *Multiculturalism in a Democratic and Jewish State,* ed. Menachem Mautner, Avi Sagi, and Ronen Shamir (Tel-Aviv: Ramot, Tel-Aviv University, 1998), 133, 141–42.

6. For further information, see "Pork Import and Saudi Arabia," available at http://www.american.edu/projects/mandala/TED/saudpork.htm.

7. See: The Palestine Order in Council, 1922, The Laws of Palestine, vol. 3, p. 2569.

8. Ibid., Article 51.

9. Kosher meat is potentially more expensive because it can only be obtained from animals declared ritually fit and slaughtered according to religious law by properly trained personnel, who can also declare carcasses ritually unclean after an inspection process performed following slaughter (see also the text accompanying n. 16, *infra*). The competitive import of nonkosher meat (be it from ritually prohibited animals or, at least, from animals slaughtered without religious supervision), could therefore lead to lower prices for the relatively large public willing to buy such meat in Israel. Observant Jews would then have to purchase kosher meat in a market with far fewer players and much reduced competition.

10. See: HC 3872/92, *Mitrael Ltd. v. Prime Minister and Minister of Religious Affairs,* 47 (5) PD 485. This decision was based on earlier holdings making it illegal for an administrative authority to take into consideration religious factors when exercising its powers regarding import permits and other business licenses. See: CA (Civil Appeal) 6/66, *Kalo v. Municipality of Bat-Yam,* 20 (2) PD 327 (discrimination between kosher and nonkosher butcher shops concerning the imposition of a business tax); HC 231/63, *Retef, Food Supplies Ltd. v. Minister of Trade and Industry,* 17 PD 2730 (restriction of imports on grounds of ritual fitness).

11. The enactment of the Meat and Meat Products Law of 1994 was accompanied by an amendment to the Basic Law: Freedom of Occupation, which

incorporated an "override provision" modeled after section 33 of the Canadian Charter of Rights and Freedoms, enabling legislation that contradicts constitutional provisions. This law was recognized as constitutional in HC 4676/94, *Mitrael Ltd. v. Israel Knesset,* 50 (5) PD 15. For more details on the new Basic Laws and the precedents interpreting them, see chapter 8.

12. See "Torah Judaism's Motion for a Vote of No Confidence in the Prime Minister at the End of the Debate on Basic Law: Social Rights," 123rd session of the 14th Knesset, 21 July 1997, 165 DK 8235, 8236. Other matters in this area deal with the question of who is entitled to sell food as kosher. For rulings issued in petitions filed in respect of the refusal to grant kashrut certificates, see: HC 465/89, *Raskin v. Jerusalem Religious Council,* 44 (2) PD 673 (refusal to grant a kashrut certificate to a venue hosting "immodest" shows); HC 22/91, *Orly S. 1985 Ltd. v. Chief Rabbi of Yavne,* 45 (3) PD 817 (refusal to grant a kashrut certificate to a plant bearing the same name as nonkosher restaurants); HC 5009/94, *Mitrael Ltd. v. Council of the Chief Rabbinate of Israel,* 48(5) PD 617 (refusing a permit for kosher meat imports to someone who also imported nonkosher meat); HC 3944/92, *Marbek Abattoir Ltd. v. Chief Rabbinate of Netanyah,* 49 (1) PD 278 (refusal to grant a kashrut certificate to meat from animals slaughtered at a distant abattoir); HC 7201/00, *Aviv Osochlansky Delicatessen Ltd. v. Council of the Chief Rabbinate of Israel,* 56 (2) PD 196 (refusal to grant a kashrut certificate to an abattoir selling ritually unfit meat surpluses); HC 351/04, *Peles Hotel Ltd. v. Chief Rabbinate, Religious Council Netanyah,* 59(2) PD 433 (refusal to grant a kashrut certificate to a hotel that leases an adjacent area to a nonkosher restaurant). For a precedent from the mandatory period, see *Federman v. District Commissioner, Jerusalem, Southern District* (1925) 1 PLR, 57.

13. For the concept of collective memory, see: Amos Funkenstein, "Collective Memory and Historical Consciousness," *History and Memory* 1 (1989): 5; Paul Connerton, *How Societies Remember* (New York: Cambridge University Press, 1989); Yosef Hayyim Yerushalmi, *Zakhor: Jewish History and Jewish Memory* (Seattle: University of Washington Press, 1982). In his work, Yerushalmi emphasizes the tension between memory and modern historiography: "The historian does not simply come to replenish the gaps of memory. He constantly challenges even those memories that have survived intact" (94).

14. Labor Hours and Rest Law of 1951.

15. For example: Cr A 217/68, *Yizramax Ltd. v. State of Israel,* 22 (2) PD 343 (overruling a bylaw mandating the closing of gas stations on the Sabbath); HC 5016/96, *Horev v. Minister of Transportation,* 51 (4) PD 1 (controversy surrounding a decision to restrict driving through a religious area in Jerusalem during prayer time).

16. See: David Nirenberg, *Communities of Violence: Persecution of Minorities in the Middle Ages* (Princeton, N.J.: Princeton University Press, 1996), 170–72.

17. The involvement of kibbutzim in pig-related economic activities highlights the potential for mixing ideological and economic considerations in this area.

Originally the leadership of the kibbutzim, inspired by the socialist ideology dominant in the first decades of the Zionist movement, opposed pig-related restrictions as part of its secular ideology. But the choice of several kibbutzim to develop pig-breeding farms and a meat industry specializing in pork processing affected the scope of their later opposition to legal prohibitions in this area. See chapter 7.

18. See, for instance: Ronen Shamir, "Suspended in Space: Bedouins in Israeli Law," *Law & Society Review* 30 (1996): 231.

19. Paul W. Kahn, *The Cultural Study of Law* (Chicago: University of Chicago Press, 1999), 112: "the object of cultural study is the community in its appearance as single, historical subject."

20. See: Joseph R. Gusfield, "Moral Passage: The Symbolic Process in Public Designations of Deviance," *Social Problems* 15 (1967): 175, 178. Another perspective on law and culture perceives law as rhetoric rather than as a system of rules. See: James Boyd White, "Law as Rhetoric, Rhetoric as Law: The Arts of Cultural and Communal Life," *University of Chicago Law Review* 52 (1985): 684.

21. See: Eric A. Posner, "Symbols, Signals, and Social Norms in Politics and Law," *Journal of Legal Studies* 27 (1998): 765. This article focuses on the function of the symbol as a signal through which the players express their loyalty to the community.

22. On the German approach, see *Crucifix in the Classrooms Decision* BVerfGE 93, 1 (1995), as discussed by Sabine Michalowski and Lorna Woods, *German Constitutional Law: The Protection of Civil Liberties* (Aldershot, England: Ashgate, 1999), 187–91. On the American approach, see: *County of Allegheny v. American Civil Liberties Union, Greater Pittsburgh Chapter* 492 U.S. 573 (1989). In the United States, the controversies in this area centered on the application of the constitutional prohibition on the establishment of religion, which also applies to government adoption or promotion of religious symbols. See also: Janet L. Dolgin, "Religious Symbols and the Establishment of a National 'Religion,'" *Mercer Law Review* 39 (1987–88): 495; Kenneth L. Karst, "The First Amendment, the Politics of Religion and the Symbols of Government," *Harvard Civil Rights—Civil Liberties Law Review* 27 (1992): 503.

23. On the dispute around the display of the picture *Piss Christ,* see: Damien Casey, "Law and the Sacred: Sacrifice, Piss Christ, and Liberal Excess," *Law/Text/Culture* 5 (2000): 19; Michael Casey, Anthony and Hayden Ramsay, "Law and the Sacred: After Serrano Ethics, Theology and the Law of Blasphemy," *Law/Text/Culture* 5 (2000): 35; Damien Casey, "Law & the Sacred: After Serrano Sacrifice and Church Politics," *Law/Text/Culture* 5 (2000): 55. A non-religious symbol that was discussed in relation to its desecration is the American national flag, "the visible symbol embodying the Nation." *Texas v. Johnson* 491 U.S. 397, 429 (1989) (Chief Justice Rehnquist, dissenting). See also Ute Krudewagen, "Political Symbols in Two Constitutional Orders: The Flag Desecration Decisions of the United States Supreme Court and the German Constitutional Court," *Arizona Journal of International & Comparative Law* 19 (2002): 679.

24. Clifford Geertz, *The Interpretation of Cultures* (New York: Basic Books, 1973), 127. The halakhic discussion on the symbolic aspect of the commandments makes for an interesting comparison. See Rabbi Samson Raphael Hirsh, *The Commandments as Symbols,* trans. from German Aviazri Wolf (Jerusalem: Mosad Harav Kook, 1984) [in Hebrew]. This book does not include a symbolic analysis of all 613 commandments, but offers a basis for discussion by reference to a number of central examples: circumcision, *tsitsit* [fringed garment], *tefillin* [phylacteries], as well as the Temple and its utensils.

25. See: Geo. D. Ferguson, "The Development of Law during the Middle Ages, Especially in France and England," *Albany Law Journal* 63 (1901–2): 419, 420; R. Vashon Rogers, "Pigs," *Green Bag* 14 (1902): 374, 374–76.

26. Other animals were also brought to trial and sentenced, but the trials of pigs, usually for wounding or even killing young children, were the most common. See: E. P. Evans, "Bugs and Beasts before the Law," *Green Bag* 11 (1899): 33, 33–36; Rogers, *supra* n. 25, at pp. 376–77; Esther Cohen, *The Crossroads of Justice: Law and Culture in Late Medieval France* (New York: E. J. Brill, 1993), 110–17; Paul Schiff Berman, "Rats, Pigs, and Statues on Trial: The Creation of Cultural Narratives in the Prosecution of Animals and Inmate Objects," *New York University Law Review* 69 (1994): 288, 298–301.

27. *Aldred's Case* (1610) 77 ER, 816; *R v. Wigg* (1705) 92 ER, 269.

28. *Village of Euclid v. Ambler Realty Co.,* 272 U.S. 365, 388 (1926).

29. Hendrik Hartog, "Pigs and Positivism," *Wisconsin Law Review* (1985): 899. A more recent debate relates to the relatively new phenomenon of keeping pigs as pets. See Andrea Hart Herbster, "More than Pigs in a Parlor: An Exploration of the Relationship between the Law and Keeping Pigs as Pets," *Iowa Law Review* 86 (2000–2001): 339.

30. Marco d'Eramo, *The Pig and the Skyscraper—Chicago: A History of Our Future,* trans. Graeme Thomson (New York: VERSO, 2002), 25–40.

31. See: John D. Burns, "The Eight Million Little Pigs—A Cautionary Tale: Statutory and Regulatory Responses to Concentrated Hog Farming," *Wake Forest Law Review* 31 (1996): 851.

32. See Peter Stallybrass and Allon White, *The Politics and Poetics of Transgression* (Ithaca, N.Y.: Cornell University Press, 1986), 44.

33. For a broader discussion, see: Robert Malcolm and Stephanos Mastoris, *The English Pig: A History* (Rio Grande, Ohio: Hambledon Press, 1998).

34. George Orwell, *Animal Farm* (New York: Harcourt, Brace, 1946).

35. *The Qur'an,* trans. M. A. S. Abdel Haleem (Oxford: Oxford University Press, 2004), ch. 5, "The Feast," para. 3, p. 67.

36. Ibid., ch. 16, "The Bee," para. 115, p. 173. See also the text accompanying *supra* n. 2. For a Muslim source referring to the slaughter of both Jews and pigs on the Day of Judgment, see also: Nirenberg, *supra* n. 16, at 197. Exploiting Islam's abhorrence of pigs, Jewish extremists have used heads of pigs or illustrations of pigs in several acts of provocation against Muslims in recent years. See: Cr. F.

(Criminal File) (Jerusalem) 108/98 *State of Israel v. Askin,* P. M. 1999 (2) 289; Cr. F. (Jerusalem) 109/98 *State of Israel v. Pekovitz* (unpublished) (placing a pig's head in a Muslim cemetery); and Cr. A. (Criminal Appeal) 697/98 *Sosozkin v. State of Israel,* 52 (3) PD 289 (distributing a leaflet containing a sketch of a pig wrapped in a *kafiah* trampling on an open *Koran*). The Muslim abhorrence of pigs has recently been associated in Israeli public consciousness with the suicide bombers who believe their actions turn them into religious martyrs. Some Jews have proposed burying Muslim suicide bombers in pigskins in order to deter potential terrorists. See: Yuval Karni, "A Fault in an Explosives Belt Saved Tens of Customers," *Yedi'ot Aharonot,* 24 February 2003. Karni writes: "Shortly after the attempted strike in Efrat, two of the town's settlers travelled to a shop selling nonkosher meat in Jerusalem and purchased about three kilograms of pig skin. The settlers claim they placed the pig skin on the terrorist's body, but the police say they know nothing about this." Similar reports appeared in other newspapers. See: Hanan Shlein, "The Terrorist Failed to Detonate Himself, and Was Shot Dead," *Ma'ariv,* 24 February 2002; Amos Harel, Jonathan Liss and Nadav Shraga'i, "Failure of Attempted Suicide in Efrat Supermarket," *Haaretz,* 24 February 2002. The matter was discussed in *Haaretz* the following day, quoting Muslim religious leaders who stated that placing a pig's skin on a body after the person's spirit had already departed it is religiously meaningless. See Amira Hass and Nadav Shraga'i, "Religious Leaders: Even in a Pig's Skin, a *Shahid* Ascends to the Garden of Eden," *Haaretz,* 25 February 2002. B. Michael noted the irony in this use of pigs by Jews, and especially by Jews who oppose the sale of pork. See: B. Michael, "Wrappers of Pig Skin," *Yedi'ot Aharonot* (Supplement), 1 March 2002.

37. Lawrence Friedman indicates that "beyond a doubt, the jewel in the crown of the moral revolution was national Prohibition." Lawrence M. Friedman, *Crime and Punishment in American History* (New York: Basic Books, 1993), 339.

38. V. P. Bharatiya, *Religion-State Relationship and Constitutional Rights in India* (New Delhi: Deep & Deep Publications, 1987), 210–11; R. I. Chaudhari, *The Concept of Secularism in Indian Constitution* (New Delhi: Uppal Pub. House, 1987), 160–61.

39. *Mohd. Hanif Quareshi v. Bihar* (1959) S. C. R. 629.

40. *Abdul Hakim Quraishi v. Bihar* (1961) 2 S. C. R. 610. For an analysis of Indian case law, see: Durga Das Basu, *Shorter Constitution of India* (10th ed., 1988), 277; H. M. Seervai, *Constitutional Law of India: A Critical Commentary* (4th ed.) vol. 1 (1991), 834–38; and vol. 2 (1993), 1946–48; J. N. Pandey, *Constitutional Law of India* (39th ed., 2003), 155; Bharatiya, *supra* n. 38, at pp. 212–14; Chaudhari, *supra* n. 38, at pp. 162–64.

41. For a critical discussion of the Indian prohibitions on the slaughter of cows, see: Gunnar Myrdal, *Asian Drama: An Inquiry into the Poverty of Nations,* vol. 1 (New York: Pantheon, 1968), 89–93.

42. Basic Law: Freedom of Occupation, and Basic Law: Human Dignity and Liberty, both enacted in 1992.

43. HC 953/01 *Solodkin v. Municipality of Beth Shemesh*, 58 (5) PD 595.

2. PIG PROHIBITIONS IN JEWISH AND ISRAELI CULTURE

1. On the complex relations between nationalism and religion, see: Anthony D. Smith, *Chosen Peoples* (New York: Oxford University Press, 2003).

2. See: Sherry Ortner, "On Key Symbols," *American Anthropologist* 75 (1973): 1338.

3. See: Mary Douglas, *Purity and Danger: An Analysis of the Concepts of Pollution and Taboo* (New York: Routledge, 1966). The third chapter of the book, devoted to "The Abominations of Leviticus," contains the main discussion on the subject. See pp. 54–55. In her later writings, however, Douglas qualified her original argument by pointing to the cultural bias of the anthropologist who traces anomalies: "It is obviously wrong to say that a thing is anomalous by using our own categories. It is not even enough to argue from our idea of nature to natural anomalies." See: Mary Douglas, *Thought Styles: Critical Essays on Good Taste* (Thousand Oaks, Calif.: Sage Publications, 1996), 127. In addition, Douglas seems to argue now that the explanation for the negation of nonkosher animals has to take into consideration the broader context of biblical laws. The dietary prohibitions were meant to apply only to Jews and, therefore, should not be interpreted as reflecting universal norms. According to this later version of Douglas, the relationship between God and its people is the model for the relationship between them and their domestic animals. These animals were considered chosen, just as the people of Israel were God's chosen. Only these animals were allowed to be sacrificed and, accordingly, only they were allowed for eating. See: Mary Douglas, *Leviticus as Literature* (New York: Oxford University Press, 1999).

4. See: Marvin Harris, *Cows, Pigs, Wars, and Witches: The Riddles of Culture* (New York: Random House, 1974). For a later and broader version, see: Marvin Harris, *The Sacred Cow and the Abominable Pig: Riddles of Food and Culture* (New York: Simon & Schuster, 1985). In the third chapter of his book, dealing with the "abominable pig," Harris sums up his view as follows: "The danger which it posed to its owner was very real, and this suffices to explain its status" (62). On the same approach, see: Melinda A. Zeder, "Pigs and Emergent Complexity in the Ancient Near East," in *Ancestors for the Pigs: Pigs in Prehistory,* ed. Sarah M. Nelson (Philadelphia: University of Pennsylvania Museum of Archaeology and Anthropology, 1998), 108. In the same volume, see also Richard A. Lobban, "Pigs in Ancient Egypt," 137.

5. See: James George Frazer, *The Golden Bough: A Study in Magic and Religion* (New York: Macmillan, 1922), 472.

6. See: Yael Katz, "The Meaning of the Jewish Abomination of the Pig" [in Hebrew], (M.A. thesis, Tel Aviv University, 2000).

7. Israel Finkelstein and Neil Asher Silberman, *The Bible Unearthed: Archeology's New Vision of Ancient Israel and the Origin of Its Sacred Texts* (New York: Free Press, 2001), 120.

8. See: Brian Hesse and Paula Wapnish, "Pig Use and Abuse in the Ancient Levant: Ethnoreligious Boundary-Building with Swine," in *Ancestors for the Pigs*, 123.

9. Baruch Rosen, "Swine Breeding in Eretz Israel after the Roman Period," *Cathedra* 78 (1997): 25 [in Hebrew].

10. TB Hulin 59a.

11. *Midrash Rabbah*, Genesis, ed. H. Freedman and Maurice Simon, trans. S. M. Lehrman (London: Soncino Press, 1939), 65:1, vol. 2, p. 581.

12. *Midrash on Psalms*, trans. William G. Braude (New Haven, Conn.: Yale University Press, 1959), vol. 2, 80:6, p. 51

13. On the juxtaposition between sacred and profane in religious culture, see: Emile Durkheim, *The Elementary Forms of the Religious Life*, trans. Joseph Ward Swain (New York: 1965), 53–54.

14. Isaiah 66:17. See also: "eat swine's flesh" (Isaiah 65:4); "as if he offered swine's blood" (Isaiah 66:3).

15. Proverbs 11:22. See also *Ethics of the Fathers* 6:2.

16. See, for instance, TB Berakhot 25a.

17. *Guide of the Perplexed*, trans. Shlomo Pines (Chicago: University of Chicago Press, 1963) 3:48, p. 599.

18. M. Bava Kamma 7:7.

19. *Shulkhan Arukh, Hoshen Mishpat*, 409.

20. TB Sotah 49b; see also TB Bava Kamma 72b; TB Menahoth 64b.

21. *The Fathers According to Rabbi Nathan*, trans. Judah Goldin (New Haven, Conn.: Yale University Press, 1955), chapter 34, p. 138. See also TB Sotah 49b. The pig also represents Edom (*Leviticus Rabbah* 13).

22. TB Shabbat, 129b. See also *Tosefot* on Sanhedrin 26b, *s.v. okhlei davar aher pesulin leha'id* ["eaters of the other thing are incompetent to testify"]: "You need not interpret 'eaters of the other thing' to mean eaters of pork." In this case, then, the exegete wishes to dispel the prevalent interpretation, which reads "eaters of the other thing" as synonymous with eaters of pork (which he claims is not applicable in the present context).

23. "'And my statutes shall ye keep' [Leviticus 18:4], meaning such commandments for which Satan and the nations of the world have answers [and Rashi explains: 'Satan's answers mislead the people of Israel, telling them that the Torah is not true, since what could be the purpose of all these commandments?'] and they concern: eating pork, wearing mixed web clothing, levirate marriage, the purification of the leper, and the sending away of the he-goat. And you might

think these are vain things, therefore Scripture says, 'I am the Lord' [Leviticus 18:4] meaning I, the Lord, have made it a statute and you have no right to criticize it" (TB Yoma 67b).

24. 1 Maccabees 1:1. For a full account, see: 1 *Maccabees,* trans. Jonathan A. Goldstein (Garden City, N.Y.: Doubleday, 1976), 1:1–47, 206.

25. See: *The Life and Works of Flavius Josephus,* trans. William Whiston (Philadelphia: John C. Winston Company, 1957); *Antiquities of the Jews,* 12:5, 363. Another report of these events appears in Howard Fast's historical novel *My Glorious Brothers* (Boston: Little, Brown, 1948), which describes the Maccabean revolt: "We went into the Holy of Holies, the inner house of God, where the shewbread and the candelabra are. It stank like a butcher's stall. The altar was filthy with dry blood and a pig's head set there. Staring open-eyed at us. A great urn of pork stood to one side, and assorted filth lay on the floor" (48).

26. 2 Maccabees 7:1. The story appears in: 2 *Maccabees,* trans. Jonathan A. Goldstein (Garden City, N.Y.: Doubleday, 1983) 7:1–42, 289–91. Another chapter tells the story of old Eleazar: "One of the leading sages was Eleazar . . . repeatedly they tried to force him to open his mouth and eat pork. He, however, preferred death with glory to life with defilement" (6:18–31, 281–82.

27. Mary Douglas, *Natural Symbols* (New York: Routledge, 1996), 40.

28. Peter Garnsey, *Food and Society in Classical Antiquity* (New York: Cambridge University Press, 1999), 82–83. See also: Audrey Briers, *Eat, Drink, and Be Merry* (Oxford: Ashmolean Museum, 1990), 12; Emily Gowers, *The Loaded Table: Representations of Food in Roman Literature* (New York: Oxford University Press, 1993), 69. Romans regarded a pig's paunch as a special treat. See: Briers, *Eat, Drink,* 13; Kenneth McLeish, *Food and Drink* (Boston: Allen & Unwin, 1978), 52.

29. See: *Life and Works of Flavius Josephus, Antiquities of the Jews: Against Apion, Book II,* 14, 889.

30. Cornelius Tacitus, *The Histories,* trans. W. H. Fyfe, ed. D. S. Levene (New York: Oxford University Press, 1997), 5:4, 235.

31. *All the Writings of the Gaon Rabbi Yitzhak Isaac Halevy Herzog: Rulings and Writings,* ed. Shlomo Shapira, vol. 2 (Jerusalem: Mosad Harav Kook, 1989), section 120 (555, 558) [in Hebrew].

32. Marguerite Yourcenar, *Memoirs of Hadrian,* trans. Grace Frick (London: Readers Union, Secker and Warburg, 1955), 206–7. For additional sources dealing with the Roman criticism of the Jewish abstention from pork, see: Zeev Gotholler, "Kashrut in the Theology of Judaism," *Mahanayim: For IDF Soldiers on the Subject of Kashrut* 88 (1964): 12 [in Hebrew].

33. Claudine Fabre-Vassas, *The Singular Beast: Jews, Christians, and the Pig,* trans. Carol Vol (New York: Columbia University Press, 1997). See also: Janet Leibman Jacobs, "Stigma and Deception: The Jewish Other in European Consciousness," *Religious Studies Review* 27 (2001): 127.

34. Fabre-Vassas, *Singular Beast,* 6.

35. Ibid., 7.

36. Peter Stallybrass and Allon White, *The Politics and Poetics of Transgression* (Ithaca, N.Y.: Cornell University Press, 1986), 53–55.

37. Fabre-Vassas, *Singular Beast*, 5–7, 93–94, 134. See also: Esther Cohen, *The Crossroads of Justice: Law and Culture in Late Medieval France* (New York: E. J. Brill, 1993), 90; Annette Donnier-Troehler, "Ogres, loup-Garous et autres hors-la-loi alimentaires de l'imaginaire occidental," in *Gastronomie, alimentation et droit: Melanges en l'honneur de Pierre Widmer,* ed. by Alberto Aronovitz (Zurich: Schulthess, 2003): 365, 372.

38. Fabre-Vassas, *Singular Beast*, 108, 126, 135; Cohen, *Crossroads of Justice*, 91; Stallybrass and White, *Politics and Poetics of Transgression*, 54.

39. Nahum T. Gidel, *Jews in Germany: From the Roman Period to the Weimar Republic* (Jerusalem: Gefen Books, 1997), 159 [in Hebrew].

40. Fabre-Vassas, *Singular Beast*, 126.

41. See: Fabre-Vassas, *Singular Beast*, 127; Cohen, *Crossroads of Justice*, 92; Gidel, *Jews in Germany*, 49.

42. David M. Gitlitz, *Secrecy and Deceit: The Religion of the Crypto-Jews* (Philadelphia: Jewish Publication Society, 1996), 534–35.

43. Ibid., 535–40; Fabre-Vassas, *Singular Beast*, 120–21; Yosef Kaplan, *The Western Sephardic Diaspora* (Tel Aviv: Misrad ha-Bitahon, 1994), 21 [in Hebrew].

44. Fabre-Vassas, *Singular Beast*, 123–24; Kaplan, *Western Sephardic Diaspora*, 16.

45. See: Moshe Sneh, "A Jewish Voice of Warning," in *Moshe Sneh: Writings*, vol. 1, trans. from Yiddish by Mordechai Halamish (Tel Aviv: Am Oved, 1995), 185–88 [in Hebrew]. Similar legislation, claiming compassion for the slaughtered animals, is currently in force in several European countries. See: Brian Barry, *Culture and Equality: An Egalitarian Critique of Multiculturalism* (Cambridge, Mass.: Harvard University Press, 2001), 35.

46. Scholem Aleichem, *Adventures of Mottel the Cantor's Son,* trans. Tamara Kahana (New York: H. Schuman, 1953, 1999). When describing the horse market he adores, Mottel speaks of his love for all young animals, except pigs: "I like everything that's little. Except pigs. I hate pigs even when they're small" (50). Their neighbor, Pessie, refers to the ignorant father-in-law of Mottel's brother as a "pig" (47). When Mottel and his friend travel on a train, his friend quarrels with a Gentile who mocks them for the onions and vegetables they are eating. They answer back, saying to him: "And how can you bear to eat pork?" (117). After emigrating to America with his family, Mottel still retains these associations. He says: "Here in America, they hate beards. They hate beards more than a pious Jew hates a pig" (194–95).

47. Zalman Shneur, *The People of Shklov* (Tel-Aviv: Am Oved, 1951) [in Hebrew]. The title of one of the chapters is "Treatise on Flagellation" ["Masekhet Makkot"] (after the eponymous Talmudic source) and another is "A Pig and its Rider" ["Hazir ve-Rokhvoh"].

48. Ibid., 59.

49. Ibid.

50. "Elohei Avi Goyim," in Uri Tzvi Greenberg, *Rehovot ha-Nahar* (Jerusalem and Tel-Aviv: Shoken, 1951), 249, 251.

51. Primo Levi, *The Periodic Table,* trans. Raymond Rosenthal (New York: Schocken Books, 1984), 19.

52. Arieh Eckstein, *Auntie Esther* (Jerusalem: Keter, 1992), 36 [in Hebrew].

53. Ibid., 158

54. "A Woman and a Girl Feed Pigs at Sundown," in Allen Grossman, *How to Do Things with Tears* (New York: New Directions, 2001), 53. The poem elaborates on the famous vow: "If I forget thee, o Jerusalem, let my right hand forget its cunning" (Psalms 137:5).

55. "The Pig" by Robert Southey. The poem is included in *The Symbolic Pig: An Anthology of Pigs in Literature and Art,* ed. Frederick Cameron Sillar and Ruth Mary Meyler (Edinburgh: Oliver and Boyd, 1961), 104–5.

56. George Orwell, *Down and Out in Paris and London* (London: Secker & Warburg, 1986), 133.

57. Tom Segev quotes from an interview he conducted: "When Moshe Aram, of Mapam, ended a sharp speech in favor of sanctioning the breeding of pigs in Israel and the sale of their flesh in the markets, he stopped for a moment by Kalman Kahana, a member of Po'alei Agudat Israel. 'Don't worry,' he said to him, according to Kahana, 'in my home you won't find it. Even you can eat at my place'" (Tom Segev, *1949: The First Israelis* [Jerusalem: Domino, 1984], 229 [in Hebrew]). This quote does not appear in the English translation, *1949: The First Israelis,* ed. Arlen Neal Weinstein (London: Collier Macmillan, 1986).

58. Berl Katsanelson's stance, whereby pig-breeding in a Jewish state was a matter of national significance, was also cited in parliamentary debates on this issue. See remarks by Mapai MK Israel Yeshayahu Shar'abi, in a debate on a motion to the agenda on the Pig-Breeding Prohibition Bill, 1953, 183rd session of the 2nd Knesset, 4 February 1953, 13 DK 639, 641; remarks by Agudat Israel MK Yehuda Meir Abramowicz when presenting the Pig-Raising Prohibition (Amendment) Bill, 1981, 432nd session of the 9th Knesset, 11 March 1981, 91 DK 2050; remarks by Agudat Israel MK Abraham Shapira during the first reading of the Pig-Raising Prohibition (Amendment) Bill, 1985, 116th session of the 11th Knesset, 30 July 1985, 102 DK 3833; remarks by National Religious Party MK Shaul Yahalom during the Knesset debate (on the motion to the agenda on "The Minister of the Interior's Statement on Summer Time and the Sale of Pork"), 186th session of the 15th Knesset, 14 March 2001, 203 DK 3493, 3494.

59. Berl Katsanelson, "In the Zionist Executive" (Jerusalem, 9 Nissan, 5694), *Writings of B. Katsanelson,* ed. S. Yavniely (Tel-Aviv: The Party of Workers in the Land of Israel Publishing, 1947), vol. 6, 203, 213 [in Hebrew].

60. Jewish children conscripted to the czarist army in Russia and placed in

conditions intended to force them to adopt Christianity. The name derives from *cantonments* [barracks].

61. See Berl Katsanelson, "How Far Does the Love of Israel Extend? In the Wake of a Hanukkah Controversy," *Writings of B. Katsanelson,* vol. 12, *Last Writings* (1950), 55, 57 [in Hebrew].

62. See: Berl Katsanelson, "Destruction and Detachment," *Writings of B. Katsanelson,* vol. 6, 365 [in Hebrew].

63. See: Anita Shapira, *Berl: A Biography* (Tel-Aviv: Am Oved, 1981), 548 [in Hebrew]. This quote does not appear in the English version of the book: *Berl: The Biography of a Socialist Zionist,* trans. Haya Galai (New York: Cambridge University Press, 1984).

64. Natan Alterman, "Freedom of Opinion and the Hooves," *The Seventh Column* (Tel-Aviv: Hakibuts ha-Me'uchad, 1975), Book Two (1954–1962), 237, 238 [in Hebrew] (originally published in *Davar,* 20 July 1956).

65. "There will be no *Kulturkampf,*" ibid., 129, at 244. For additional quotes from secularists who, at the time, supported the adoption of pig-related prohibitions in the State of Israel, or at least showed understanding for them, see "In the Struggle to Uproot the Pig Bane in Israel," *Sheluhot: A Monthly for Religious Youth,* Adar B 5714 (1954), 4–7 [in Hebrew] (the issue is in File No. 34-(3) 7 in TAMA). The article quotes Yehoshua Manoah from kibbutz Degania Alef; Moshe Kol, Chairman of the Progressive Party; Yitzhak Maor, who relies on Berl Katsanelson; and M. Zohar, the Mapai Mayor of Tiberias.

66. For the definition of pork as "white meat," see Dahn Ben-Amotz and Netivah Ben-Yehuda, *The World Dictionary of Hebrew Slang* (Jerusalem: E. Lewin-Epstein, 1972), 44 [in Hebrew]. See also Amnon Dankner and David Tartakover, *Where Were We and What Did We Do: Treasury of the 1950s and 1960s* (Jerusalem: Keter, 1996) [in Hebrew], where Leviko-Moshiko (the name of a once very popular steak house) is defined as follows: "Cuisine at its height. One of the first steakhouses in the country . . . the height of sin was white meat—white!—in a pita" (99). Advertisements published by the Tiv Ta'am food stores chain, which specializes in nonkosher food, also refer to pork as "white meat," although explicitly mentioning other kinds of nonkosher meat (such as rabbit, crab, lobster, and squid). See: Tiv Ta'am advertisement in the Tel Aviv weekly *Ha'ir,* 9 September 2004.

67. Erich Kastner, *The Goat at the Barber,* trans. Yaakov Adini (Tel-Aviv: Israel, 1965).

68. "Yielding to Ultra-Orthodox Pressure: Pigs Out of a Children's Toy," www.news.walla.co.il, 10 December 2002.

69. "The Land of Lamentation (Draft for a Mutiny)," in David Avidan, *Impossible Poems* (1968), 92 [in Hebrew].

70. The quote is from the famous "rabbits and swine" speech that Rabbi Shakh delivered to a vast crowd at the Yad Eliyahu Sports Stadium, at the opening of the Degel ha-Torah national conference in 1990. The text of the speech appears in *"In This I Trust": Letters and Papers on Current Events by the Gaon Rabbi Eliezer*

Menachem Man Shakh (Bnei Brak: Published by the Rabbi's Students, 1993) [in Hebrew], in a chapter entitled "Only Through the Power of Faith and the Torah Will We Survive War" (80). On the impact of this speech on public opinion, see, for instance: Menachem Rahat, "Great in Torah, Great in Politics," *Ma'ariv*, 4 November 2001.

71. Yigal Even-Or, *Fleisher* [in Hebrew]. A copy of the play is preserved in the archives of the Cameri Theatre. The play was first staged on 20 May 1993.

72. This work, together with a number of controversial views that Tomarkin expressed on this subject, served as grounds for a petition to the Israeli Supreme Court against the decision to grant him the prestigious Israel Prize. The petition was dismissed on the basis of a policy of minimal intervention in professional decisions regarding prizes and grades. See: HC 2769/04 *Yahalom v. Minister of Education, Culture and Sports* (not published, 19.4.04).

3. TOWARD INDEPENDENCE

1. See: Assaf Likhovski, "Between 'Mandate' and 'State': Rethinking the Periodization of Israeli Legal History," *Mishpatim* 29 (1999): 689 [in Hebrew].

2. Ronen Shamir, *The Colonies of Law: Colonialism, Zionism, and Law in Early Mandate Palestine* (New York: Cambridge University Press, 2000).

3. Dan Horowitz and Moshe Lissak, *Origins of the Israeli Polity: Palestine under the Mandate,* trans. Charles Hoffman (Chicago: University of Chicago Press, 1978), 149.

4. See: Arieh Morgenstern, "The Establishment of the Chief Rabbinate in Eretz-Israel" [in Hebrew], in *Collection of Articles in Celebration of Seventy Years since the Establishment of Israel Chief Rabbinate,* ed. Itamar Warhaftig and Rabbi Shmuel Katz, vol. 3 (Jerusalem: Heichal Shlomo Publicationsm, 2002), 1027; S. Zalman Abramov, *Perpetual Dilemma: Jewish Religion in the Jewish State* (Rutherford, N.J.: Fairleigh Dickinson University Press, 1976), 92–97; Menachem Friedman, *Society and Religion: The Non-Zionist Orthodox in Eretz-Israel 1918–1936* (Jerusalem: Yad Yitshak Ben- Ben-Tsvi. 1977), 110–28 [in Hebrew]; Shamir, *The Colonies of Law,* 64–66.

5. See: *The Attorney General v. Altshuler* (1928) 1 PLR. 283.

6. A bylaw later passed by the Tel Aviv municipality ordering shops to close on Saturdays took into consideration that people of other religions could open their stores on Saturdays and close them on other days. See: Tel Aviv (Opening and Closing of Shops), Bylaw, 1937, PG 1937, Supp. 2, p. 799

7. Slaughter House Rules, The Laws of Palestine, vol. 3, p. 1644 (from 1927) applied to "swine" as well. Animal Quarantine Rules, The Laws of Palestine, vol. 3, p. 1622 (from 1931) were also applicable to imports of "swine" that were permitted from several countries, including Egypt, Turkey (both Muslim countries!), and Great Britain. Carcasses from European Countries (Prohibition) Rules, 1938, PG 1938, Supp. 2, p. 427, which imposed veterinary restrictions on the import of

meat, applied to "cattle, sheep, goat, pig, and their meat" in accordance with the definition of a "carcass" in Regulation 2. The same definition appears in Import of Carcasses from European Countries Rules, 1938, PG 1938, Supp 2, p. 785. Rule 5 of the Public Health (Imported Meat) Rules, 1938, PG 1938, Supp. 2, p. 1390, which regulated the wrapping of imported meat cuts, requiring every piece of chilled or frozen pork to be wrapped in "one muslin cloth wrapper." Further allusions to pig-breeding and pork sales appear in the Notice Regarding Purchase of Slaughter Swine by Government PG, 1945, p. 249. The notice includes detailed guidelines concerning government purchases of swine for slaughter at three urban centers (Haifa, Jerusalem, and Lydda), at specified prices.

8. See: Haim Broide, *Netivei Haim: Pirkei Havai ve-Yezirah* [Paths of Life: Events and Endeavors] (Tel Aviv: published by the author, 1977), 177 [in Hebrew]. Israeli novelist Meir Shalev, who has used the agricultural endeavors of early Zionism as the setting for several of his works, alludes to a practice common among German Templars who, in their farms, used to breed pigs beside other animals. See: Meir Shalev, *Fontanella* (Tel Aviv: Am Oved, 2002), 218, 226 [in Hebrew]. Even more significantly, we are told about one of the Jewish characters that she raised pigs in the neighboring Templar village and did not dare do so in her own community, although it was not a religious settlement (313).

9. Broide, *Netivei Haim: Pirkei Havai ve-Yezirah*. On the secularization of the public space in Palestine in the 1930s, including the opening of nonkosher restaurants, see: Friedman, *Society and Religion,* 335.

10. Letter from P. Steinwaks to the Industry Department of the Jewish Agency, 2 May 1938.

11. *Gazette of the Tel Aviv Municipality* [in Hebrew], fourteenth year, Elul 5704–Tishrei 5705 (1940–1945), issues 5–6, p. 62 (TAMA). The column "Answers to Questions in the Council" includes the following report: "On the bringing of pork into Tel Aviv. 14 May 1944. Concerning the comment of Mr. D. Z. Pinkas on the bringing of pork into Tel Aviv for sale in butcher shops and branding it with the stamp of the city abattoir, the mayor stated he would ask the High Commissioner to ban pork from admittance into Tel Aviv for selling purposes." Note that Katsanelson's article on pig-breeding was also written at this time. See *supra,* chapter 2, nn. 60–61.

12. Broide, *Netivei Haim,* 176.

13. Rabbi Shmuel Katz, "Diary of the Activities of the Chief Rabbinate in the Years 1921–1993" [in Hebrew], in *Collection of Articles,* Warhaftig and Katz, vol. 3, 1157, 1254.

14. Ibid., 1279.

15. See chapter 2, n. 20.

16. PG 1934, Supp 1, p. 1. This ordinance is still part of Israeli law, in a new version issued in 1964: Municipal Corporations Ordinance [New Version] (hereafter the Municipal Corporations Ordinance).

17. Section 96(12) of the Ordinance provided: "As regards animals: to regulate

or prevent the keeping of swine, and regulate the keeping of animals and birds so that their keeping shall not be a public nuisance or injurious to health." See also: Section 96(12) of the Municipal Corporations Bill, 1933, PG 1933, p. 1209, 1236. The Hebrew version of this bill, however, did not explicitly specify the verb "prevent" regarding the rearing of swine, and referred only to the "regulation" of this activity (Municipal Corporations Bill, 1933, PG 1933 [Hebrew version], p. 1089).

18. The explanatory notes accompanying the proposed Municipal Corporations Ordinance dealt with the principles of the proposed legislation only generally, without considering the details of the regulations. On the powers of municipalities, the explanatory notes only stated: "the duties and powers of councils are set out in detail." See: Municipal Corporations Bill, 1267.

19. See: Chaman P. Shelah, "Freedom of Religion and Conscience in Israeli Law" [in Hebrew] (Thesis submitted for the Degree Doctor Juris, Hebrew University, 1978), 353–54.

20. HC 194/54 *Axel v. Mayor, Councilors, and Residents of Netanyah,* 8 PD 1524, at 1535.

21. HC 72/55 *Fridi v. Municipality of Tel Aviv* 10 PD 734, at 742.

22. See chapter 1, n. 27.

23. Bylaws prohibiting the keeping of pigs near residential housing have been held to be reasonable in a town (see: *Wanstead Local Board of Health v. Wooster* [1873] 38 JP 21), but unreasonable in the country (see: *Heap v. The Rural Sanitary Authority of the Burnley Union* [1884] 12 QBD 617).

24. See: Minutes of the JNF Board Meeting, Jerusalem, 9 July 1930.

25. For further elaboration, see: Shlomo Haimovitz, "The Jewish National Fund and Religious Jewry" [in Hebrew], in *Religious Zionist Annual,* ed. Shmuel Borenstein (Jerusalem: Mesilot, 1984), 135; "R. Kook and the Jewish National Fund" [in Hebrew], in *Year by Year: 1992 Annual,* ed. R. Haim Menachem Levitas (Jerusalem: Heichal Shlomo Publications), 526. See: Haim Y. Peles, "The Relationship between the Jewish National Fund and the Mizrachi between the Two World Wars" [in Hebrew], in *The History of the Jewish National Fund at the Eleventh World Congress of Jewish Studies* (Jerusalem: The Institute for Research of the History of the Jewish National Fund, Land and Settlement, 1993), 23; Haim Y. Peles, "The Reactions of R. A. Y. Kook to Sabbath Desecrations on JNF Land (1927–1933) According to 'New' Sources," *Sinai* 115 (1995): 180 [in Hebrew]; Neriah Gutal, "Rules and Proceedings of the JNF and the Settlement Circle in R. Kook's Correspondence," *Sinai* 121 (1998): 103 [in Hebrew].

26. Agudat Israel and Po'alei Agudat Israel MK Kalman Kahana stated in a Knesset speech: "I read there [in *Be-Terem*], that according to the contract with the JNF they are forbidden to breed pigs. Why do they not honor their signatures?" See in: "The Continuation of the Debate on the First Reading of the Local Authorities (Special Enablement) Law, 1956," 162nd session of the 3rd Knesset, 24 July 1956, 20 DK 2400, 2403. Similarly, Ha-Po'el ha-Mizrahi MK Zerah Warhaftig notes: "The board of the Jewish National Fund included a provision

in its standard contract with the settlers on its lands, stating: 'It is prohibited to raise pigs on the nation's land.'" Zerah Warhaftig, *A Constitution for Israel: Religion and State* (Jerusalem: Mesilot, World Center of Ha-Mizrachi—Ha-Poel ha-Mizrachi, 1988), 294.

27. Letter on "Breeding pigs on JNF land," Y.B.G./D223, 23 November 1952.

28. Both letters are dated 27 November 1952.

29. SI. YAA/DH, 9 December 1952.

30. SI. YAA/SH, 9 December 1952. This correspondence is located in File KKL 19065 in the Central Zionist Archive.

31. Rabbi Shmuel Katz, "Diary of the Activities," 1157, 1354.

32. "British Jews Demand an End to Pig-Breeding," *Herut,* 30 October 1956.

33. The contract is dated 27 July 1952.

34. The contract is dated 1 January 1953.

35. In both cases, the prohibition appears in para. 15 entitled "Religious and Social Requirements." Adv. Eyal Sternberg, who researched the rights of agricultural lessees on lands of the Israel Land Administration, provided me with these contracts.

36. Leviticus 25:1–7.

37. See: Menachem Friedman, "The Chronicle of the Status Quo: Religion and State in Israel" [in Hebrew], in *Transition from "Yishuv" to State 1947–1949: Continuity and Change,* ed. Varda Pilowsky (Haifa: University of Haifa, Herzl Institute for Research in Zionism, 1990), 47; Charles S. Liebman and Eliezer Don-Yehiya, *Religion and Politics in Israel* (Bloomington: Indiana University Press, 1984), 31–34.

4. The Establishment of the State and the Politics of Nation-Building

1. See: 14th session of the Provisional State Council, *Provisional State Council,* vol. A, 7.

2. 16th session of the Provisional State Council, *Provisional State Council,* vol. A., 7. A third question in this matter was raised by council member Levenstein from Agudat Israel, and the minister answered by referring to his earlier responses. 19th session of the Provisional State Council, *Provisional State Council,* vol. A, 27.

3. See: Discussion on Meat Imports, 31st session of the Provisional State Council, *Provisional State Council,* vol. B, 20–27; Discussion on Meat Imports, 33rd session of the Provisional State Council, *Provisional State Council,* vol. B, 9–19, 24–41.

4. See: 31st session of the Provisional State Council, *Provisional State Council,* vol. B, 21.

5. Aviad Hacohen, "'The State of Israel: This Is a Holy Place!' Forming a 'Jewish Public Domain' in the State of Israel" [in Hebrew], in *On Both Sides of the*

Bridge: Religion and State in the Early Years of Israel, ed. Mordechai Bar-On and Zvi Tsameret (Jerusalem: Yad Yitshak Ben-Tsvi, 2002), 144.

6. See: Yair Sheleg, *The New Religious Jews: Recent Developments among Observant Jews in Israel,* (Jerusalem: Keter, 2000), 287 [in Hebrew]. For Knesset debates on the activities of this underground movement, see, for instance, a question on "religious fanatics torching cars in Jerusalem," 120th session of the 1st Knesset, 30 January 1951, 8 DK 913; motion to the agenda on "burning cars in Jerusalem," 235th session of the 1st Knesset, 7 March 1951, 8 DK 1295; motion to the agenda on "terror and religious coercion," 253rd session of the 1st Knesset, 16 May 1951, 9 DK 1777 (the burning of a butcher shop by the Orthodox underground, beside other activities, is mentioned by the minister of police, Bekhor Shitreet, ibid., 1779). See also: Isser Har'el, *Security and Democracy* (1989) 180 [in Hebrew].

7. See: Peter Fitzpatrick, *The Mythology of Modern Law* (New York: Routledge, 1992), 111–18; Peter Fitzpatrick, *Modernism and the Grounds of Law* (New York: Cambridge University Press, 2001), 111–45.

8. Fitzpatrick *Modernism and the Grounds of Law,* 130.

9. Haim Broide, *Netivei Haim: Pirkei Havai ve-Yezirah* [Paths of Life: Events and Endeavors] (Tel Aviv: published by the author, 1977), 199 [in Hebrew].

10. *All the Writings of the Gaon Rabbi Yitzhak Isaac Halevy Herzog: Rulings and Writings,* ed. Shlomo Shapira, vol. 4, section 39 (Jerusalem: Mosad Harav Kook, 1989), 121 [in Hebrew]. R. Herzog's responsum, dated 7 Tamuz 5712 (1952), is addressed to "my friend the minister, Mr. Moshe Shapira" and relates to "the question he asked me last night when leaving the house late at night that, to the best of my recollection, was the following: given that the government was given the opportunity to purchase a huge quantity of two million boxes, including ritually unfit meat and also pork, can this forbidden meat be given to non-Jews in the country, and can the forbidden meat be given to Jews to feed fowl for which there is currently little food." Rabbi Meshulam Ratta also referred to this question in a response from the same period and cited R. Herzog. See: *Responsa Kol Mevaser,* part 1, chapter 33, dated 10 Tamuz, 5712 (1952) [in Hebrew].

11. See: First reading of the Local Authorities (Special Enablement) Law 1956, the 161st session of the 3rd Knesset, 24 July 1956, 20 DK 2384, 2385. Warhaftig resorted to this interpretation in his book as well. See: Zerah Warhaftig, *A Constitution for Israel: Religion and State* (Jerusalem: Mesilot, World Center of ha-Mizrachi—Ha-Poel ha-Mizrahi, 1988) 294–95 [in Hebrew].

12. See chapter 2, n.3.

13. "Consumption of Meat Imported from Poland," 165th session of the 1st Knesset, 12 July 1950, 6 DK 2175, p. 2176.

14. 451st session of the 2nd Knesset, 30 June 1954, 16 DK 2084. These figures were also mentioned as a source of reference in the debate on the Prohibition on Raising Pigs in Israel Bill, 1956, 122nd session of the 3rd Knesset, 23 May 1956, 20 DK 1835.

15. William I. Miller, *The Anatomy of Disgust* (Cambridge, Mass.: Harvard University Press, 1997), 50.

16. See chapter 5.

17. Charles S. Liebman and Eliezer Don-Yehiya, *Civil Religion in Israel: Traditional Judaism and Political Culture in the Jewish State* (Berkeley: University of California Press, 1983), 82.

18. The concept of civil religion as used here follows the formulation coined by Robert Bellah. See: Robert N. Bellah, "Civil Religion in America," *Daedalus* 96 (1967): 1; Robert N. Bellah, *The Broken Covenant: American Civil Religion in Time of Trial*, 2nd ed. (Chicago: University of Chicago Press, 1992).

19. Liebman and Don Yehiya, *Civil Religion in Israel*, 81–122.

20. Flag and Emblem Law, 1949.

21. Liebman and Don-Yehiya, *Civil Religion in Israel*, 113.

22. Clifford Geertz, *The Interpretation of Cultures* (New York: Basic Books, 1973), 89.

23. Liebman and Don-Yehiya, *Civil Religion in Israel*, 107–8.

24. Ibid., 91.

25. Anita Shapira, "Religious Motifs of the Labor Movement," in *Zionism and Religion*, ed. Shmuel Almog, Jehuda Reinharz, and Anita Shapira (Hanover and London: University Press of New England, 1998), 251; David Knaani, *The Second Aliyah and Its Attitude toward Religion and Tradition* (Tel Aviv: ha-Makhon le-hikre 'avodah ve-hevrah, 1976) [in Hebrew].

26. This distinction between "religion," "tradition," and "Yiddishkeit" in the context of the labor movement was developed by Anita Shapira. See: Shapira, "Religious Motifs in the Labor Movement," 253–54.

27. Liebman and Don-Yehiya, *Civil Religion in Israel*, 90.

28. See chapter 5.

29. See chapter 2.

30. Shapira, "Religious Motifs in the Labor Movement," 264; Nili Arieh-Sapir, "The Procession of Lights: Hanukkah as a National Festival in Tel-Aviv 1909–1936," *Cathedra* 103 (1992): 131 [in Hebrew]; Shmuel Dotan, "From the Festival of Hanukkah to the 'Festival of the Hasmoneans': The Birth of a Zionist 'National Festival,'" *Holiday Studies: Journal of Jewish Culture* 10 (1998): 29 [in Hebrew]; Eliezer Don-Yehiya, "Hanukkah and the Myth of the Maccabees in Ideology and in Society," in *Israeli Judaism*, ed. Shlomo Deshen, Charles S. Liebman, and Moshe Skokeid (New Brunswick, N.J.: Transaction Publishers, 1995), 303.

31. See: Rabbi Shmuel Katz, "Diary of the Activities of the Chief Rabbinate in the Years 1921–1993" [in Hebrew], in *Collection of Articles in Celebration of Seventy Years since the Establishment of Israel Chief Rabbinate*, ed. Itamar Warhaftig and Rabbi Shmuel Katz, vol. 3 (Jerusalem: Heichal Shlomo Publications, 2002), 1157. In 1952, the Council of the Chief Rabbinate decided to issue a protest to all places involved in pig-breeding and issue a declaration on the severity of

this prohibition (ibid., 1341), and later published a strong ruling on this matter (ibid., 1343). In 1953, the Council of the Chief Rabbinate decided to call on the government to prohibit pig-breeding (ibid., 1345). At the beginning of 1954, members of the Council of the Chief Rabbinate participated in a "state emergency conference" that was also attended by municipal heads of kashrut departments and by representatives of religious parties at municipal councils. The conference demanded the legislation of two laws, one prohibiting pig-breeding, and another prohibiting nonkosher meat (ibid., 1347–48). In 1955, the Council of the Chief Rabbinate decided it would demand from Knesset members of all political parties to legislate a law banning pig-breeding and pork trading (ibid., 1350). In 1956, the Council of the Chief Rabbinate decided that expanding pig-breeding could ruin kashrut in the country, and Knesset members should act vigorously to pre-empt this danger by legislating a countywide law prohibiting pig-breeding and pork distribution (ibid., 1354).

32. M. N. Naphtali, "On a Shameful and Disgraceful Affair," *Ha-Modi'a,* 9 September 1953, Rosh Hashanah edition

33. A. Na'aman, "Its Claws Are Still Stuck," *Ha-Modi'a,* 17 July 1956.

34. A. N. Miletsky, "Everything Is Conceivable in This Country," *Ha-Modi'a,* 13 July 1956.

35. A. Nedivi, "For Another Year: Praise and Thanksgiving," *Ha-Modi'a,* 27 November 1956.

36. "Hed Hayom" (editorial), *Ha-Modi'a,* 8 July 1953; "The Interior Committee Discussed Agudat Israel's Proposal to Ban Pig Breeding," *Ha-Modi'a,* 29 July 1953; A. Abarav "'After the Closing of the Knesset Session," *Ha-Modi'a,* 30 July 1953.

37. "A Law and Not By-Laws" (editorial), *Ha-Tsofeh,* 1 May 1956; "Compromise and Principles" (editorial), *Ha-Tsofeh,* 27 July 1956.

38. Interview with the author, 14 December 2003.

39. Meir A. Bareli, "On the Question of Pig-Breeding in Israel," *Davar,* 15 July 1956.

40. A. Shamir "Tolerance—Yes, Coercion—No!" *Davar,* 26 September 1956.

41. Nathan Alterman, "Freedom of Opinion and the Hooves," *Davar,* 20 July 1956. See also chapter 2, n. 64.

42. Brakhah Havas, "A Different Tone in the Debate on the Pig," *Davar,* 8 July 1956

43. Secularist trends, however, were also found within the right wing of the political spectrum, though certainly not as the dominant approach. An ironic piece describing a visit of a pig to the Knesset in the course of the legislative debates on pig prohibitions illustrates this minority view in the Zionist right. See: Y. Nets, "An Interview with 'the Other Thing,'" *Herut,* 27 July 1956.

44. H. Koev, "The Hooves of Impurity," *Herut,* 7 August 1956.

45. Israel Eldad, "Jews, 'Israelites' and Pig Riders," *Ha-Boker,* 9 March 1962.

5. Laying the Foundations

1. See: Basic Law: The Knesset and the Knesset Elections Law [Combined Version], 1969. Details regarding the political parties mentioned in the book are included in Appendix 2.

2. Zvi Tsameret, "Yes to a Jewish State, No to a Clericalist State: The Mapai Leadership and Its Attitude to Religion and Religious Jews" [in Hebrew], in *On Both Sides of the Bridge: Religion and State in the Early Years of Israel,* eds. Mordechai Bar-On and Zvi Tsameret (Jerusalem: Yad Yitshak Ben-Tsvi, 2002), 175.

3. On the constitutional debate in the early years of the state, see: S. Zalman Abramov, *Perpetual Dilemma: Jewish Religion in the Jewish State* (Rutherford, N.J.: Fairleigh Dickinson University Press, 1976), 135–43; Daphne Barak-Erez, "From an Unwritten to a Written Constitution: The Israeli Challenge in American Perspective," *Columbia Human Rights Law Review* 26 (1995): 309, 312–22.

4. 2nd Knesset, 1953, 13 DK 654 (Annexes).

5. Ibid., 655.

6. Motion to the agenda on the "Pig-Raising Prohibition Bill, 1953," 183rd session of the 2nd Knesset, 4 February 1953, 13 DK 639.

7. Ibid., 640.

8. Question on "Publicizing Pig-Breeding in Israel," 266th session of the 2nd Knesset, 8 July 1953, 14 DK 1866.

9. Debate on a motion to the agenda on "Pig-Breeding in Israel," 266th session of the 2nd Knesset, 8 July 1953, 14 DK 1873.

10. Ibid.

11. Ibid., 1874.

12. Conclusions of the Knesset Interior Committee on pig-breeding in the State of Israel, 19 August 1953, 14 DK 2596 (Annexes).

13. Ibid.

14. Ibid., 2597.

15. PG 1944, Supp. 2, p. 939. These were eventually repealed upon the enactment of the Commodities and Services (Control) Law, 1957.

16. The minister of trade and industry, Peretz Bernstein, clarified that the government has no confiscation powers in this context (in response to a question by MK Michael Hazani, who criticized the government for the increasing availability of pork products). See: Question on "The Government's Implementation of Decisions Concerning Pig-Breeding," 350th session of the 2nd Knesset, 6 January 1954, 15 DK 583. See also the statements of the minister of justice, Pinhas Rosen, during the debate on the motion to the agenda in "Raising and Selling Pigs," 524th session of the 2nd Knesset, 29 December 1954, 17 DK 454, 456.

17. KT [Kovets Takkanot—Regulations Compendium] 933.

18. PG 1942, supp. 1, p. 5.

19. As the minister of justice, Pinhas Rosen, explained in a debate on a motion to the agenda in "Raising and Selling Pigs," 456.

20. See: "The Composition of a New Government and Its Plan (Sequel of Discussion)," 360th session of the 2nd Knesset, 25 January 1954, 15 DK 733, 734.

21. Motion to the agenda in "Raising and Selling Pigs," 455. See also question on "Food Parcels Containing Non-Kosher Meat," 382nd session of the 2nd Knesset, 1 March 1954, 15 DK 1002 (a question by Agudat Israel MK Shlomo Lorenz).

22. See: 6th Council of the Tel Aviv Municipality, 689th session, 29 August 1948, questions (TAMA).

23. 7th Council of the Tel Aviv Municipality, 105th session, 7 December 1952, questions (TAMA).

24. The 7th Council of the Tel Aviv Municipality, 128th session, 5 July 1953, questions and motions to the agenda (TAMA). See also: "Agudat Israel's Representative Demands an End to the Spreading Pig Scandal in Tel Aviv," *Ha-Modi'a*, 6 July 1953.

25. H. Agami, "Poster Wars in the Streets of Tiberias," *Ha-Tsofeh*, 26 July 1956 (referring to an event that had taken place three years earlier).

26. HC 194/54 *Axel v. Mayor, Councilors, and Residents of Netanyah*, 8 PD 1524.

27. Adv. Silbiger in a letter to the secretary of the Haifa religious council on the issue of "pork," No. 4282-5/7/K/MS, 11 March 1954 (TAMA File 34-7[3]).

28. The letter is a request by Deputy Mayor Boyer to a member of the Rishon Le-Zion municipal council, asking him to intervene in the function of the municipal veterinary surgeon. No. 4760-5/7/K, 18 March 1954 (TAMA File 34-7[3]). These letters refer to Rule 8 of the Slaughterhouse Rules, which stated that "no animal intended for food shall be slaughtered outside a public slaughterhouse nor shall any meat be exposed for sale which does not bear the official stamp."

29. Haim Broide, *Netivei Haim: Pirkei Havai ve-Yetsirah* [Paths of Life: Events and Endeavors] (Tel Aviv: published by the author, 1977), 200 [in Hebrew].

30. A file at TAMA entitled "Protest Letters Supporting the Prohibition of Pig-Breeding and Pork Sales" includes dozens of letters sent to the municipality by religious activists and representatives of congregations and synagogues, calling for a ban on pigs. Most of them are dated 3 January 1954.

31. (TAMA File 34-7[3]). Compare with the precedent-setting Mandate bylaw forbidding business activity on the Sabbath, which was also enacted in Tel Aviv. See chapter 3, nn. 5–6.

32. Local Councils Order (A) 1950, KT 178.

33. Local Councils Order (A) (Amendment No. 9), 1955, KT 593. This amendment added sub-section (8A) to section 71 of the Local Councils Order (A). Following other amendments made in the order, this provision is now known as section 146(9) of the Local Councils Order (A).

34. See chapter 3, nn. 16–17.

35. The main precedent is *Axel v. Mayor*.

36. Ibid.

37. Ibid., 1531.

38. Ibid., 1528.

39. See: Opinion of Adv. Silbiger on "Pigs and Pork: Licenses under the Trades and Industries (Regulation) Ordinance," 352 / A-2429, 13 December 1954 (TAMA File 34-7[3])

40. HC 72/55 *Fridi v. Municipality of Tel Aviv*, 10 PD 734.

41. Ibid., 752. Note that this petition was filed because the bylaw in this matter had definitely become a nuisance to owners of butcher shops. For examples of rulings at the Tel Aviv–Jaffa municipal court, see: *Compilation of Selected Judgments in Cases Concerning the Municipality of Tel Aviv–Jaffa 5708-5719 (May 1948– September 1959)* (hereinafter: *Tel Aviv Judgments*). See Cr. F. (T-A) 5135/55 *Attorney General v. Treibish, Tel Aviv Judgments,* 158; See Cr. F. (T-A) 6817/55 *Attorney General v. Blumenfeld, Tel Aviv Judgments,* 160; See Cr. F. (T-A) 6821/55 *Attorney-General v. Isaac, Tel Aviv Judgments,* 162 (all from June 1955).

42. Yitzhak Olshan, *Din u-Devarim* (Jerusalem: Shoken, 1978), 330.

43. 8th Council of the Tel Aviv Municipality, 25th session, 2 May 1956, questions and motions to the agenda (TAMA).

44. Note the explanatory notes to the Local Authorities (Special Enablement) Bill, 1956, HH 165, clarifying that the bill follows from the Supreme Court ruling stating that restrictions on the sale of pork must be anchored in legislation.

45. Cited in Menachem Elon, *Religious Legislation* (Tel Aviv: Ha-Kibuts ha-Dati, 1968), 192–93 [in Hebrew]. Quotation is from paragraph 7 of the letter. Prime Minister Ben-Gurion reiterated this undertaking in the Knesset, when reporting on the contents of the coalition agreements. 21st session of the 3rd Knesset, 3 November 1955, 19 DK 284 (also cited in Elon, 194). Subsequently, MK Yitzhak Raphael asked Minister of Justice Pinhas Rosen "whether he considers bringing to the Knesset a law authorizing local authorities to enact bylaws prohibiting pig-breeding and pork sale within their precincts." The minister answered, "This bill has no direct bearing on the Ministry of Justice. It was submitted to the government by the minister of religions and will be submitted to the Knesset after the government completes discussions on it." See: Question on "Prohibition of Pig-Breeding and Sale of Pork," 118th session of the 3rd Knesset, 21 May 1956, 20 DK 1775.

46. Pig-Raising Prohibition in Israel Bill, 1956, proposed by MK Benjamin Mintz (from Agudat Israel and Po'alei Agudat Israel) and the Prohibition on Pig-Raising Bill, 1956, recorded in DK as proposed by MK Y.S. Rosenberg. (This is probably a typographical error, since there was no MK by that name in the 3rd Knesset. Possibly, reference was to MK Aharon Yaakov Greenberg from the Mizrachi and Ha-Po'el ha-Mizrahi). See 3rd Knesset, 1956, 20 DK 1851 (Annexes). Excerpts from Greenberg's speech in the Knesset in this matter were published in *Ha-Tsofeh*. See: Yaakov Greenberg, "The Pig Bane: The State's Disgrace," *Ha-Tsofeh*, 27 May 1956.

47. Motion to the agenda: "The Pig-Raising Prohibition in Israel Bill, 1956," 122nd session of the 3rd Knesset, 23 May 1956, 20 DK 1835.

48. Ibid., 1836.

49. See chapter 2, n. 20.

50. Motion to the agenda: "The Pig-Raising Prohibition in Israel Bill of 1956," 1838.

51. First reading of the Local Authorities (Special Enablement) Law 1956, 161st session of the 3rd Knesset, 24 July 1956, 20 DK 2384; continuation of the debate on the first reading of the Local Authorities (Special Enablement) Law 1956, the 162nd session of the 3rd Knesset, 24 July 1956, 20 DK 2400; continuation of the debate on the first reading of the Local Authorities (Special Enablement) Law 1956, the 162nd session of the 3rd Knesset, 24 July 1956, 20 DK 2407; continuation of the debate on the first reading of the Local Authorities (Special Enablement) Law 956, the 163rd session of the 3rd Knesset, 25 July 1956, 20 DK 2428.

52. Olshan, *Din u-Devarim*, 332–33.

53. First reading, *supra* n. 51, at 2387.

54. Ibid., 2428.

55. Ibid. This emotional appeal—"Honor thy father and thy mother"—was the title used by *Herut*, Begin's party newspaper, for the report on his speech. See: "Remember the Commandment: Honor thy Father and thy Mother," *Herut*, 26 July 1956.

56. First reading, *supra* n. 51, at 2401.

57. Ibid.

58. Ibid., 2396.

59. Ibid., 2403.

60. Ibid., 2409, 2433.

61. Ibid., 2392.

62. Ibid., 2393.

63. Ibid., 2397.

64. Second and third reading of the Local Authorities (Special Enablement) Law 1957, the 193rd session of the 3rd Knesset, 26 November 1956, 21 DK 326 ff.

65. N. Stern, "A Byzantine Debate (On the Pig Law Debate)," *Ha-Tsofeh*, 27 July 1956; "The Knesset Ratified the Law against the Pig," *Ha-Tsofeh*, 17 November 1956.

66. HC 98, 105/54 *Lazarovitz v. Food Controller*, 10 PD 40.

67. Ibid., 56.

68. An undated document found in the archives of the United Kibbutz Movement lists more than sixty kibbutzim that had bred pigs in the past (UKM, Division 2, Farmstead, Container 56, File 6).

69. For instance, HC 199/60 *Reif v. Commissioner of the Northern District*, 15 PD 869. The petitioner, a breeder who did not want to bring his pigs to the municipal abattoir but wanted to slaughter them himself, argued that other pig-breeders had been allowed to do so and that therefore he was a victim of discrimination. This claim indicates that a pig market was at work at the time.

70. Rabbi Shmuel Katz, "Diary of the Activities of the Chief Rabbinate in the Years 1921–1993" [in Hebrew], in *Collection of Articles in Celebration of Seventy Years since the Establishment of Israel Chief Rabbinate*, ed. Itamar Warhaftig and

Rabbi Shmuel Katz, vol. 3 (Jerusalem: Heichal Shlomo Publications, 2002), 1157, 1354.

71. Ibid., 1359.

72. Ibid., 1363.

73. Some documents in the archives of the United Kibbutz Movement show that the kibbutzim were pressured to liquidate this branch of activity. Minutes of a meeting held by the coordinating secretariat of the United Kibbutz Movement on 19 May 1957, include a brief report entitled "Liquidating Pig Herds": "Inform the kibbutzim not to sign any commitment to liquidation, appeal the decision of the Merkaz ha-Hakla'yi [Agricultural Division] to impose sanctions on the kibbutzim, appeal the decision of Tnuva not to market the milk of these kibbutzim" (UKM, Division 1B, Container 11, File 62, including minutes of meetings of the kibbutz secretariat between 17 January 1957 and 9 January 1958).

74. Coalition agreement after elections to the 5th Knesset (dated 20 January 1961). Cited in: Elon, *Religious Legislation*, 197–98.

75. Olshan, *Din u-Devarim*, 333.

76. For a detailed analysis of the arguments raised in the Knesset in favor of the bill, see: Uri Milstain, "Religious Argumentation in Legislative Process in Israel (As Expressed in Three Groups of Laws)" (Ph.D. dissertation, Hebrew University of Jerusalem, 1972), 43–51 [in Hebrew].

77. Pig-Raising Prohibition Bill, 1962, HH 110.

78. The first reading of the Pig-Raising Prohibition Law of 1962, 95th session of the 5th Knesset, 19 February 1962, 33 DK 1307.

79. Ibid., 1307–8.

80. Ibid., 1308.

81. Ibid., 1311.

82. Hereinafter: Pig-Raising Prohibition Law. See also: "The Knesset Has Passed the Law Prohibiting Pig-Breeding," *Davar*, 24 July 1962.

83. Jonah Ben-Amitai, "The Long Struggle for a Law against Pigs Has Finally Ended," *Ha-Tsofeh*, 27 July 1962.

84. It is interesting to compare the sharp phrasing of the law with alternative formulations proposed at the meetings of the kibbutz movement in preparation for the Knesset debates on the bill ("Notes for Members Participating in the Committee to Discuss the 'Pig-Raising Prohibition Law, 1962,'" UKM, Yad Tabenkin, Division 15, Container 23, File 1). One concerned changing the name of the law from "Pig-Raising Prohibition" to "Allocating Places for Pig-Raising" or "Restricting Locations for Pig-Raising," and qualifying the prohibition stating "No pigs will be raised" by adding "except in places listed in the schedule." The original bill also included reference to a schedule where the prohibition would not apply. The alternative drafts were designed to make the bill a regulatory rather than a prohibitive statute.

85. See section 10 of the Pig-Raising Prohibition Law.

86. The schedule does not list all Christian areas in the country. Note that the

amendments document in the archives of the United Kibbutz Movement had required adding to the proposed schedule "every Christian settlement in the rest of the country," including "the Jaffa neighborhood of Tel Aviv."

87. According to section 11 to the Pig-Raising Prohibition Law: "The minister of the interior will, by order, delete the name of any locality from the schedule to this law if that locality is a local authority, and its council decides to request the deletion of its name."

88. Pig-Raising Prohibition (Seizure and Destruction) Regulations, 1963. For a halakhic view on the topic of killing seized pigs, see the responsum of Rabbi Eliezer Yehuda Waldenberg in "Destroying Confiscated Pigs," *Tehumin: Torah Society and State, Halakhic Compilation* 10 (1989): 140–41 [in Hebrew].

6. FORMATIVE BATTLES OF ENFORCEMENT

1. HC 72/55, *Fridi v. Municipality of Tel Aviv*, 10 PD 734, discussed in chapter 5.

2. See Letter from Adv. Silbiger to the deputy mayor on "Local Authorities (Special Enablement) Law, 1956—Bylaw Concerning Pigs and Pork," No. 352/A-3808, 10 December 1956 (TAMA File 143-7[9]).

3. See 8th Council of the Tel Aviv Municipality, 48th session, 6 January 1957, Authorization of Tel Aviv Municipality (Pigs and Pork) Bylaw, 1957 (TAMA).

4. Ibid.

5. Ibid.

6. See the letter from Mayor Haim Lebanon to the minister of the interior, 8 January 1957.

7. See "Does the Bylaw on the Removal of Pork Require Endorsement by the Minister of the Interior? Lawyers Claim That the Enablement Law Is Exempt from Additional Endorsement (From Our Correspondent in Jerusalem)," *Ha-Tsofeh*, 10 January 1957.

8. No. 352/A-3830, 12 December 1956 (TAMA File 143-7[9]).

9. Letter, "Submitting the Tel Aviv Bylaw on Pigs and Pork," 13 January 1957.

10. Letter, "Bylaw on Pigs and Pork: On Submitting for Endorsement to the Minister of the Interior," No. 352/A-160, 15 January 1957.

11. Letter from A. Boyer to the deputy minister of religious affairs, Zerah Warhaftig, 27 April 1954 (TAMA File 2951-4).

12. Letter from the minister of the interior, Israel Bar-Yehuda, 61531/87, dated 14 February 1957.

13. See "Tel Aviv Municipality Rejects the Minister of the Interior's Comments on the Enforcement of the Pig Law," *She'arim*, 19 February 1957; "Lebanon Is Considering Amendments to the Pig Law," *Lamerhav*, 19 February 1957; "Minister of the Interior Tries to Thwart Pig Law: Demands Amendments in the Tel Aviv Pig Law," *Ha-Tsofeh*, 18 February 1957; "Minister of the Interior Demands Amendments in Tel Aviv Pig Law," *Davar*, 18 February 1957; "Minister of the Interior

Sends Back Pig Law to Tel Aviv Municipality for Fundamental Amendments,"
Ha-Boker, 18 February 1957; "Minister of the Interior's Obstructions," *Ha-Tsofeh,*
19 February 1957.

14. Letter from Mayor Haim Lebanon to the minister of the interior, 3813-
5/7/K/MS, 25 February 1957. Minister's reply 61531/87, dated 1 March 1957.

15. MKs from religious parties began working against the minister of the interior on this issue. See question raised by MK Ben-Yaakov on "the endorsement
of the Tel Aviv bylaw prohibiting pork sales," 251st session of the 3rd Knesset, 25
February 1957, 21 DK 1163 (the question raised on 12 February stated that more
than a month had already elapsed since the promulgation of the bylaw, which
"most of the citizens of this country had hoped and yearned for . . . and the law
has not yet been implemented because the minister of the interior has failed to
add the required endorsement," ibid., 1164); question by MK Mintz on the "Minister's Endorsement of Bylaws Enacted by Local Authorities," 268th session of
the 3rd Knesset, 21 March 1957, 22 DK 1412 (the question, dated 21 February, was
addressed to the minister of justice objecting to the requirement of endorsement by the minister of the interior). For newspaper reports on this parliamentary exchange, see "Demands Debate on Minister of the Interior's Requests
from Tel Aviv Municipality: The Pig Bylaws Resonate in the Knesset," *Haaretz,*
19 February 1957, and "Question on the Pig Law," *Lamerhav,* 26 February 1957.

16. "B. G. [Ben Gurion] Mediates on the 'Pig Dispute,'" *Ma'ariv,* 13 March 1957.

17. Letter from the minister of the interior, 61531/87, 25 March 1957.

18. Tel Aviv-Jaffa (Pigs and Pork) Bylaw, 1957. The Tel Aviv municipality ratified the bylaw in its amended version on 7 April 1957. See 8th Council, 55th session, 7 April 1957. See also "Tel Aviv Municipality Ratified the Pig Law with the
'Amendments' of the Minister of the Interior," *She'arim,* 8 April 1957.

19. See: Jerusalem (Pigs and Pork) Bylaw, 1957; Ramle (Pigs and Pork) Bylaw,
1957; Rishon le-Zion (Pigs and Pork) Bylaw, 1957; Petah Tikvah (Pigs and Pork)
Bylaw, 1957; Netanyah (Pigs and Pork) Bylaw, 1957; Modi'im (Pigs and Pork) By-
law, 1957; Nahal Soreq (Pigs and Pork) Bylaw, 1957; Holon (Pigs and Pork) Bylaw,
1957; Rehovoth (Pigs and Pork) Bylaw, 1957; Ef'al (Pigs) Bylaw, 1958; Ramat Gan
(Pigs and Pork) Bylaw, 1958; Gederah (Pigs and Pork) Bylaw, 1958; Haderah (Pigs
and Pork) Bylaw, 1958; Lod (Pigs and Pork) Bylaw, 1958; Tiberias (Pigs and Pork)
Bylaw, 1958; Beth She'an (Pigs and Pork) Bylaw, 1958; Ashkelon (Pigs and Pork)
Bylaw, 1958; Or Yehuda (Pigs and Pork) Bylaw, 1958; Zikhron Yaakov (Pigs and
Pork) Bylaw, 1958; Yavneh (Pigs and Pork) Bylaw, 1958; Nes-Ziona (Pigs and Pork)
Bylaw, 1958; Afula (Pigs and Pork) Bylaw, 1958; Yavneh District (Pigs and Pork)
Bylaw, 1959; Ramat ha-Sharon (Pigs and Pork) Bylaw, 1959; Tel Mond (Pigs and
Pork) Bylaw, 1959; Kiryat Shemonah (Pigs and Pork) Bylaw, 1959 (joined later by
the Kiryat Shemonah (Pigs and Pork) Bylaw, 1993; Herzliyah (Pigs and Pork)
Bylaw, 1960; Binyamina (Pigs and Pork) Bylaw, 1960; Givatayim (Pigs and Pork)
Bylaw, 1960; Lakhish (Pigs and Pork) Bylaw, 1960; Ofakim (Pigs and Pork) By-
law, 1960; Or Akiva (Pigs and Pork) Bylaw, 1960; Kiryat Ata (Pigs and Pork)

Bylaw, 1960; Kiryat Gat (Pigs and Pork) Bylaw, 1960; Gan Yavneh (Pigs and Pork) Bylaw, 1960; Pardes Hannah-Karkur (Pigs and Pork) Bylaw, 1960; Sderot (Pigs and Pork) Bylaw, 1960; Nesher (Pigs and Pork) Bylaw, 1960; Shafir (Pigs and Pork) Bylaw, 1960; Tirat ha-Carmel (Pigs and Pork) Bylaw, 1961; Azur (Pigs and Pork) Bylaw, 1961; Kiryat Yam (Pigs and Pork) Bylaw, 1961; Ashdod (Pigs and Pork) Bylaw, 1961 (which was later replaced by Ashdod [Pork] Bylaw, 1976); Rosh Pinah (Pork) Bylaw, 1964; Kiryat Ono (Pork) Bylaw, 1968; Dimonah (Pigs and Pork) Bylaw, 1993; Yahud (Pigs and Pork) Bylaw, 1994. In Haifa, which has a mixed Arab and Jewish population, the local bylaw distinguishes between various districts of the city. See Haifa (Pigs and Pork) Bylaw, 1959. A distinction between the borders of the city and the industrial area appears in the Carmiel (Pork) Bylaw, 1978, stating that the prohibition relates only to "the residential area." A formula whereby pork sales are forbidden outside the "public market," and hence permitted inside the market, was once part of the bylaws enacted before the Special Enablement Law. See Tel Aviv–Jaffa (Pigs and Pork) Bylaw, 1954 (invalidated by *Fridi*); Safed (Pigs and Pork) Bylaw, 1955 and the Acre (Pigs and Pork) Bylaw, 1955.

20. Haim Broide, *Netivei Haim: Pirkei Havai ve-Yetsirah* [Paths of Life: Events and Endeavors] (Tel Aviv: published by the author, 1977), 200 [in Hebrew]. Press reports from the time tell a similar tale. See, for example: "The Battle 'Against the Pig' Has Begun in Tel Aviv—Butchers: We Shall Continue Marketing the Meat," *Lamerhav*, 2 July 1957. The article also reports on the training of a municipal unit of inspectors specifically for this purpose and clarifies that, until the beginning of enforcement, pork trade had been fairly common in Tel Aviv: "Established butchers report that, in Tel Aviv alone, 1,200 pigs are slaughtered every month, supplying 120 tons of meat monthly." See also "Sellers of the Profane Meat Attacked Municipal Inspectors," *Ha-Tsofeh*, 5 December 1957; "Legal Proceedings Brought against Five-Hundred Pork Sellers in Tel Aviv," *Ha-Tsofeh*, 13 March 1958.

Municipal files contain monthly reports from the markets department (headed by Haim Broide) on the various enforcement activities. See, for example, Monthly Report for January 1958, Inspections for the Elimination of Pork, 6 January 1958 (TAMA File 28-7[1]). According to the report, "1,510 businesses were visited in the course of the month," and pork was confiscated in sixty-three of them.

The municipality began to deploy for enforcement immediately after the enactment of the first bylaw on this matter, rescinded in *Axel*. See letter from Adv. Silbiger to the chief municipal inspector, No. 352/A-79, 19 January 1955, which includes explanations for the implementation of the bylaw (File 2951-4, 19 January 1955). See also Minutes signed by Deputy Mayor Boyer and by H. Broide, secretary, "further to the discussion on the implementation of (Pigs and Pork) Bylaw held by Deputy Mayor Boyer in his office on Thursday 10.3.55" (TAMA File 34-7[3]).

21. As noted, this issue first arose in the discussions preceding the promulgation of the bylaw.

22. HC 129/57 *Manshi v. Minister of the Interior and the Municipality of Tel Aviv–Jaffa*, 12 PD 209.

23. See Letter from Haim Broide, head of the market division, on "Searching Clients' Packages," 14 February 1958 (TAMA File 28-7[1]).

24. See Letter from the Mayor to the head of the church in Jaffa, 12134-5/17/K, 11 July 1957

25. *Manshi, supra* n. 22, at 223.

26. See Haifa (Pigs and Pork) Bylaw, 1959.

27. HC 111/62, *Zilber v. Municipality of Haifa*, 16 PD 1160.

28. HC 163/57, *Lubin v. Municipality of Tel Aviv–Jaffa*, 12 PD 1041. Given the importance of this decision as a precedent, the question was reconsidered in a further hearing that upheld the original decision. See FH 13/58 *Municipality of Tel Aviv–Jaffa v. Lubin*, 13 PD 118. In this sense, the early reservations of Minister of the Interior Bar-Yehuda on the scope of confiscatory powers were later accepted. See the text following *supra* n. 12. By contrast, another ruling held that attachment (seizure) powers, which are temporary by nature, may be implemented even in the absence of a court ruling. See HC 219/58 *"Farga" Butcher's Shop and Sausage Factory v. Municipality of Haifa*, 13 PD 41.

29. HC *Lubin*, 1065.

30. FH *Lubin*, 130.

31. See: in Cr. A. 217/68, *Yizramax Ltd. v. State of Israel*, 22 (2) PD 343.

32. Ibid., 355.

33. See Letter from the mayor on the appointment of inspectors as police officers, 14344-5/7/K/MS, 11 August 1957; Letter from the minister of police to the attorney general on the appointment of municipal inspectors as police officers, 3968-221/22, 17 November 1957; opinion of Attorney General Haim Cohn on "Tel Aviv–Jaffa (Pigs and Pork) Bylaw, 1957," 1/4/557, 8 December 1957.

34. HC *Lubin*, 1048. Besides cases involving general matters of principle, hearings were also conducted on cases hinging on factual questions. See, for example: Cr. A. (T-A) 165/58, *Yungstein v. Attorney-General, Tel Aviv Judgments* 157 (a district court ruling dismissing the appellant's contention that the meat seized in his shop had not been pork).

35. HC 149/57, *Karl Berg and Co. Ltd. v. Municipality of Tel Aviv–Jaffa*, 12 PD 447.

36. HC 230/57, *Rapaport v. Municipality of Tel Aviv–Jaffa*, 12 PD 1037, 1040.

37. Ibid., 1038.

38. Cr. F. (T-A) 9431/61 *Attorney-General v. Bekher* (7 June 1961, files of Tel Aviv municipality).

39. Broide, *Netivei Haim*, 200.

40. For examples of reports signed by Y. Polak, Coordinator of the Pig Control Department, see TAMA File 196-7 (3).

41. Decision of Minister of Finance Pinhas Sapir from January 1964. The decision referred to the recommendations of a committee appointed by the minister

in a letter from 28 July 1963. On 27 January 1964, the Department for Agricultural Development at the Ministry of Agriculture issued a specific order to transfer grants to kibbutzim that had liquidated their pig herds (documents available at the Lavon Institute archive).

42. This agreement was mentioned in a later decision which dealt with a petition submitted by the partnership against the Iblin locality. See: HC 4264/02 *Iblin Breeders Partnership v. Municipality of Iblin* (to be published 12 December 2006), discussed in chapter 8.

43. *Zilber*, discussed above.

44. HC 176/64, *Halon v. National Inspector Implementing the Pig-raising Prohibition Law*, 18 (4) PD 790; HC 103/65, *Gornstein v. Minister of the Interior*, 19 (2) PD 618.

45. *Gornstein*, ibid., 622–23.

46. In HC 261/63, *Megidovitz v. The Planning Commission for the Northern District, Nazareth*, 18(2) PD 287.

47. Animal Diseases (Slaughter of Animals) Regulations, 1964. According to Schedule 13 of these regulations, as originally enacted, the three legal abattoirs for pigs were located in Nazareth and Iblin for the north, and in the research institute at Kibbutz Lahav for the south.

48. In HC 153/64, *"The Breeders" Registered Partnership v. Minister of the Interior*, 18(4) PD 388, the court dealt with a petition against a bylaw imposing a particularly high tax on the pig breeding business. The court dismissed the petition, saying it could not rule that the tax was unreasonable because the breeders marketed their products beyond the permitted breeding area as well. In HC 228/63, 193/64, *"The Breeders" v. The Head of the Municipality of Iblin*, 19(1) PD 617, the petition hinged on a demand from several pig breeders to operate their abattoir themselves (and not through the municipality) and on their arguments against the high fees they were required to pay for its use. The alternative of using another abattoir located elsewhere was probably problematic, given previous rulings that had restricted the transport of pigs through areas where their breeding was prohibited, as detailed above.

49. The control of food supply for animals was regulated according to the Emergency Regulations (Maintenance of Essential Supplies and Services) (Extension of Validity) Law, 1957, which served as the basis for the Emergency Order (Use of Bread and Flour for Feeding Animals), 1957. This order prohibited the use of bread and flour for feeding animals without a permit. In practice, using bread was not permitted with regard to breeding pigs. The order remained valid even after the law under which it had been issued was replaced by the Commodities and Services (Control) Law 1957. See "'We Did Not Sell Bread for Feeding Pigs but for Feeding Poultry,' Argues the Secretary of Moshav Komemiyut," *Ha-Tsofeh*, 4 April 1962.

50. "The Abattoir's License to Sell Pork Was Revoked in Haifa," *Davar*, 9 April 1962.

51. HC 14/65, *Basal v. Minister of the Interior and Local Council of Kafr Yasif* 19(2) PD 322.

52. HC 8/63, *Bazul v. Minister of the Interior* 19(1) PD 337.

53. Ibid., 349.

54. Ibid., 356.

7. FROM STATUS QUO TO POLITICAL CONFLICT

1. Interview with the author, February 2002.

2. TAMA File No. 16-17 / CL 31 May 1970

3. Section 3 of the Special Enablement Law and Sections 3–4 of the Pig-Raising Prohibition Law.

4. C. F. (Petah Tikvah) 2514/86 *Agudat Keren Kohav-Zaslovsky v. Pikovsky,* P. M. 1992 (4) 249.

5. Ibid., 252.

6. Ibid., 250–51.

7. Section 2 (2) of the Pig-Raising Prohibition Law.

8. HC 229/63 *Institute for Livestock Science and Research at Kibbutz Lahav v. Minister of the Interior,* 18 (2) PD 185.

9. The exchange of letters between Rosen and Justice Berenson was later published. See: Dov Rosen, "Exchange of Letters on the Enforcement of the Law Prohibiting Pig-breeding" [in Hebrew], in *Year by Year: 1981 Annual* (Jerusalem: Heichal Shlomo Publications, Aharon Halevi Fitsnik ed.), 339. Rosen had actually asked the question concerning the destruction of confiscated pigs (mentioned in chapter 5, n. 88). At the time, Rosen was also in charge of matters connected with the promulgation of bylaws on the sale of pigs under the Special Enablement Law. In a column entitled "From the Diary of a Junior Religious Civil Servant" [in Hebrew], in *Year by Year: 1983 Annual,* Rosen published "The Owner of 'The Other Thing' Retreats" (380–81). See also: "The Minister Refused To Sign the Enablement Law on the Matter of the Pig" [in Hebrew], in *Year by Year: 1987 Annual* (Jerusalem: Heichal Shlomo Publications, Aharon Halevi Fitsnik ed.) 313, 314–15.

10. Although the national prohibition on alcohol had initially enjoyed public backing, support waned after a few years. See Kenneth M. Murchison, *Federal Criminal Law Doctrines: The Forgotten Influence of National Prohibition* (Durham, N.C.: Duke University Press, 1994), 9–10; Richard B. Bernstein and Jerome Agel, *Amending America: If We Love the Constitution So Much, Why Do We Keep Trying to Change It?* (New York: Times Books, 1993), 175.

11. Lawrence M. Friedman, *Crime and Punishment in American History* (New York: Basic Books, 1993), 339–40.

12. Ibid., 339.

13. Dan Horowitz and Moshe Lissak, *Trouble in Utopia: The Overburdened Polity of Israel,* trans. Charles Hoffman (Albany: State University of New York Press, 1989), 58.

14. These issues are comprehensively discussed in Menachem Mautner's writings. See Menachem Mautner, *The Decline of Formalism and the Rise of Values in Israeli Law* (Tel-Aviv: Ma'gele da'at, 1993), 127–28 (reference to "the renewed strug gle over Israel's character") [in Hebrew]. See also: Menachem Mautner, "The 1980s: Years of Anxiety," *Tel-Aviv University Law Review* 26 (2002): 645 (discussing the collapse of Labor hegemony) [in Hebrew].

15. Government Decision from 2 May 1982.

16. HC 347/84, *Municipality of Petah Tikvah v. Minister of Interior* 39(1) PD 813.

17. Cr. F. (Jerusalem) 3471/87 *State of Israel v. Kaplan* 1988(2) PM 265.

18. See Naomi Gutkind-Golan, "The Heikhal Cinema Issue: A Symptom of Religious-Non-Religious Relations in the 1980s," in *Religious and Secular: Conflict and Accommodation between Jews in Israel,* ed. Charles S. Liebman (Jerusalem: Keter, 1990), 67.

19. Municipal Corporations Ordinance Amendment (No. 40) Law, 1990, which inserted Section 264A into the Municipal Corporations Ordinance (New Version).

20. Letter on "Suspending the Filing of Legal Proceedings Linked to the Municipal Bylaw on Pig Eradication," 11 April 1978 (TAMA).

21. Letter on "Filing Legal Proceedings on Pig Eradication," 352/A 940, 1 May 1978 (TAMA).

22. See Letter on "Ceasing the Filing of Legal Proceedings Related to the Municipal Bylaw on Pig Eradication," 31 July 1978 (TAMA File 16-17 / CL).

23. In the letter, he refers to this as "Rabbi Shazransky's proposal." See Letter on "Activities against Pork Sales," 12/A-456, 4 March 1980 (TAMA).

24. Letter on "Enforcement of the Law for the Eradication of Pigs," 25 March 1980 (TAMA).

25. Yair Sheleg characterized this period as a time of transition "from a secular offensive to an orthodox offensive." See Yair Sheleg, *The New Religious: Recent Developments among Observant Jews in Israel* (Jerusalem: Keter, 2000), 290 [in Hebrew].

26. For the presentation of the law, see: Debate on Festival of Matzot (Prohibition of Leaven) Bill, 1985, the 69th session of the 11th Knesset, 12 March 1985, 101 DK 2037; first reading of Festival of Matzot (Prohibition of Leaven) Law, 1985, the 113th session of the 11th Knesset, 22 July 1985, 102 DK 3631; second and third readings of Festival of Matzot (Prohibition of Leaven) Law, 1986, the 234th session of the 11th Knesset, 4 August 1986, 105 DK 3970. For an account considering these two examples of legislation together, see statements of MK Meir Kahana during the debate on "Polarizing Relationships between Orthodox and Secularists," 136th session of the 11th Knesset, 12 November 1985, 103 DK 410, 418 ("A law against the pig? They oppose it. Like with like. A law against leaven? It is only natural for one who is 'wholly leaven' [impure] to fight for its own kind.")

27. As emphasized by MK David Libai. See: Pig-Raising Prohibition (Amendment) Bill, 1985, 117th session of the 11th Knesset, 30 July 1985, 102 DK 3833, 3942.

28. See Pig-Raising Prohibition (Amendment) Bill, 1981, 432nd session of the 9th Knesset, 11 March 1981, 91 DK 2050 (presentation of the bill by MK Yehuda Meir Abramowicz of Agudat Israel) and the Pig-Raising Prohibition (Amendment) Bill, 1981, 432nd session of the 9th Knesset, 11 March 1981, 91 DK 2051 (presentation of the bill by NRP MKs Yehuda Ben-Meir, Abraham Melamed and Sarah Stern-Katan). For the text of the bill, see Pig-Raising Prohibition (Amendment) Bill, 1981, 91 DK 2085 (Annexes) and Pig-Raising Prohibition (Amendment) Bill, 1981, 91 DK 2086 (Annexes).

29. 91 DK 2050.

30. Ibid., 2051, 2052.

31. Ibid., 2053.

32. Ibid.

33. Pig-Raising Prohibition (Amendment) Bill, 1981, HH 254.

34. Debate on Pig-Raising Prohibition (Amendment) Bill, 1981, 100th session of the 11th Knesset, 19 June 1985, 102 DK 2980.

35. Debate on the Pig-Raising, Marketing, and Distribution Prohibition (Amendment) Bill, 1985, 100th session of the 11th Knesset, 19 June 1985, 102 DK 2983.

36. Ibid., 2987.

37. First reading of the Pig-Raising Prohibition (Amendment) Bill, 1985, 116th session of the 11th Knesset, 30 July 1985, 102 DK 3833.

38. Yehoshua Shofman, "Pig-Raising Prohibition (Amendment) Bill, 1985," *Civil Rights* 13–14 (1986): 15 [in Hebrew].

39. Pig-Raising Prohibition (Amendment) Bill, 1985 (first reading), 145th session of the 11th Knesset, 3 December 1985, 103 DK 727.

40. Notice by Michael Eitan, House Committee chairperson, 152nd session of the 11th Knesset, 18 December 1985, 103 DK 915.

41. This criticism was voiced in the context of another parliamentary debate regarding bills from the former Knesset, to which the government did choose to apply the rule of continuity. See: Motion of the Democratic Front for Peace and Equality and Agudat Israel against the Abstention from Applying the Law of Continuity on Bills, 25th session of the 12th Knesset, 23 May 1989, 112 DK 636, 637.

42. See Pig-Raising Prohibition (Amendment) Bill, 1990, 178th session of the 12th Knesset, 21 May 1990, 117 DK 3506.

43. Ibid., 3508–9.

44. See: Coalition agreements, 117 DK 3975 (appendixes). The agreement, dated 8 June 1990, included the following parties: Likud, Shas, NRP, Movement for the Advancement of the Zionist Ideal, Tehiyah, Tsomet, Degel ha-Torah, Minister R. Yitzhak Peretz, and MK R. Eliezer Mizrahi.

45. Ibid., 3976.

46. See: Coalition agreements, 119 DK 747 (appendixes). The agreement is dated 18 November 1990. The parties included were Likud and Agudat Israel.

47. Ibid.

48. See: Rubik Rosental, "I Love Pork," *Al ha-Mishmar,* 24 May 1990; "Turbid Legislation" (editorial) *Haaretz,* 9 January 1990.

49. Ran Kislev, "The Political Pig," *Haaretz,* 21 June 1990.

50. Gadi Yatsiv, "Taboo, Totem, and Pig," *Al ha-Mishmar,* 30 November 1990.

51. Avi Ganor, "Back to Russia," *Haaretz,* 22 November 1990.

52. Dan Margalit, "When White Meat Turns Black," *Haaretz,* 8 January 1991.

53. Yehuda Koren, "On the Whole, It Has an Image Problem," *Haaretz* (Supplement), 1 June 1990.

54. Yoram Bar, "Monsignor in the Interior Committee: Why Only Pig? Why Not Shrimp?" *Al ha-Mishmar,* 18 July 1990. Christians in the north of the country had traditionally been involved in pig-breeding and made their livelihood from this industry. See: Yehuda Tsur, "Pig Business: Law or No Law, We Will Go On Selling," *Al ha-Mishmar,* 24 May 1990.

55. For newspaper articles focusing on a demand to compensate pig breeders see, for instance: Baruch Bracha, "A Pig When He Treads" [a pun on Deuteronomy 25:4: "Thou shalt not muzzle the ox when he treads out the corn"], *Haaretz,* 19 June 1990; Avraham Tal, "Hast Thou Coerced and Also Robbed?" [after 1 Kings 21:19: "Hast thou killed, and also taken possession?"], *Haaretz,* 2 December 1990; Betsalel Amikam, "Death Blow," *Al ha-Mishmar,* 21 December 1990; Yoram Bar, "Everybody Understands How Superfluous This Is," *Al ha-Mishmar,* 18 December 1990; Betsalel Amikam, "Mizra against the Knesset: I Do Not Want Matsa and His Friends Deciding on Our Way of Life," *Al ha-Mishmar,* 20 December 1990.

56. Aviva Luri, "Kibbutz Lahav: This Is a Swinish Law," *Ma'ariv,* 23 November 1990; Tsvia Ben-Shalom, "Swinishness *Oblige*" [a pun on noblesse oblige], *Al ha-Mishmar,* 23 November 1990; Betsalel Amikam, "Get Out of Our Plates," *Al ha-Mishmar,* 27 December 1990; Idit Pelekh, "They Are No Longer Alone," *Al ha-Mishmar,* 27 December 1990.

57. "Swinishness" (editorial), *Al ha-Mishmar,* 5 December 1990; "The Pig Law: Redundant" (editorial), *Al ha-Mishmar,* 19 December 1990.

58. Betsalel Amikam, "The Coalition Lashed Its Whip and the Law Passed," *Al ha-Mishmar,* 8 January 1991.

59. Pig-Raising Prohibition Order, 1988, KT 924, issued under section 11 of the Pig-Raising Prohibition Law. Raineh, omitted from the schedule to the law by this order, was the village of the petitioners in HC 8/63 *Bazul v. Minister of the Interior* 19(1) PD 337. See chapter 6.

60. See Municipalities (Fines Offences) (Amendment No. 34) Order, 1989, KT 434.

61. As noted, this idea had been proposed by Basok already in 1980.

62. Dr. Galin, the municipal veterinary surgeon, was asked about it in February 2002 by Adv. Gabi Priel, from the legal counsel office at the Tel Aviv municipality. Dr. Galin indicated that, as far as he could remember, the unit had been disbanded about twelve years previously.

63. The title was criticized in an article that praised approaches to which *Davar* had provided a forum in the past, and focused on Alterman's poem "Freedom of Opinion and the Hooves" (see chapter 2, n. 64). See Akiva Tsimerman, "The Pig Prohibition for Alterman," *Ha-Tsofeh,* 1 January 1991.

8. The Renewed Challenge

1. The use of this term was promoted by Aharon Barak, Chief Justice of the Israeli Supreme Court. See Aharon Barak, "The Constitutional Revolution: Protected Human Rights," *Mishpat U-Mimshal* 1 (1992–93): 9 [in Hebrew].

2. Although freedom of occupation is not expressly protected in all constitutional traditions, Israel is not alone in providing constitutional safeguards for its protection. For instance, Article 12 of the German Basic Law entitled "Right to Choose a Trade, Occupation or Profession," states: "All Germans shall have the right to freely choose their trade, occupation, or profession, their place of work, and their place of training."

3. *Unified Hamizrahi Bank v. Migdal Cooperative Village,* 49(1) PD 221.

4. See: Cr. F. H 2316/95 *Ganimat v. State of Israel,* 49(4) PD 589.

5. See: HC 3872/92 *Mitrael Ltd. v. The Prime Minister and the Minister of Religious Affairs,* 47 (5) PD 485.

6. See: HC 4676/94 *Mitrael Ltd. v. Israeli Knesset,* 50 (5) PD 15.

7. Section 2 of Basic Law: Freedom of Occupation and Section 1a of Basic Law: Human Dignity and Liberty. This wording is a variation on section 1 of the Canadian Charter of Rights and Freedoms, which relates to a "free and democratic society."

8. Asher Cohen and Bernard Susser, *Israel and the Politics of Jewish Identity: The Secular-Religious Impasse* (Baltimore: Johns Hopkins University Press, 2000), 111.

9. Yair Sheleg, *The New Religious: Recent Developments among Observant Jews in Israel,* (Jerusalem: Keter, 2000) 291 [in Hebrew].

10. Sheleg's description of the developments during the 1990s is worth noting, although it is inaccurate from a legal perspective. He states: "In 1990, the 'Pig Law' was enacted, preventing the marketing and distribution of pork except in cities with a Christian majority. This law was enacted following the large immigration wave from the former Soviet Union, which brought with it a high demand for pork, after the breeding of pigs had already been forbidden in the early years of the State" (291). Later he adds that: "The 'Pig Law,' passed in 1990, was the last statute enacted at the initiative of the religious parties. This law reflected their sense that this too was a symbolic matter, a standard issue for most Jews" (294). Although this description of the legal situation is wrong, since the various legislative initiatives of the 1980s and early 1990s to amend the laws on pork trading and pig breeding were unsuccessful, it is accurate from a social perspective. The pig question became a renewed legal issue during the 1990s

due to impact of the demand for pork among new immigrants from the former USSR.

11. According to a report in a local Tel Aviv magazine, a new bar called Babe offers, besides drinks, only variations on one dish: pork spareribs. See: Matan Tsuri, "A Wild Boar Discovered in Jaffa," *Zeman Tel Aviv,* 4 June 2004.

12. A gourmet butcher shop of this kind opened up in 1988 in Jerusalem, catering to a clientele that also includes MKs, judges, and journalists. See: Lauren Gelfond, "The Secret Life of Pigs," *Jerusalem Post,* 4 January 2004.

13. See Gabi Zohar, "It's OK, the Shop Is Closed on the Sabbath," *Haaretz,* 3 December 1997 (on the arson of a butcher's shop selling pork, against the background of the conflict between the city's immigrant and ultra-Orthodox communities). See also: Eli Ashkenazi, "In Tiberias, They Have Not Yet Acknowledged the New Immigrants," *Haaretz,* 16 December 2003.

14. Question on "Marketing of Non-Kosher Products," 35th session of the 13th Knesset, 9 December 1992, 127 DK 1039 (the original question was dated 6 August 1992).

15. Motion to the agenda, "Increasing Sales of Pork and Ritually Unclean Meat," 94th session of the 13th Knesset, 19 May 1993, 130 DK 4979.

16. Ibid., 4980.

17. Ibid.

18. Ibid., 4981.

19. Question on "Sale of Nonkosher Meat," 267th session of the 13th Knesset, 2 November 1994, 140 DK 1141 (the original question was dated 21 March 1993).

20. Ibid.

21. Question on "Immigrants from Russia: Registration of Non-Jews as Jews and Their Sale of Pork" 152nd session of the 14th Knesset, 3 December 1997, 167 DK 1295 (the original question was dated 9 July 1997).

22. Ibid.

23. Question on "Shops for the Sale of Ritually Unfit Products" 196th session of the 14th Knesset, 4 March 1998, 173 DK 6606.

24. HC 129/57 *Manshi v. Minister of the Interior and the Municipality of Tel Aviv-Jaffa,* 12 PD 209. See chapter 6, nn. 22–25.

25. Cr. F. (Netanyah) 1310/95 *State of Israel v. Rubinstein* (unpublished, 23 October 1996).

26. Ibid., 16.

27. Ibid., 21.

28. Uzi Fogelman was appointed district court judge in 2000, and Meni Mazuz was appointed attorney general in 2004.

29. The meeting took place on 28 November 1996. A detailed report of the participants' positions and of the summary by the attorney general are cited in the opinion of Yaakov Shapira, from the office of the deputy attorney general (advice) on the "Acre (Pigs and Pork) Bylaw, 1997," dated 30 July 1997. The quote is from this opinion, p. 4.

30. See: Letter from Deputy Attorney General Meni Mazuz on "Acre (Pigs and Pork) Bylaw, 1997," dated 31 July 1997, endorsing Shapira's opinion, ibid.

31. Letter on "Bylaws Prohibiting the Sale of Pork and Pork Products" signed by Deputy Attorney General Meni Mazuz, dated 9 March 1998.

32. Letter from Deputy Attorney General Meni Mazuz on "By-laws Prohibiting the Sale of Pork," dated 19 February 1998.

33. Cr. F. (Ashkelon) 260/95 *State of Israel v. Shmukler* (unpublished, 8 March 1995) (hereafter: *Shmukler-Magistrate*).

34. At the time, a petition was also submitted to the High Court of Justice against the Ashkelon bylaw on pigs. See: HC 1387/95 *Spokvini v. Mayor of Ashkelon*. The petitioners stated that about 25 percent of Ashkelon's residents were immigrants from the former Soviet Union. Ultimately, no decision on the merits was rendered in this case. In a brief judgment of a few lines issued on 25 September 1997, the court explained that a ruling was unnecessary given the hearing on this matter in the Ashkelon Magistrate's Court.

35. *Shmukler-Magistrate,* p. 8 of the ruling, legal CD-ROM *Dinim ve-Od.*

36. Ibid., 11.

37. Ibid., 10.

38. Motion to the agenda on "The Ruling of an Ashkelon Judge Allowing the Municipality to Enforce the Law Regarding Pork Sales," 195th session of the 14th Knesset, 173 DK 6469.

39. Appeal was the defendants' last resort, after their earlier request for the disqualification of Judge Yitzhak had been rejected. This request was based on the argument that the judge was known to be a religious Jew. See: Aliza Arbeli, "An Ashkelon Court: The Reason for Banning Pork Sales Is Historical and National," *Haaretz,* 11 March 1998.

40. Cr. A. (Beer-Sheba) 7182/98 *Shmukler v. State of Israel-Municipality of Ashkelon* (unpublished, 27 October 1999).

41. Ibid., page 23 of the ruling, legal CD-ROM *Dinim ve-Od.*

42. Ibid.

43. Letter on "Prohibition on the Sale of Pork and Pork Products in Carmiel" by Amnon De-Hartog, head of the section of legal advice and legislation to Shlomo Geva, legal advisor to the Carmiel municipality, 28 August 2000.

44. Ibid., 3.

45. Cr. F. (Petah Tikvah) 1004-1011/97 *State of Israel v. Mutsmacher* (unpublished, 8 July 2001).

46. Improving the Efficiency Standards of Bylaws Publication (Amendment of Legislation) Bill, 1999 (submitted by MK Amnon Rubinstein), 150th session of the 15th Knesset, 8 November 2000, 199 DK 311.

47. HC 194/54 *Axel v. Mayor, Councilors and Residents of Netanyah,* 8 PD 1524 and 72/55 *Fridi v. Municipality of Tel Aviv,* 10 PD 734, discussed in chapter 5 above.

48. HC 8182/00 *Varmus v. Municipality of Ramat Gan,* at p. 3.

49. Ibid., page 8 of the petition.

50. HC 8182/00 *Varmus v. Municipality of Ramat Gan* (unpublished, 20 December 2000).

51. For a report on the demonstration, see Rivka Freilich, "Shas Activists: 'The Russians—Lewdness, Abomination, and Impurity,'" *Ma'ariv,* 22 November 1999.

52. Motion to the agenda on "Statements by Rabbis and Public Figures in Beth-Shemesh against Immigrants from Russia," 52nd session of the 15th Knesset, 24 November 1999, 188 DK 1746.

53. Ibid., 1750.

54. Beth Shemesh (Pigs and Pork) Bylaw, 2000.

55. HC 963/01 *Solodkin v. Municipality of Beth Shemesh.* The court's ruling on this matter is discussed below.

56. Ibid., para. 4 of the petition.

57. HC 1355/01 *Shinui/Secular Movement v. Minister of the Interior.* The court's ruling on this matter is discussed below.

58. Ruling issued on 9 March 2001.

59. HC 7406/01 *Solodkin v. Municipality of Carmiel.* The court's ruling on this matter is discussed below.

60. Ibid., page 5 of the petition.

61. Ruling issued on 22 October 2001.

62. HC 2283/02 *Mania Delicatessen Meat Products and Sausages Industries Co. Ltd. v. Mayor of Tiberias.* The court's ruling on this matter is discussed below. Originally, a petition had been filed against the same bylaw a year earlier. On this petition, a brief ruling was issued that the city council would consider the contents of the bylaw and the possibility of changing it while preserving the petitioner's right to petition the court anew, according to the outcome of these deliberations. See: HC 9533/00 *Mania Delicatessen Meat Products and Sausages Industries Co. Ltd. v. Mayor of Tiberias* (unpublished, 7 November 2001). Since the city council decided not to change the bylaw, the new petition was filed.

63. An *order nisi* was issued by the court on 14 March 2002, and an interim order was issued on 4 January 2004. See also Yuval Yoaz, "High Court of Justice to the Municipality of Tiberias: Not to Prohibit Sale of Pork," *Haaretz,* 5 January 2004.

64. Debate on "Transfer of the Electricity Company's Generator on the Sabbath," 99th session of the 15th Knesset, 1 February 2000, 192 DK 5066, 5073–74.

65. Question on "Pig Breeding in Kibbutz Lahav," 129th session of the 15th Knesset, 10 July 2000, 197 DK 9662.

66. Question on "Sale of Ritually Unfit Meat as Beef," 211th session of the 15th Knesset, 18 June 2001, 206 DK 554.

67. See: Cr. F. (Beer-Sheba) 3042/97 *State of Israel v. Kibbutz Lahav* (unpublished, 3 June 1999). Note that the indictment was not based on offenses committed under the Pig-Raising Prohibition Law, but rather under business licensing laws.

68. Motion to the agenda on "Declaration by the Minister of the Interior on

Summer Daysaving Time and the Sale of Pork," 186th session of the 15th Knesset, 14 March 2001, 203 DK 3493.

69. Ibid., 3494.

70. Ibid.

71. Ibid., 3495.

72. Ibid., 3496.

73. Ibid. These comments by Minister Eli Yishai refer to the elections on 6 February 2001.

74. Oral questions on "Police Filming of Demonstrations," 122nd session of the 15th Knesset, 21 June 2000, 196 DK 8939, 8940.

75. Debate on Meat and Meat Products (Amendment—Repeal of the Law) Bill, 2000 (proposal by a group of MKs), 247th session of the 15th Knesset, 14 November 2001, 210 DK 962, 963.

76. Michal Goldberg, Tovah Tsimuki, and David Regev, "Poraz to the High Court: Enable Pork Sales," *Yedi'ot Aharonot*, 7 March 2003. The article quotes from the letter that the minister wrote to the attorney general: "It is inappropriate for a municipal authority to enact bylaws limiting pork sales. Authorities that enacted bylaws limiting pork sales within their precincts exceeded the boundaries of reasonableness." See also: Mazal Mu'alem, "Poraz: I Will Abolish Municipal By-Laws Limiting Pork Sales," *Haaretz*, 7 March 2003.

77. Supplementary Statement to the Court on behalf of the Attorney General, 10 March 2003.

78. Ruling issued on 28 April 2003.

79. Assaf Zelinger, "Justice Cheshin: 'Where Do You Want Pork to Be Sold, in the Fields?'" *Ma'ariv*, 8 December 2003.

80. Haim Shibi, "Complaint against MK Porush: Referred to a Supreme Court Justice as 'Pig,'" *Yedi'ot Aharonot*, 10 December 2003.

81. Request submitted by the Movement for Quality Government in Israel to join proceedings as *amicus curiae*, 16 February 2004.

82. Prof. Aviezer Ravitzky, a renowned scholar of Jewish philosophy, and three rabbis.

83. HC 953/01 *Solodkin v. Municipality of Beth Shemesh*, 58 (5) PD 595. The ruling notes that the request submitted by the Movement for Quality Government in Israel to join the proceedings as *amicus curiae* was dismissed both due to its late submission and on its merits, without further explanations (at 604).

84. Ibid., 608–10.

85. Ibid., 613.

86. Ibid., 613–15.

87. Ibid., 615–16.

88. Ibid., 616–20.

89. Ibid., 621–22.

90. Legal advisors and politicians at the municipal level who had taken an active role in the proceedings throughout the years did express frustration about the

ruling's failure to bring closure. See: Michal Goldberg and Rami Chazut, "Every Neighborhood Will Decide," *Yedi'ot Aharonot*, 15 June 2004.

91. Previously, the court had decided that the appeal in the *Shmukler* case (discussed *supra*) would be considered after its ruling on the petitions against the validity of the bylaws. Cr. A. 8708/99 *Shmukler v. State of Israel* (decision from 27 December 2001). Following the *Solodkin* ruling, the state notified the court of its agreement to an acquittal in this case, so the court held in this matter without any further deliberation. See: Cr.A. 8708/99 *Shmukler v. State of Israel-Municipality of Ashkelon* (unpublished, 21 December 2004).

92. As emphasized by Gideon Sapir, "Much Ado about Nothing," *Ma'ariv*, 15 June 2004.

93. Ze'ev Segal, "Neither Victors nor Vanquished," *Haaretz*, 15 June 2004. See also Yael Gevirtz, "Not 'According to the Cry of It'" [hinting at Genesis 18:20–21], *Yedi'ot Aharonot*, 15 June 2004.

94. Menachem Mautner, "Ratifying a Correct Principle," *Yedi'ot Aharonot*, 16 June 2004.

95. Rabbi Yuval Sherlo criticized the decision precisely due to its failure to give any weight to Israel's character as a Jewish state. According to Sherlo, pork trading prohibitions should be maintained because they express Israel's Jewish identity rather than because of individual feelings. See: Yuval Sherlo, "What Does Pork Have to Do with the HCJ," *Haaretz*, 16 June 2004. Sherlo presented a similar argument in the opinion he gave for supporting the *amicus curiae* request submitted to the Court in this matter. See *supra* nn. 81–83 and the accompanying text.

96. Quoting Proverbs 11:22.

97. For reports on the different reactions to *Solodkin*, see: Goldberg and Chazut, "Every Neighborhood Will Decide"; Rami Chazut and Chaim Shibi, "Pig with the HCJ's Sanction," *Yedi'ot Aharonot*, 15 June 2004; Samuel Mitelman et. al, "The HCJ Brought the Pig Back," *Ma'ariv*, 15 June 2004; Gideon Alon and Yuval Yoaz, "Yishai: A Nail in the Coffin of Jewish Identity," *Haaretz*, 15 June 2004.

98. *Solodkin v. Municipality of Beth Shemesh*, 621. In a procedural decision that preceded the final judgment, the court ordered both the petitioners and the respondents to provide data regarding the population distribution and the residential areas in the cities involved in the litigation (ruling issued on 19 June 2002). It specifically asked for data concerning areas populated by "secular" residents, thus intimating that prohibitions on pork trade would not be relevant to these areas. Ultimately, however, the court did not make any concrete decisions based on the data available.

99. Eli Ashkenazi, "The Residents Referendum Planned by Tiberias' Mayor Will Also Address Pork Sales," *Haaretz*, 15 June 2004; Dani Brenner, Merav Daviv, and Moran Katz, "Tiberias: Residents' Referendum Will Decide," *Ma'ariv*, 15 June 2004.

100. Goldberg and Chazut, "Every Neighborhood Will Decide."

101. See: Adam Baruch, "HCJ, the Neighborhood, The Deal (Pig)," *Ma'ariv,* 18 June 2004. According to Baruch, the Court's decision professed to detach itself from the political culture of deals over matters of religion and state although, in fact, it merely shifted the deal from the state to the neighborhood level.

102. Nir Arnon and Abraham Peled, "A Matter of Taste," *Ma Ba-Petah: The Newspaper of Petah-Tikvah,* 27 February 2004; Moshe Micha'eli "'The 'Other Thing' Dug Its Hooves in Petah-Tikvah . . . ," *Hamodi'a* (Supplement), 26 March 2004.

103. Including the Sonia butchery that, according to the reports, had been operating in the city for over fifty years. See: Arnon and Peled, "A Matter of Taste." The unsuccessful eviction action against this butchery was discussed in chapter 7.

104. According to estimates, the scope of nonkosher meat purchases in Israel is about a billion NIS (over $200 million), from which 300 million NIS (over $60 million) go to the purchase of fresh pork. See Yehudit Yahav and Navit Zomer, "A Billion NIS a Year," *Ma'ariv,* 15 June 2004.

105. Government Decision 1825 (KL/34) entitled "The Place of Slaughter-houses and Abattoirs: Amendment of Government Decision 279 (PS/3) from 16 December 1979," from 5 June 2000, which approved the necessary changes in Schedule 13 to the Animal Diseases (Slaughter of Animals) Regulations, 1964, omitting Nazareth and adding Ma'liyeh.

106. Debate on Animal Diseases (Regulating the Movement of Animals in Israel) (Amendment) Notice, 2002, Economics Committee of the 15th Knesset, 28 January 2002.

107. See chapter 6, nn. 43–45.

108. As in the letter from Deputy Attorney General Meni Mazuz on "Prohibition on Pig Transport without Veterinary Permit," from 11 April 2002. This document was discussed at the following meeting of the economics committee. Debate on Animal Diseases (Regulating the Movement of Animals in Israel) (Amendment) Notice, 2002, Economics Committee of the 15th Knesset, 3 June 2002.

109. Animal Diseases (Regulating the Movement of Animals in Israel) (Amendment) Notice, 2002.

110. As the then chairman of the Economics Committee, Abraham Poraz from Shinui, repeatedly and bluntly told the religious MKs participating in the debate.

111. HC 11597/04 *Iblin Breeders v. The Supervisor of the Southern District at the Ministry of the Interior* (pending).

112. See chapter 7.

113. Cr. App. (Haifa) 2633,2890/02 *State of Israel-Ministry of the Environment v. Araf* (unpublished, 22 January 2003).

114. P. C. A. (Petition for Civil Appeal) 8965/02 *Municipality of Iblin v. Dr. Nir* (unpublished, 27 January 2003).

115. HC 4264/02 *Iblin Breeders Partnership v. Municipality of Iblin* (to be published 12 December 2006. See chapter 6, n. 42.

116. Iblin (Abattoir) Bylaw 1964.

117. This argument, as well as some other details mentioned in the text, were derived from the petition of the breeders in this matter (and not from the final decision, cited in n. 115 *supra*).

9. NATIONAL SYMBOL OR RELIGIOUS CONCERN?

1. On the concept of tradition, its authoritative status, the resistance to it, and its modification over time, see Edward Shils, *Tradition* (Chicago: University of Chicato Press, 1981).

2. See: Jonathan Shapira, *Politicians as an Hegemonic Class: The Case of Israel*, (Tel-Aviv: Sifriyat Po'alim, 1996), 54 [in Hebrew].

3. Ibid., 62. On the connection between religion and nationalism in the Zionist movement and in the State of Israel, see also: Baruch Kimmerling, "Religion, Nationalism, and Democracy in Israel," *Zmanim* 50–51 (1994): 116 [in Hebrew].

4. Surveys of observance levels among Israeli Jews have concentrated on the consumption of kosher food in general, without addressing pork consumption separately. The leading survey in this context is the so-called Guttman Report prepared by the Guttman Center, affiliated with the Israel Democracy Institute, upon the request of the AVI CHAI foundation. The first Guttman Report was based on research conducted in 1991 and the second on research conducted in 1999 (see *A Portrait of Israeli Jewry* [Jerusalem: Israel Democracy Institute, 2000] [in Hebrew]). A survey specifically touching on the traditional pig prohibition was conducted in the 1970s. This survey also included questions regarding so-called religious legislation and addressed, among other issues, the prohibition on pig breeding. This survey reported that 54 percent supported such a prohibition (against 46 percent who opposed it). See Peri Kedem, "Dimensions of Jewish Religiosity," in *Israeli Judaism: The Sociology of Religion in Israel*, ed. Shlomo Deshen, Charles S. Liebman, and Moshe Skokeid (New Brunswick, N.J.: Transaction Publishers, 1995), 33, 43.

5. See *To Be Citizens in Israel—a Jewish and Democratic State* (civics for high-school students in the general and religious schools, updated edition, Jerusalem: Ma'a lot, August 2001), 306 [in Hebrew]. One of the exercises illustrating the religious schism cites a newspaper report dealing with the polemic surrounding the *Rubinstein* ruling (*infra* n. 18). Ibid., 313–14.

6. See Uri Yablonka, "New in the Occupied Territories: 'Watchpigs,'" *Ma'ariv*, 28 October 2003; Uri Binder, "The Sow for the War on Terror," *Ma'ariv*, 18 March 2004.

7. Note that this initiative emerged in religious circles, whereas Shalev himself is known as a hard-line secular intellectual. See: Meir Shalev, "Innovations and Inventions," *Yedi'ot Aharonot* (Shabbat supplement), 31 October 2003.

8. See: Menachem Mautner, "Regime and Law in a Multicultural Society" [in Hebrew], in *The Conflict: Religion and State in Israel*, ed. Nahum Langental and Shuki Friedman (Tel-Aviv: Yedi'ot Aharonot, 2002), 59, 76–77.

9. CA 294/91 *Hevrah Kadisha Jerusalem Community v. Kastenbaum*, 46(2) PD 464.

10. Ibid., 501–2.

11. For an explanation of this process, see: Asher Cohen and Barukh Susser, "Changes in the Relationship between Religion and State: Between Consociationalism and Resolution" [in Hebrew], in *Multiculturalism in a Democratic and Jewish State*, ed. Menachem Mautner, Avi Sagi, and Ronen Shamir (Tel-Aviv: Ramot, Tel-Aviv University, 1998), 675.

12. This argument challenges the view of the Ministry of Justice, whereby "the national component does not rule out the duty incumbent on the local authority seeking to prohibit or restrict the sale of pork products within its jurisdiction to exercise its power in a reasonable and proportional manner, while also considering the option of adopting only a partial prohibition or restriction at the initial stage, in line with the composition, customs, and needs of the population." See: Summary of the debate on "By-Laws Prohibiting the Sale of Pork and Pork Products" drafted by deputy attorney general Meni Mazuz, 18 March 2001.

13. HC 953/01 *Solodkin v. Municipality of Beth Shemesh*, 58 (5) PD 595.

14. According to Heroes' Remembrance Day (War of Independence and Israel Defense Army) Law, 1963.

15. According to the Martyrs and Heroes' Remembrance Day Law, 1953.

16. On the perception of red-light districts as anomalies, see: Gerald L. Neuman, "Anomalous Zones," *Stanford Law Review* 48 (1996): 1197, 1206–14; William Ian Miller, "Sanctuary, Red Light Districts, and Washington DC: Some Observations on Neuman's Anomalous Zones," *Stanford Law Review* 48 (1996): 1235.

17. On the resistance to red-light districts in the United States, see: Lawrence M. Freedman, *Crime and Punishment in American History* (New York: Basic Books, 1993), 328–32.

18. Cr. F. (Netanyah) 1310/95 *State of Israel v. Rubinstein* (unpublished, 23 October 1996) discussed in chapter 8.

19. Cr. F. (Ashkelon) 260/95 *State of Israel v. Shmukler* (unpublished, 8 March 1995) and Cr. A. (Beer-Sheba) 7182/98 *Shmukler v. State of Israel–Municipality of Ashkelon* (unpublished, 27 October 1999) discussed in chapter 8.

20. See also: Danny Statman, "Offending Religious Feelings" [in Hebrew], in *Multiculturalism in a Democratic and Jewish State,* ed. Mautner, Sagi, and Shamir, 133.

21. See: Avi Sagi, *Society and Law in Israel: Between a Rights Discourse and an Identity Discourse* (Ramat Gan: Zivion, Bar-Ilan University, 2001).

22. Referring to HC 5016/96 *Horev v. Minister of Transportation,* 51(4) PD 1.

23. Sagi, *Society and Law in Israel,* 29.

24. Gideon Alon and Mazal Mu'alem, "Poraz: I Will Not Authorize Inspectors to Prevent Leaven Sales in Public Places," *Haaretz,* 7 April 2003; Mazal Mu'alem, "The Ministry of Interior Will Not Enforce the Leaven Law this Year," *Haaretz,*

15 April 2003; Mazal Mu'alem et al., "Leaven Sales Are Expanding This Year in the Absence of Official Enforcement," *Haaretz,* 18 April 2003; Yuval Karni, "No Longer Selling Bread through the Back Door," *Yedi'ot Aharonot,* 20 April 2003; Uri Yablonka et. al., "The Leaven Dam Has Broken," *Ma'ariv,* 20 April 2003; Nehamah Du'ek and Shirley Golan-Meiri, "Rage in the NRP and Shas Following the 'Leaven Celebrations,'" *Yedi'ot Aharonot,* 21 April 2003.

25. Emuna Elon, "Whose Passover Is This?" *Yedi'ot Aharonot,* 20 April 2003.

26. See: Yair Sheleg, *The New Religious: Recent Developments among Observant Jews in Israel,* (Jerusalem: Keter, 2000), 297 [in Hebrew].

27. Prohibition of Opening Entertainment Centers on the Ninth of Av (Special Enablement) Law, 1997.

28. See: Prohibition of Opening Entertainment Centers on the Ninth of Av (Special Enablement) (Amendment) Law, 2002.

29. As noted (chapter 2, n. 62), one of Katsanelson's well-known articles deals with the approach toward the Ninth of Av as a national day of mourning. See: Berl Katsanelson, "Destruction and Detachment" [in Hebrew], in *Writings of B. Katsanelson,* ed. S. Yavniely, vol. 6 (Tel-Aviv: The Party of Workers in the Land of Israel Publishing, 1947), 365.

30. Ahad Ha'am, "Sabbath and Zionism" [in Hebrew], in *At the Crossroad,* ed. Yirmiyahu Frenkel, vol. 2 (Tel-Aviv and Jerusalem: Dvir and Hebrew Publishing, 1979), 139.

31. For example, see: Cr. F. (Jerusalem) 3471/87 *State of Israel v. Kaplan* (1988) P.M., Vol. 2, 265.

32. For example, it is the policy of Tiv Ta'am, the nonkosher food chain, to open its stores on the Sabbath. In Petah Tikvah the municipality sought a judicial order against the opening of the local Tiv Ta'am store on the Sabbath because this violates the provisions of a municipal bylaw on business hours. See Moti Zaft, "Pork Only on Weekdays . . ." *Ha-Shavu'a be-Petah Tikvah,* 29 March 2004 (in his personal column titled "Stories in Brief"). Tiv Ta'am's request that this order be abolished was dismissed. See DR [Different Request] (Petah Tikvah) 1003/04 *Tiv Ta'am Chains Ltd. v. State of Israel* (unpublished, 30 March 2004); CA (TA) 2071/04 *Tiv Ta'am Chain Ltd. v. State of Israel* (unpublished, 5 July 2004).

33. See chapter 5.

34. Municipal Corporations Ordinance Amendment (No. 40) Law, 1990 which inserted Section 264A into the Municipal Corporations Ordinance [New Version]. See chapter 7.

35. The importance of local legislation on this issue, although conveying a weaker symbolic message, is not entirely negligible in its symbolic value. As discussed in chapter 1, in India too, limitations on cattle slaughter are legislated by the states and are therefore not identical throughout the country.

36. See: HC 129/57 *Manshi v. Minister of the Interior and the Municipality of Tel Aviv-Jaffa,* 12 PD 209, 223. See chapter 6, *supra,* nn. 22–25.

37. For a general discussion of the development of Jewish cultures with

different nuances in Israel and in the largest Diaspora community in the world (in the United States), see Charles S. Liebman and Steven M. Cohen, *Two Worlds of Judaism: The Israeli and American Experiences* (New Haven: Yale University Press, 1990).

38. Arend Lijphart, *The Politics of Accommodation* (Berkeley: University of California Press, 1968); Arend Lijphart, *Democracy in Plural Societies* (New Haven: Yale University Press, 1977).

39. Eliezer Don-Yehiya, "The Resolution of Religious Conflicts in Israel," in *Conflict and Consensus in Jewish Political Life,* ed. Stuart A. Cohen and Eliezer Don-Yehiya (Ramat-Gan: Bar-Ilan University, 1986), 203.

40. Asher Cohen and Bernard Susser, *Israel and the Politics of Jewish Identity: The Secular-Religious Impasse* (Baltimore, Md.: Johns Hopkins University Press, 2000); Asher Cohen and Bernard Susser, *From Accommodation to Escalation: The Secular-Religious Divide at the Outset of the Twenty-first Century* (Jerusalem: Shoken, 2003) [in Hebrew].

41. Cohen and Susser, *Israel and the Politics of Jewish Identity,* 86–93; Cohen and Susser, *From Accommodation to Escalation,* 97–102.

42. HC 3267/97, 715/98 *Rubinstein v. Minister of Defense,* 52 (5) PD 481.

43. Law on Service Deferments for Full-Time Yeshivah Students, 2002.

44. HC 2751/99 *Paritsky v. Minister of Education and Culture* (unpublished, 23 January 2000); HC 10296/02 *Teachers' Union (High Schools, Seminars, and Colleges) v. The Minister of Education, Culture and Sports,* 59(3) PD 224.

45. Cohen and Susser, *From Accommodation to Escalation,* 138–48.

46. Yaron London, "My Sacred Cow and His Unclean Cow," *Yedi'ot Aharonot,* 22 June 2004.

47. Aviezer Ravitzky, "Religious and Secular Jews in Israel: A Kulturkampf?" (Jerusalem: Israeli Democracy Institute, Position Paper No. 4), 17.

48. Ibid., 19.

Index

Locators in bold indicate supplementary descriptions in appendices.

enforcement of pig related legislation:
  (*continued*)
  65–66, 70–71, 95, 103; privacy
  issues, 53, 64, 92; seizures of pork,
  63–64, 66, 70, 125, 162n33
entertainment venues, prohibitions
  on opening, 72–73, 115, 116
environmental impact of pig-breeding,
  9, 103, 174n113
euphemisms for pork, ix, 24–25, 78,
  79, 107, 146n66

fallen soldiers remembrance day, 111
family law, 4–5, 32, 81, 118, 120–21
Federman decision, 137n12
fines, 46, 70, 71, 74, 91, 124
flag, Israeli, 36–37, 120
Fogelman, Uzi, 87, 169n28
folklore, Jewish, 19, 21, 23, 144n46
Food Control legislation, 46, 54
food shortages and rationing, 33–35,
  151n10
food supply for pigs, 67, 163n49
Foundations of the Law Act of 1980, 74
Frazer, James, 16
freedom of conscience, 56
freedom of movement, and Sabbath
  transportation, 6, 34, 72, 75, 113,
  116, 137n15
Freedom of Occupation (Basic Law),
  115, 168n2; import of nonkosher
  meat, 136n11; municipal bylaws
  and, 86, 88; Ninth of Av, 115; pig-
  breeding, 103–4, 174n108; pig-
  related legislation and, 81–82, 85,
  97–98, 104
Fridi decision, 49, 91, 135n1

Gafni, Yehuda, 5
Geertz, Clifford, 8, 36
General Zionists, 52, 53, *130,* 131, 132
German settlements in Palestine,
  pork production in, 28, 148n8

gourmet culture, 83–84, 169nn11, 12
Granot, Avraham, 30–31
Granot, Eliezer, 76
Greeks, ancient, ix, 6, 18–19, 52, 101
Greenberg, Uri Tsvi, 22
Grossman, Allen, 22
Gush Emunim, 72
Guttman Report, 175n4

Haifa: Arab population in, 160n19;
  bylaw, municipal, 160n19; districting
  for pork sales in, 63, 86; religious
  council of, 47
Halakhah: distribution of pork to
  non-Jews, 35; immigrants from the
  USSR as Jews, 83, 120; pigs in
  halakhic sources, 17–18; symbolic
  aspects of the commandments,
  139n24
Ha-Modi'a (newspaper), 39
Hannah and her seven sons, ix, 19, 23,
  108
Hanukkah, 18–19, 23, 143n25
Ha-Po'el ha-Mizrahi, 46, 49, 50, 51,
  130, 133
Ha-Po'el ha-Tsa'ir, *130,* 132
Harari, Yizhar, 53
Harris, Marvin, 16, 141n4
Hartog, Hendrik, 9, 139n29
Hasmoneans, 18–19, 23, 50, 143n25
Ha-Tsofeh (newspaper), 39, 53, 56, 67
hegemony, 43, 72, 79
Heikhal cinema (Petah Tikvah),
  72–73
Herut, 47, *130, 131,* 132; Menachem
  Begin, 52, 56, 119, 131, 157n52; on
  pig prohibitions, 52, 94; Pig-Rais-
  ing Prohibition Law, 56, 119, 158n77;
  on pork sales in Tel Aviv, 47
Herzog, Isaac, Rabbi, 19, 34–35, 151n10
holocaust remembrance day, 22, 52,
  83, 111
Horev decision, 113, 176n22